QUALITY IN HEALTH CARE

In memory of Professor Mo Malek, 1949-2001

Professor Mo Malek – 1949–2001 – A Dedication

This text is dedicated to Professor Mo Malek, Professor of Health Care Policy, Planning and Management at the University of St Andrews, and founder of the *Strategic Issues in Health Care Management* (SIHCM) conferences. Sadly, Mo passed away on 12 March 2001 after a short illness. Our thoughts are with his family, especially his wife Linda, and children Rebecca, Ali, Miriam and Gemma. Mo went to school in Switzerland and obtained his first degree, in economics, at the University of Tehran. He taught in Iran for a couple of years before coming to Queen Mary College of London University, first as a postgraduate student, then research assistant, then temporary lecturer. Mo moved to St Andrews in 1981, as a Lecturer in Economics, being promoted to Reader in 1991, and being awarded a Chair in Health Policy, Planning and Management in 1995.

Mo contributed much, both internationally and across disciplines. However, it is perhaps for his work in pharmacoeconomics that he is best known, much of it conducted through the PharmacoEconomics Research Centre (PERC), which he founded and directed. For many people though, it is through the SIHCM conferences that Mo was first encountered.

Mo organised the first SIHCM conference in 1993. Further meetings followed in 1994 (on the theme of *Setting Priorities in Health Care*), 1998 (*Managing Quality, Controlling Costs*) and 2000 (*Efficiency, Quality and Access in Health Care*). Mo's work continues after him as the fifth meeting is planned for April 2002 (on *Policy, Finance and Performance in Health Care*).

Throughout these meetings many hundreds of people from dozens of countries encountered Mo's great hospitality and warmth. The SIHCM meetings were a source of some pride for Mo, and he delighted in the eclectic mix of disciplines and cultures in attendance. He was also concerned that as many as possible should be given a chance to share their work – and many a delegate gave their first ever conference presentation at an SIHCM meeting.

Mo was a tireless worker for his subject area, his institution, and his colleagues. He cared greatly about the development of health care and the appropriate use of health technologies, especially in developing nations. It is with great sadness that we record his death; and it is to his boundless energy, enthusiasm and generosity that this text, which explores some of these issues, is dedicated.

Huw Davies, Manouche Tavakoli, Rosemary Rushmer
SIHCM editors

Quality in Health Care

Strategic issues in health care management

Edited by
HUW T.O. DAVIES, MANOUCHE TAVAKOLI AND MO MALEK

Ashgate

Aldershot • Burlington USA • Singapore • Sydney

Published by
Ashgate Publishing Ltd
Gower House
Croft Road
Aldershot
Hants GU11 3HR
England

Ashgate Publishing Company
131 Main Street
Burlington, VT 05401-5600 USA

Ashgate website: http://www.ashgate.com

British Library Cataloguing in Publication Data
Quality in health care : strategic issues in health care
    management
    1.Medical care - Quality control
    I.Davies, Huw T. O. II.Tavakoli, Manouche III.Malek, Mo,
    1949-
    362.1'068

Library of Congress Control Number: 2001089067

ISBN 0 7546 1613 4

Printed and bound in Great Britain by MPG Books Ltd, Bodmin, Cornwall

Contents

List of Figures

List of Tables and Boxes

Acknowledgements

We wish to thank, first of all, participants in the Fourth International Conference on *Strategic Issues in Health Care Management* held at the University of St Andrews, Scotland in spring 2000. Over 20 countries were represented from many disciplines, and this eclectic mix ensured rich and varied debates on the problems facing health care as we enter the new millennium. Special thanks go to our plenary speakers, Professors Andrew Bindman and Thomas Rundall from the University of California (in San Francisco, and at Berkeley, respectively), and Sir David Carter, Chief Medical Officer at The Scottish Executive. Their contributions, which both opened and closed the conference, set the tone for some thoughtful discussions throughout. In addition, we are particularly grateful to the session chairs, manuscript reviewers and contributors for their efforts in shaping the material in this volume.

Appreciation is also due to our colleagues in the Department of Management, and the School of Social Sciences, at the University of St Andrews. We are likewise grateful for the excellent support provided by Reprographics, Printing, and Residential and Business Services at St Andrews. These capable and friendly people assisted in preparing conference materials and ensured the smooth running of the conference. Central to the conference planning and management was our conference secretary, Claire Topping. Claire performed wonders before, during and after the meeting, for which we are eternally grateful. In addition, Mehran Zabihollah, Eli Brock, Barbara Lessels and Liz Brodie also contributed to the conference management, and we thank them for their assistance.

Finally, Pat FitzGerald contributed great skill and considerable patience in the preparation of the text, and our publishers Ashgate greatly smoothed the production process: we thank them both.

Of course, none of the above can be held responsible for the final product. Responsibility for the presence of any errors or omissions lies solely with the editors and the contributing authors.

Huw Davies
Manouche Tavakoli
Mo Malek

Editors' Preface:
Challenges and Choices in Health Care

Introduction

The *Fourth International Conference* on *Strategic Issues in Health Care Management* took place in St Andrews in spring 2000. Delegates from over 20 countries heard around 100 presentations covering a wide range of issues – from national health systems reform and measuring performance in the health sector, to the human problems of developing a patient-focused culture. The three days intense activity provided a venue not only for expanding professional networks and encouraging collaborative work between health researchers/managers and professionals from a wider economy, but also the making new friends. Also produced were three eclectic collections of papers on key issues facing health services development: managing quality; developing organisations; health reforms; and choices in care. The papers in this volume, selected from nearly 100 original high quality submissions, reflect the upsurge of challenging and innovative work currently taking place on *health policy and economics*. Papers in companion volumes examine issues in health care quality. (*Quality in Health Care: Strategic Issues in Health Care Management*, Ashgate, 2001), and the challenges of organisational development in health care (*Organisational Development: Strategic Issues in Health Care Management*, Ashgate, 2001).

System Issues

The first two chapters in this collection examine some 'big picture' issues in health care. First, Thomas Rundall from Berkeley explains the role of integrated delivery systems in improving quality and efficiency in health care. These systems seek integration of preventive services, acute medical care and long-term care into a seamless system. From a review of the major efforts to create integrated health care delivery in the US and the UK, Rundall extracts five key lessons learned and devises a conceptual framework to guide future research and programme development.

The paper by Mattia Gilmartin and David Melzer looks further at innovative services but from a very different tack. They point to the stark differences in incentive structures (and hence investment in development and testing) between those that exist around new clinical technologies (especially drugs) and those around innovative care processes (including, for example, new ways of integrating service delivery). In doing so, they highlight potentially huge lost opportunities to improve both quality and efficiency in health care.

Bringing about Quality Improvement

Much of this text is, broadly speaking, about quality in health care: its system precursors, its assessment, and its perception. This middle swathe of six papers focuses specifically on the structures and processes of quality improvement.

Andrew Bindman sets the scene by comparing and contrasting US and UK approaches to influencing physician behaviour change and tackling practice variation. In the US, much of the charge has been led by managed care organisations – using gate-keeping, utilisation review, physician profiling, and financial incentives (including risk-sharing). Such market-dominated mechanisms have largely been eschewed by the UK in favour of 'physician networking and increased professional accountability'. Bindman concludes that each country may have lessons for the other from consideration of these diverse strategies.

From North America we move next to Central America and Ghana. Here Victoria Doyle and David Haran explore the difficulties of promoting bottom-up quality improvements in developing nations. Their explication of the quality process has much to offer middle- and low-income countries facing a need for visible quality improvement within very tight resource constraints. Taking a similarly pragmatic line, Peter Buckley and James Watkins describe the pitfalls and lessons learnt from the implementation of a balanced scorecard performance management system. This took place within an independent charitable group of hospitals operating in mental health, a traditionally difficult arena for quality improvement activity. A third contribution to a triptych of papers describing practical experience comes from Ruth Boaden and colleagues. Here they explore in depth bed management in UK hospitals, taking a bench-marking approach to identify good practice and uncover areas for future research.

The final two papers in this section tackle some of the larger policy issues around the quality improvement agenda. Carmel Hughes asks of those in pursuit of quality improvement in health care: should we legislate or educate? Hughes illuminates this question by developing a detailed case-study of quality of care in nursing homes. Using a substantial 'minimum data set' collected on patients in nursing homes in the US, Denmark, Iceland, Italy, Japan and Sweden, she shows that legislation may bring about some improvements whilst still leaving much to be desired. Hughes concludes that multiple approaches, carefully balanced, may be more appropriate rather than an over-reliance on a single legislative strategy. This theme is taken up again by Huw Davies who identifies some of the major strategies used to drive change and concludes that none in isolation has provided the sort of breakthrough in quality required.

Exploring Variations in Health Care

Much of the impetus for quality improvement activity – and an issue that drives quality to the fore in policy circles – comes from the presence of substantial practice variations in health care. Documenting and explaining these has been a preoccupation of health researchers for over a quarter of a century. This section contains four papers: two of which describe and attempt to explain service variation, and two of which discuss the ways in which such knowledge of variation may be used to encourage change.

Rebecca Duffy and Harry Staines explore the wide variations in emergency medical admission rates between different primary care practices. Whereas crude figures showed almost twofold variations between practices, much of this could be explained by differences between practices in sociodemographic factors such as age structure and levels of deprivation. In contrast, Catherine O'Donnell explores variations in general practitioner (family doctor) referral rates from primary to secondary care. Her review of the literature uncovers 88 empirical papers from which she summarises that patient characteristics explain less than 40 per cent of the observed variation in referral rates and primary doctor characteristics explain less than 10 per cent. Her conclusion that variations in referral rates remain largely unexplained poses significant challenges both for researchers in this area and for those who would use these kinds of data as performance yardsticks.

That variations in either process or outcomes may reflect underlying differences in the quality of care is an enduring and appealing notion. Because of this, many nations have made significant efforts at gathering, analysing, and distributing comparative data on clinical practice. In his paper 'Going Public on Clinical Performance', Martin Marshall examines more than a decade's experience in the US of what has become known as 'the report card movement'. His findings, from an extensive literature view, reveal two things. First, that there is a paucity of data to support what is, in fact, very significant activity around the public release of performance data. Second, that the evidence currently points to health care *provider* organisations as being the main engine for change in the light of variations in performance. This second point is picked up and developed by Russell Mannion and colleagues as they explore the role in health care of performance measurement systems based around quantitative comparative data. Such systems, they conclude, require caution in design and implementation if benefits are to be maximised and drawbacks minimised.

Incorporating User Views

The final four papers all provide a different take on the incorporation of user views in developing packages of care. Petra Kliempt and colleagues explore expectations about the important outcomes from health and social care held by both older people and health and social care professionals. They reveal both areas of consistency and some surprising areas of contrast. Yaniv Poria and colleagues use qualitative techniques to elicit the views and preferences that lesbians and gay men hold about health care services. This study, carried out in the UK and Israel, provides some clear messages for health services striving to meet the expectations of all its user communities. Further work from New Zealand by Lynette Stewart and colleagues, demonstrates not only the importance, but also the feasibility, of developing health services appropriate to marginalised groups – in this case the indigenous people of New Zealand, the Maori. In contrast, Janet Tucker and colleagues present a rather sombre assessment of the ability to effect consumer-oriented change in health services. They document the evidence of both the demand for, and the effectiveness of, different models of maternity care, but then go on to show the inertia in the system in providing more than just limited access to these alternative models of care.

Concluding Remarks

Improving access, controlling costs, and maintaining health care quality remain at the top of the agenda in many developed nations, with developing nations now also paying greater attention to these issues. The rising costs of health provision and the ever-increasing demand by citizens upon health care have brought about the reality that decision-makers now have to make hard choices. This has resulted in an ever-increasing rate of production of guidelines with economic evaluation being central to the decision-making process. We hope that you enjoy these contributions to the debate, and we look forward to welcoming you to SIHCM 2002 – to be held in St Andrews in spring of 2002.

Manouche Tavakoli, Huw Davies, Mo Malek
Department of Management
University of St Andrews

SECTION ONE
SYSTEM ISSUES

Chapter One

The Sisyphean Challenge:
Health Services Integration

Thomas G. Rundall

Introduction

The integration of health care services is intended to improve the continuity, quality and efficiency of care provided to patients. This is a challenging goal and presumes that there is much about the current health care system that needs improvement. Indeed, health care delivery could be substantially improved. A case study illustrates the complexity of health services delivery and the potential of integrated service delivery to improve the patient's experience with the health system.

Ms Deborah Myers was a 66-year-old woman living alone in a retirement community. On 1 February, she was found unconscious in her apartment and was taken to the emergency room of the local hospital. Even though she had been a patient in that hospital a few months earlier, her medical record was not available for physicians to review at the time of this admission. The emergency department physician conducted an assessment of Ms Myers' condition, and transferred her to the hospital's medical unit.

The medical unit staff conducted a second assessment and developed a nursing plan. Ms Myers' condition improved over the next few days, and she was transferred to the rehabilitation unit, where a third assessment was done and a second nursing plan was developed. While in the rehabilitation unit, Ms Myers developed a urinary tract infection and was readmitted to the medical unit, where still another assessment and nursing plan were developed. Three days later she was discharged to a home care programme, where yet another assessment and care plan were prepared.

Two weeks later, Ms Myers was readmitted to the emergency department with an elevated temperature and dehydration. At this time she received her sixth assessment and was admitted to the medical unit. In the medical unit she was again evaluated and received yet another nursing plan. Two days later

Quality in Health Care: Strategic Issues in Health Care Management, H.T.O. Davies, M. Tavakoli and M. Malek (eds), Ashgate Publishing Ltd, 2001.

she was discharged to the Good Samaritan Nursing Home and received her eighth assessment and sixth nursing plan. On the fourth day in the nursing home, Ms Myers complained of shortness of breath and was readmitted to the emergency department, where despite all efforts she died.

This episode of illness lasted over a month, during which Ms Myers' health deteriorated while sporadic, and at times heroic, attempts were made to reverse the course of her illnesses. Indeed, Ms Myers received a lot of care. During the 38 days during which Ms Myers was under medical treatment she experienced caring medical and nursing staffs, state-of-the-art technology, eight assessments, six nursing care plans, eight admissions, 14 attending physicians and 24 separate bills. Moreover, Ms Myers (and her family and friends) had to coordinate services from an ambulance, emergency room, hospital medical unit, rehabilitation centre, nursing home, homemaker agency, pharmacy, outpatient clinic and various transportation companies.

Clearly, Ms Myers was not being cared for in an integrated delivery system. Each of the health care organisations and individual providers did a responsible job. However, each acted independently. The task of coordinating all these activities fell to Ms Myers herself, and it was so overwhelming an informal care network of family, friends and neighbours had to make many of the arrangements for Ms Myers' care. Not only was the experience frustrating and exhausting for all concerned, the lack of coordination and shared communication among those caring for Ms Myers may have contributed to the worsening of her condition and eventually to her death.

Unfortunately, Ms Myers' experience is all too common. While exceptions can be found in some health care systems, for the most part health and medical care services are not organised in a way that provides comprehensive, integrated care on an ongoing basis. The following description of an ideal integrated system of health care helps clarify what is missing in most contemporary health systems and will serve as a key referent for the remainder of this chapter:

> An integrated health system is a client-oriented system composed of both a continuum of services and integrating mechanisms that guides and tracks patients over time through a comprehensive array of health, mental health, and social services spanning all levels of intensity of care (Evashwick, 1987, p. 28).

In most communities the current organisations that provide medical care do not approach the ideal. Each community has its own combination of services and in each community there are numerous formal and informal arrangements by which patients enter the system and navigate its complex array of programmes and resources. Most people with complex or chronic health problems are subjected to multiple intake assessments and enrolment procedures for each service they use, and then they receive services in an uncoordinated way. Typically, the patients themselves, albeit lacking clinical or administrative expertise, serve as the information conduit across the different service providers, sharing information about the services they are receiving and the treatment plan each provider has developed for them.

Hence service integration holds forth the promise of adding considerable value for the patient/consumer. Table 1.1 lists the potential benefits for consumers of integrating health services.

Table 1.1 The promise of integrated delivery systems: adding value for the consumer

- Reducing fragmentation by offering a continuum of services
- Improving coordination of care
- Improving quality of care
- Improving outcomes for individuals
- Distributing risk across providers to encourage more appropriate utilisation of services
- Reducing redundancy in administration and service provision (economies of scope)
- Reducing production costs through standardisation and bulk purchasing (economies of scale)
- Reducing transaction costs (hassles, delays, uncertainty, lack of trust, etc.)
- Increasing flexibility in the use of funds to purchase patient services that are not covered by standard benefit packages

As health organisations integrate a continuum of services into a system, patients are able to seek out and use preventive services, early detection, primary care, disease management, acute care, rehabilitation, long-term care and other services more easily and within a familiar organisational environment. This reduces the fragmentation of services that occurs when multiple services are provided by different organisations and independent health care professionals. Having the continuum of services housed within a single organisational framework makes it easier for providers across the entire range of services to communicate with one another, thereby improving the coordination of care and the quality of care being provided. Moreover, in integrated systems with consolidated budgets, financial risk is distributed across all providers, thus discouraging either inappropriate referrals or over-utilisation as means to increase revenue. In this idealised system, due to improved coordination, more appropriate use of services and improved quality of care, one would expect patient outcomes to be better than in a fragmented care system. Integration of services also has the potential to improve the efficiency of service provision by reducing redundancy in administration and service provision, reducing production costs through standardisation and bulk purchasing and reducing transaction costs. Finally, it should be noted that integrated delivery systems add value to clients through their ability to purchase patient services that are not covered under standard benefit packages due to the flexibility such systems typically have to purchase services across the normal acute–chronic–mental–social service boundaries (Rundall and Evashwick, 2001; Shortell et al., 2000).

Efforts to Integrate Health Services in the US and the UK

Over the past two decades a number of private and public sector efforts have emerged in the United States and the United Kingdom to create integrated health care systems (Leutz, 1999). In the United States, three generic models have emerged:

*   systems that integrate acute care services;
*   systems that integrate long-term care services; and
*   systems that integrate both acute and long-term care.

The integration of acute care services in the US is most clearly developed in health maintenance organisations (HMOs). HMOs provide a continuum of services including disease prevention, primary, secondary and tertiary acute care services, in exchange for a fixed membership fee per member per month. In the United States, HMOs have been created in the private and public sectors for three health care markets: a) the commercial market (persons under the age of 65 years who can afford to purchase, or have their employer purchase for them, a private health plan; b) the Medicare market (persons over the age of 65 years who are eligible for the federal government's Medicare programme); and c) the Medicaid market (persons with incomes sufficiently low to qualify them for the free state/federal government Medicaid programme). In each case, the available HMOs include not-for-profit and investor-owned HMOs created through virtual and vertical integration (Wagner, 1996; Shi and Singh, 1998; Robinson, 1999).

Two types of programmes to integrate long-term care in the US have been implemented on a demonstration basis: gate-keeping systems and managed long-term care systems. In gate-keeping systems, a single agency manages patient entry to all sources of long-term care (Evashwick and Rundall, 1996; White and Gundrum, 1996). One example of a managed long-term care programme is the Arizona Medicaid programme, which contracts with one organisation in each of the state's counties to manage long-term care on a capitated basis (McCall and Korb, 1994).

There have been a number of efforts in the US to develop systems that integrate acute and long-term care services. These efforts have focused on the Medicare-eligible population: those over the age of 65 years. There are three basic types of such programmes: Community Care Retirement Communities (CCRC), the Program of All-Inclusive Care for the Elderly (PACE) and the Social Health Maintenance Organization (SHMO). In each case the integrated system receives permission from the Medicare programme to be offered as an alternative to the standard Medicare package of benefits.

A CCRC provides a package of services, including housing, health care, and social services, to older adults. While there is substantial variation in the arrangements, most CCRCs constitute a closed system of residential and health services that span subacute, postacute, rehabilitation and long-term custodial care for people no longer capable of independent living. Other services may include meals, organised social and recreational activities, homemaker and transportation services. After years of historical growth, new CCRC development slowed in the early 1990s, largely due to lack of capital financing. Investors have grown wary of this type of integrated system due to some well-publicised failures of some CCRCs and the fact that even in financially successful cases it takes four or five years to turn a profit (Aaronson, 1996).

The SHMO began in 1985 as a federal Health Care Financing Administration demonstration project. SHMOs provide traditional Medicare-covered services (physician services and hospital care) and long-term care services. Thus the SHMO is an innovative approach to the integration of medical and long-term care services, financed through capitation and enrollee premiums, with the SHMO being the risk-bearing agent. Providing an integrated continuum of care while controlling utilisation and cost was (and is) a major challenge for SHMOs. In general, those SHMOs that were created by health maintenance organisations, which have extensive experience in utilisation control, fared better financially than SHMOs created by long-term care providers or other types of parent organisations. However, there appears to have been biased selection among those seniors who volunteered to join the SHMOs, which caused the SHMOs to have care costs higher than expected for the general Medicare population. When adjustments are made for this biased selection, it appears that the SHMO model is a viable approach for creating an integrated delivery system (Leutz, Greenlick and Capitman, 1994; Aaronson, 1996).

PACE is a model of integrated service delivery based upon On Lok Senior Services, a demonstration project initiated in 1983 in San Francisco. PACE care systems are designed to meet the health and health-related needs of frail elderly, all of whom are certified for nursing home admission. Hence PACE differs from the CCRCs and SHMOs by 'carving out' a sub-population of the elderly; those who are frail and in need of comprehensive health services. PACE systems use multidisciplinary teams to plan, organise and deliver health care, ranging from primary care to chronic disease care. One of the goals of PACE systems is to avoid institutionalisation of the patient and maintain them in the community for as long as possible. The federal government and private foundations are funding replications and evaluations of the PACE system of care based upon the On Lok model (Aaronson, 1996).

Over the past 10 years there have been a number of policy initiatives in the UK that have attempted (among other things) to increase the integration of health and medical services. These initiatives include the Community Care Act (1990), GP fundholding (1990), total purchasing pilots (1995) and the formation of Primary Groups (1997). The Community Care Act strengthened care management in long-term care and directed health authorities to cooperate in planning and purchasing services for certain population subgroups, such as persons with learning disabilities. GP fundholding allowed private GP practices to finance and contract for home health and nursing home care. Total purchasing pilots allowed GPs to participate in planning for long-term care for frail populations. Finally, the 1997 Blair government reforms indicate that the National Health Service will modify the fundholding and internal market reforms of the early 1990s and create 500 primary groups that will be responsible for integrated health planning and could eventually become freestanding primary care trusts (Leutz, 1999). In the aggregate, these policy initiatives attempted to create internal markets for health services by 'splitting' the purchaser and provider functions within the NHS, to strengthen coordination in planning and purchasing health services and to allow private GP practices to finance and contract for home health and nursing home and become more involved in the planning of long-term care services (ibid.).

Lessons Learned from Efforts to Integrate Health Services

Although there are examples of individual programmes successfully integrating health service delivery, on the whole the various forms of integrated delivery systems have produced disappointing results. As Shortell and his colleagues (Shortell et al., 2000, pp. ix–x) have noted, in the United States,

> the performance of HMOs has been spotty, and the overall value of integration itself has been questioned. Growing consolidation among health plans, suppliers, and providers alike has led to increased levels of conflict among all parties. Overlaid on these developments, or, perhaps more accurately, as a result of these developments, has been a public backlash against certain aspects of 'managed' care, the call for greater consumer protection, and the demand for greater accountability from plans and providers alike.

In the UK, the policy changes of the early 1990s are under attack by the current government in spite of the fact that some improvements in efficiency in health services delivery appear to have been achieved (Enthoven, 1999).

Clearly, integrated delivery systems are still evolving, and innovative approaches to integrating the governance, administrative, and clinical functions are still emerging (Shortell et al., 2000). It is too early to judge whether integrated delivery systems will be successful and become the dominant mode of health services delivery. It is fair to say that to date integrated systems have not fulfilled their promise. However, there are a number of important lessons to be learned from the recent experience of integrated systems, and the remainder of this paper discusses five lessons of particular note.

Lesson Learned No. 1

We need a conceptual framework to guide our thinking, research, and actions. There has been considerable confusion in the professional and academic literatures over the meaning of integration and over what is and is not an integrated delivery system. As Leutz (1999) has noted, there are three levels of integration: linkage, coordination, and full integration. While most of the benefits of integration to patients, particularly frail or severely ill patients, emerge with full integration, most delivery systems have not implemented the integrating mechanisms necessary to be fully integrated. Despite their rhetoric, most systems are linking or coordinating systems. Table 1.2 presents my assessment of the current status of linking, coordinating and fully integrated systems with respect to eight key integrating mechanisms. This framework usefully distinguishes among different levels of integration, helping us to classify like systems together for analytical purposes, and it provides policy makers and planners with a template to guide the development of integrated systems.

Linking systems are unlikely to have collaborative leadership, integration of information systems or joint marketing of services. Other integrating mechanisms, such as client screening, case management, disease management, centralised purchasing and consolidated financial statements, may be present in some linking systems, but typically each mechanism is implemented in a way that maintains the autonomy of the individual service providers. Coordinating systems differ from linking systems by having focused screening to identify persons with special needs and much stronger case managemen, and disease management programmes. Still, with coordinating systems the leadership, information systems, marketing, purchasing and financial arrangements maintain the independence and autonomy of the network of providers to the greatest extent possible among providers with explicit referral agreements. The fully integrated system, one the other hand, incorporates all eight integrating mechanisms in ways that strengthen the interdependency of the providers and the integration of their patient care activities.

Lesson Learned No. 2

Even in what are considered the best integrated delivery systems, implementation of the key integrating mechanisms is incomplete. One way to illustrate this is to examine the extent to which integrating mechanisms have been adopted in what are popularly believed to be the best integrated delivery systems. In 1998, *Hospitals and Health Networks*, a leading professional journal in the United States, ranked integrated delivery systems based on a number of patient care and financial performance criteria. A list of the 'Top 100 Integrated Delivery Systems' was published, including the systems listed in Table 1.3 (Hospitals and Health Networks, 1998).

Data on the adoption of various integrating mechanisms by these 100 'top' systems reveals that many of the integrating mechanisms have not been adopted by these systems. In Table1.4, the percentage of the top 100 integrated delivery systems that adopted each of eight integrating mechanisms is reported. These systems had a very high adoption rate for centralised decision-making, unified marketing, unified financial bottom line and centralised purchasing. However, four integrating mechanisms essential to integrated patient care had low rates of adoption. Only 38 per cent of the top 100 systems had

Table 1.2   Implementation of integrating mechanisms in three types of service systems

Integrating mechanisms	Linking systems	Coordinating systems	Integrating systems
Collaborative leadership	Not done	Not done	Executive management team includes representatives from all facility types
Integration of information systems	Not done	Not done	Patient clinical and financial information is accessible at all sites and by all providers as needed
Joint marketing	Not done	Not done	Facilities market themselves as one system
Client screening	Screen or survey populations to identify emergent needs	Screen patients at key points (e.g. hospital discharge) to identify those with special needs	Screening is not important; case management is emphasised
Case management	Providers respond to special needs of patients and refer, sometimes follow-up	Case management roles (e.g. discharge planner) used to coordinate program of care	Multidisciplinary teams manage the care of complex cases
Disease management	Referral to other service providers	Patient education provided about primary and secondary disease prevention and referral to available services	Persons with selected diseases or risk factors are put on a disease management protocol
Centralised purchasing	Not done to avoid duplication, may be done to reduce costs through bulk purchasing	Not done to avoid duplication, may be done to reduce costs through bulk purchasing	Equipment and supplies are centrally purchased to reduce redundancy and purchase costs
Finance	Know who pays for each service and bill accordingly; each service has own bottom line	Use guidelines to decide who pays for what; each service has own bottom line	Pool funds to finance services; one financial bottom line for related facilities

Table 1.3   Examples from a list of the top 100 integrated delivery systems in the US

Promina Health System, Atlanta, GA

Allina Health System, Minneapolis, MN

Scrippshealth, San Diego, CA

Mercy Health Services, Farmington Hills, MI

Sentara Health System, Norfolk, VA

Advocate Health Care, Oak Brook, IL

Kaiser Permanente, Oakland, CA

Table 1.4   Adoption of integrating mechanisms by the top 100 integrated delivery systems in 1998

98% indicated that the system had integrated (centralised) decision-making

96% indicated that the system marketed itself as one unit

94% indicated that the organisation has one financial bottom line for related facilities

86% indicated that the system has centralised purchasing

38% indicated that the IDS had integrated information systems

38% indicated that they implemented case management

36% indicated that they implemented disease management

22% indicated that the executive management team included representatives from the full spectrum of facility types

integrated information systems and case management; 36 per cent of the systems indicated they had disease management programmes; and 22 per cent indicated that the executive management team included representatives from the full spectrum of facilities in the system.

Lesson Learned No. 3

Barriers to the implementation of integrated delivery systems are found at every level: public policy, market forces, organisational structures and individual wants and expectations. This is not surprising. Alain Enthoven (1999, pp. 1–2) has noted the inherent difficulty of organising, financing, and delivering medical care:

Medical care is extremely complex, changing rapidly, filled with uncertainties, difficult to measure results and evaluate. Medical problems are very heterogeneous and we are a long way from having common denominators to compare the relative health gains produced by one treatment versus another. There are built-in contradictions between effectiveness, efficiency, and equity. There is a clash between utilitarian ethics and the rule of rescue. There are paradoxes between the imperatives of national and local decision-making. The boundaries between medical care that ought to be provided to everyone free or at a low cost versus what people ought to pay for themselves are not clear.

There are many reports and analyses of the barriers specific to implementing integrated delivery systems (see, for example, Shortell et al., 1993; Shortell, Gillies and Mitchell, 1994; Conrad, 1993). At the policy level, one important barrier is the categorical nature of health services funding commonly found at the national and state levels. Funds are programmatically designated for prevention services, acute care, long-term care, etc. and providers do not have the authority to spend the funds outside of these 'boxes.' A long list of other barriers based on market, organisational, managerial, and professional issues has been identified by Shortell and his colleagues (Shortell et al., 1993). These include:

- failure to understand the new core business (integrated care);
- inability to overcome the hospital paradigm;
- inability to convince the 'cash cow' (usually the hospital) to accept a system strategy;
- inability of the board of directors to understand the new health care environment;
- ambiguous roles and responsibilities among managers;
- inability to 'manage' managed care;
- inability to execute the integration strategy; and
- lack of alignment of financial interests among providers.

Lesson Learned No. 4

Patience is necessary, but very hard to sustain. In the short run implementing an integrated delivery system may increase costs while not improving quality. In the long run, an IDS may reduce costs and improve quality, but politicians, payers, managers, providers, and others have shown little willingness to invest over a long enough period of time to reap the return. Although we do not know how long it will take for a new integrated delivery system to show improvements in quality of care and efficiency in comparison to the typical fragmented system, given the complexity of implementing all the integrating mechanisms identified in Table 1.2 surely five or more years of implementation are required before a reasonable assessment can be made.

Lesson Learned No. 5

The keys to success lie not in technology, but in the values and motivations people bring to their work. Four particularly important keys to success are developing:

- a focus on the patient;
- a shared vision of the purpose of integration;
- leadership committed to integration of services;
- trust among the organisations and participants involved.

Emphasising patient-focused care establishes the patient as the centre of the delivery system and supports the development of a collaborative culture among care providers. The concept of patient-focused care also provides an easily understood organisational vision, and it is important to the success of integrated delivery systems that all participants share this vision. Although participatory management and governance play important roles in the development of systems of care, without sustained supportive leadership over a period of time integration will likely fail. The established historical patterns of interaction among providers will likely re-emerge if managerial and medical staffs perceive that the leadership of the organisation is willing to allow it to happen. Finally, the changes required of all participants to create and maintain an integrated delivery system require a good deal of trust. Without this interpersonal trust, and the mutual respect that is a part of a trusting relationship, battles over power, protection of 'turf' and budgets that are so common in organisational transformations will undermine the effort to truly integrate the system.

Conclusion

This chapter has examined the efforts over the past two decades in the United States and the United Kingdom to integrate health services. It is apparent that fully integrated systems are more rare than appears at first glance. Moreover, the barriers to creating fully integrated systems are substantial. Like Sisyphus pushing his rock up to the top of the hill, organisational leaders trying to develop integrated delivery systems may feel that just as they are about to achieve their goal, some aspect of their complicated set of arrangements comes apart, leaving them back where they started. This chapter offers encouragement of two types. First, by differentiating between linking, coordinating, and fully integrating systems, it is possible to see what is minimally necessary to create linking and coordinating systems. For many populations such systems may be adequate for meeting the vast majority of their health care needs. Thus the much more challenging task of developing fully integrated systems may be reserved for those sub-populations with high levels of medical need or special circumstances (Leutz, 1999). Second, examination of barriers and facilitators in many systems suggests that human motivations and values play a central role in the development of effective systems. Since a desire to serve clients and care for patients is a fundamental value shared by nearly all health service managers and providers, we have a good foundation to build on for the future development of integrated delivery systems.

Acknowledgement

Presented at the Fourth International Conference on Strategic Issues in Health Care Management, University of St Andrews, 30 March 2000. The author would like to acknowledge the support of the Center for Health Management Studies at the University of California, Berkeley in the preparation of this chapter.

References

Aaronson, W. (1996), 'Financing the Continuum of Care: A disintegrating past and an integrating future', in C. Evashwick (ed.), *The Continuum of Long-Term Care: An integrated systems approach*, Delmar Publishers, Albany, New York.

Conrad, D.A. (1993), 'Coordinating Patient Care Services in Regional Health Systems: The challenge of clinical integration', *Hospital and Health Services Administration*, 38(4), pp. 491–508.

Enthoven, A.C. (1999), *In Pursuit of an Improving National Health Service*, The Nuffield Trust, London.

Evashwick, C. (1987), 'Definition of the Continuum of Care', in C. Evashwick and L. Weiss (eds), *Managing the Continuum of Care: A Practical Guide to Organization and Operations*, Aspen Publishers, Gaithersburg, Maryland.

Evashwick, C. and Rundall, T.G. (1996), 'Organizing the Continuum of Long-Term care', in C. Evashwick (ed.), *The Continuum of Long-Term Care: An integrated systems approach*, Delmar Publishers, Albany, New York.

Hospital and Health Networks (1998), 'The Top 100 Integrated Systems', *Hospitals and Health Networks*, 20 March, pp. 40–51.

Leutz, W.N. (1999), 'Five Laws for Integrating Medical and Social Services: Lessons from the United States and the United Kingdom', *The Milbank Quarterly*, 77(1), pp. 77–110.

Leutz, W.N., Greenlick, M.R. and Capitman, J.A. (1994), 'Integrating Acute and Long-Term Care', *Health Affairs*, 13(4), pp. 58–74.

McCall, N. and Korb, J. (1994), *Combining Acute and LTC in a Capitated Medicaid Program: The Arizona LTC system*, Laguna Research Associates, San Francisco.

Robinson, J.C. (1999), *The Corporate Practice of Medicine*, University of California Press, Berkeley.

Rundall, T.G. and Evashwick, C. (2001), 'Organizing the Continuum of Care', in C. Evashwick (ed.), *The Long-Term Continuum of Care*, 2nd edn, Delmar Publishers, Albany, New York.

Shi, L. and Singh, D.A. (1998), *Delivering Health Care in America: A systems approach*, Aspen Publishers, Gaithersburg, Maryland.

Shortell, S.M., Gillies, R.R. and Anderson, D. (1994), 'The New World of Managed Care: Creating Organized Delivery Systems', *Health Affairs*, 13(5), pp. 46–64.

Shortell, S.M., Gillies, R.R., Anderson, D.A., Mitchell, J.B. and Morgan, K.L. (1993), 'Creating Organized Delivery Systems: The barriers and facilitators', *Hospital and Health Services Administration*, 38(4), pp. 447–66.

Shortell, S.M., Gillies, R.R., Anderson, D.A., Erickson, K.M. and Mitchell, J.B. (2000), *Remaking Health Care in America, Second Edition*, Jossey-Bass, San Francisco.

Wagner, E.R. (1996), 'Types of Managed Care Organizations', in P.R. Kongstvedt (ed.), *The Managed Health Care Handbook*, 3rd edn, Asoen Publishers, Gaithersburg, Maryland.

White, M. and Gundrum, G. (1996), 'Case Management', in C. Evashwick (ed.), *The Continuum of Long-Term Care: An integrated systems approach*, Delmar Publishers, Albany, New York.

Chapter Two

Process Innovation in Health Care: A New Model for the New Knowledge Economy

Mattia J. Gilmartin and David Melzer

Introduction

Health systems around the world are faced with the challenge of improving the efficiency, effectiveness and responsiveness of service delivery. Traditionally, efforts to improve provider performance have emphasised improvements in everyday management of services and improved responsiveness from staff. Prescriptions for achieving these efficiency gains have varied between health systems, although most of the international attention has focused on the role of competition between providers (Enthoven, 1999). On the whole, however, the effects of competition, certainly within the National Health Service (NHS), were very modest.

However, a more detailed analysis of efficiency and effectiveness in health care will immediately draw attention to the role of technology. Broadly, technology is defined as knowledge about natural phenomena systematically applied to useful purposes (Quinn, 1992). Health care is now a highly technological industry, delivering durable technologies such as drugs and devices and less tangible interventions, such as advice and information. The flow of new technology is undoubtedly the main cost driver within health care (Eddy, 1993) and innovation in the technology of health care, including the technology of organising and delivering care, will undoubtedly be the main route to improved performance, as it has been in other industries.

Taking this view, the central issue in improving health care efficiency and responsiveness is that of innovation and the creation of new technologies. The demand for improved efficiency and responsiveness implies a

Quality in Health Care: Strategic Issues in Health Care Management, H.T.O. Davies, M. Tavakoli and M. Malek (eds), Ashgate Publishing Ltd, 2001.

transformation of care providers into active participants in a knowledge-based economy within health care. At the centre of the transformation of health care service is the need for a view and a structure to foster innovation to change the process of clinical care delivery. This chapter presents a model of process innovation for the health care delivery sector to support the development of wholesale service technologies/clinical care technologies within the context of a knowledge-based economy.

What is Technology and Innovation in Health Care?

Technology within health care takes many forms. The most obvious is the technology that health care buys in; the drugs, information technology and devices that abound in health care settings. In addition to this tangible technology is a wide range of therapeutic know-how – the technology of surgery, of psychological treatments, of advice on self management of chronic disease and finally the knowledge of what produces a more effective model of service organisation and delivery.

Pasmore (1989) defines organisational technology as consisting of the tools, techniques, devices, artefacts, methods, configurations, procedures and knowledge used to acquire inputs, transform inputs to outputs and provide services to clients. Services are considered knowledge technologies in that they provide clients/consumers with the necessary knowledge to perform tasks for themselves which otherwise would require the use of a service provider (Mills and Moberg, 1982). The service firm produces knowledge-based technology in a form consumable in the market that is of benefit to consumers.

Organisational Innovation, Knowledge and Service Production

Technology derives from innovation, and the innovation concept provides an overarching frame to describe the climate of service development and the diffusion of these services in the industry, community, or population that an organisation serves (Drazin and Schoonhoven, 1996). In its broadest sense, innovation refers to positive change through the application of specialised knowledge in a creative manner to solve a problem (Dewar and Dutton, 1986; Dougherty, 1990; Gilmartin, 1998). Innovation is dynamic, multidimensional, time dependent and is influenced by external market conditions and organisational characteristics.

In the evolutionary model of economic growth (Nelson and Winter, 1982) innovation is described as the progression of dominant and newly applied knowledge in the form of technology. The firm's ability to engage in a systematic search process for knowledge leading to the development of new technology shapes its competitive position in the market. Additionally, the firm engages in a search process to identify and apply public and scientific knowledge, industry, and organisational specific knowledge for new product and service development (Leonard-Barton, 1995).

Typically, the firm produces four types of innovation to support operating goals. These include:

1 product or service innovation, which reflects the introduction of new products or services that the organisation produces, sells, or gives away;
2 production-process innovation, which involves the introduction of new elements in the organisation's task, decision and information systems or its physical production or service operations, the advances in the technology of the organisation;
3 organisational structure innovation, which includes the introduction of altered work assignments, authority relations, communication systems, or formal reward systems into the organisation, and;
4 people innovation, which involves a direct change in the people or social norms within the organisation (Knight, 1967).

Examples of Innovation/Technology in Health Care

Examples of each of Knight's classes of innovation in firms are not hard to find within health care. New drugs and diagnostic equipment typify product innovation. Clinical pathways, restructuring and evidence-based medicine all address issues of production process innovation. Organisational structure innovation includes such examples as clinical governance, multidisciplinary team-based care and US managed care and integrated delivery systems. People innovations within the health sector include the emergence of a service culture, patient-centred care, core competencies and new skills for practitioners.

However, thus far much of the focus of attention in health care has been on the durable or product innovation, leading to an imbalance between bought and created technologies. An organisation's propensity for innovation has focused on the diffusion and adaptation of durable medical and pharmaceutical technologies into the clinical care routines (Meyer and Goes, 1998; Greer, 1977; Romano, 1990). In many ways, this has driven changes in the production process, organisation of service, to the extent that the organisation and clinicians adopt technologies into existing care routines.

The Obsession with Durable Technology

Socio-technical theory (Pasmore, 1989) provides a framework to examine the adaptation of new technology into the organisational routines for the delivery of clinical care. Within the clinical sphere technology is viewed as an antecedent to the complexity of care and organisational structure to support service delivery (Verran and Reid, 1987). Stevens (1989) provides a history of the interdependent relationship between the practice of medicine, the advances in durable medical and pharmaceutical technology, the growth of the acute care hospital hub, and complexity of care delivery in the twentieth century. Historically, health care services produced within hospitals have focused on the treatment of disease in the acute phase. The disease focus of service delivery has shaped organisational structures, professional practice and technology development within the service sector. In the delivery sector, technology has come to imply an object, usually in the form of durable medical equipment or pharmaceuticals. The metaphor of technology as object has shaped policy initiatives and market behaviours that have in turn shaped the diffusion and production of innovation within the delivery sector (Sandelowski, 1996).

The Roots of Success in the Durable Innovation Sector in Health Care

The main features of the durable technology sector are immediately obvious – large firms, depending heavily on intellectual property rights, compete in a knowledge-based global market. Firms survive in this market through innovation for sustained performance and profitability. The competitive market has been so successful that it has produced extraordinary levels of investment in innovation through dedicated research and development infrastructure. Investments in the research and development are protected by intellectual property rights and patent law so that the firm can recover its development investments once a new product enters the market.

However, there is a further crucial feature. From the users' point of view, the regulatory requirement for evaluation has shaped the durable technology industry, especially that for pharmaceuticals, into producing proof of the effectiveness of those innovations. In a world where most of the patients within the health care system have chronic disease (Huff et al., 2000), predicting the effects of innovation (of all sorts) is very difficult. The regulatory requirement for proof combined with a well-functioning knowledge economy of durable technology innovation has produced an extraordinarily successful flow of new and effective durable technologies.

The Cinderella Sector of Innovation

In comparison, the predominately not-for-profit service sector expresses a fundamentally different pattern of firm-based innovation production. The approach to technology development in the clinical sector has been shaped by the separation of the clinical and administrative cores of the hospital enterprise (O'Connor and Lanning, 1992). The modern health care organisation is a hierarchy of parallel management and medical structures, in which the health care professional (physicians and to a smaller extent nurses and other providers) is viewed as the innovator, with autonomy over clinical decision making and disciplinary knowledge (Reed and Evans, 1987). In this model, clinicians and academics typically work in isolation or in small groups to provide clinical services, develop and test clinical care innovations using at best small and often underpowered trials. The results of care innovations are published in the academic press or presented at professional conferences as the main channel for diffusion into clinical practice.

Unfortunately, the output of this professionally-driven, academic model of innovation does not seem up to the challenges health care now faces. Increasing cost and quality pressures in the service sector have further threatened the Academic Health Sciences Centre model of clinical research and development activities (Tanne, 1997; Neumann and Sandberg, 1998; Weisbrod and LaMay, 1999; Gaus and Fraser, 1996). The existing system of technologic innovation produces promising new services that are never developed and refined to a level at which efficacy can be demonstrated.

A recent review conducted by the NHS Research and Development Health Technology Assessment Programme (HTAP) highlights the flaws in the existing research and development model of clinical care technologies. The HTAP examined the available evidence on the effectiveness and efficacy of a variety of clinical services; a few examples include geriatric services, near patient testing and paramedic services in the field. Upon review of the existing research literature some startling results come to light about these clinical technologies.

For geriatric services, interventions after hip fracture were found to be complex and strongly influenced by local conditions. Additionally, the effectiveness of rehabilitation programmes was found to be uncertain, with a lack of comparative studies examining different treatments and the testing of strategies available in the literature are of poor to moderate quality (Faulkner et al., 1998).

An examination of patient outcomes after field intervention performed by ambulance crews with basic life support training found that the protocols used by paramedics increase the mortality from serious trauma involving bleeding injuries, but may also lead to better outcomes for survivors. The observed increase in mortality may be due to factors such as delays on the scene and inappropriate pre-hospital fluid infusion (Nicholl et al., 1998).

A review of near patient testing (NPT), the use of alternative delivery systems between laboratory and general practice, including electronic data interchange (EDI), and computerised diagnostic decision support (CDDS) in the primary care setting was undertaken to examine the availability, clinical effectiveness and cost-effectiveness of these services. The authors found that a wide variety of NPT systems have been developed. In general, the quality of the methods reported in the literature was poor and the issue of patient convenience and acceptability has not been adequately addressed. Lastly, few economic analyses on these technologies have been conducted and, if available, most were simple cost analyses. At the present time, there are insufficient data for conclusions to be drawn on the cost-effectiveness of NPT in primary care (Hobbs et al., 1997).

A New Model of Process Innovation: Could we Bring Cinderella into the Knowledge-based Economy?

The changing orientation of health care service requires new models of innovation in clinical care routines/service technologies. The shifting emphasis on the role of innovation within the health care delivery sector provides the context to examine new patterns of organisation, management, and service delivery to capitalise on the collective knowledge and expertise of practitioners (Gilmartin, 1999; Leonard-Barton, 1995). In the current environment of shrinking resources and uncertain conditions organisations are squeezing harder to find resources to support innovation (Fiol, 1996). Clearly, the existing system of technology innovation within the health sector is inadequate and neglects a whole range of innovations in service and patient care technologies that merit investment and development. While the clinical sector violates most of the basic assumptions of perfect markets in which true competition occurs, important lessons can be drawn from the more competitive sectors of the health economy to change the way in which clinical technology is developed, tested and diffused into the marketplace (Melzer, 1998; Haines and Iliffe, 1995; Stevens et al., 1999).

The principle of emergent competition (Freeman and Liedtka, 1997) provides the foundation for a new model of process innovation for clinical care technology. The principle of emergent competition states that organisations thrive because they are engaged in competition with other organisations to provide goods and services of benefit to their stakeholders. The principle of emergent competition is applied to structure groups of clinicians and researchers who would compete with one another to develop, refine, rigorously test and bring to market service technologies in the manner of pharmaceutical and durable medical technology firms. The knowledge, skill and expertise of each practitioner form the development base for clinical technologies and care technologies for a given disease or health problem.

Drawing upon the social benefits gained by the competitive dynamic of innovation production, this model seeks to overcome the adaptation of clinical care fads or practices based on tradition or poor evidence regarding treatment efficacy. The aim of the new model is to create a group of competitive, knowledge-based professional organisations dedicated to developing and disseminating process, organisational and people innovations in the health care sector.

A new model of health care innovation in the knowledge- based economy includes four components. First, a new structure of intellectual property rights is needed to support the development of a full range of 'hard' and 'soft' health care technologies. The extension of intellectual property rights for service/process innovations would extend equal protection to all classes of health technology so that investments in research and development are not distorted by arbitrary exclusions.

Second, regulatory requirements are necessary to shift the burden of proof to the developing group to demonstrate the technology's effectiveness before bringing it to market. This would be accomplished through a combination of patent/intellectual property protection and regulations to enforce the proper testing of the clinical effectiveness of new health technologies.

Third, arrangements are necessary to avoid monopoly power of the developing group in limiting the supply of the technology to patients. Namely, the developing group would license the new care technology to other providers or organisations to diffuse the technology into the marketplace. The developing organisation would recover investment costs through compulsory licensing agreements and consumers are ensured that they are purchasing an effective technology.

Lastly, institutional arrangements and funding mechanisms should change so that the research and development activities of the knowledge based professional organisations competing to bring effective clinical and organisational technologies to market are viewed as an integral component of public health policy that provides large-scale evaluation of health care technology. As a first step, new institutional arrangements and incentives to promote the development of non-patentable technologies used in health care service delivery are needed (Root-Bernstein, 1995).

Conclusion

Health care now faces intensified pressure to improve efficiency and responsiveness. To do this in any substantial way, innovation and the resulting new technology will be needed. The durable technology sector in health care, through a combination of intellectual property rights and regulatory requirements for proof of effectiveness has produced an extraordinary flow of new effective technologies. However, the process, organisational and people classes of innovation have become Cinderellas.

As the knowledge-based economy develops, it becomes ever more apparent that these Cinderella technologies could be fostered within arrangements that are analogous to those for durable health care technologies. There is ample evidence that there are many promising technologies within the nondurable sector that, under the right organisational conditions, could make major contributions to meeting the pressure for more efficiency in health care provision.

References

Dewar, R.D. and Dutton, J.E. (1986), 'The Adoption of Radical and Incremental Innovations: An empirical analysis', *Management Science*, 32, pp. 1422–33.
Dougherty, D. (1990), 'Understanding New Markets for New Products', *Strategic Management Journal*, 11, pp. 59–78.
Drazin, R. and Schoonhoven, C.B. (1996), 'Community, Population and Organisational Effects on Innovation: A multileveled perspective', *Academy of Management Journal*, 39(5), pp. 1065–83.
Eddy, D. (1993), 'Three battles to watch in the 1990s', *Journal of the American Medical Association*, 270, pp. 520–26.

Faulkner, A., Kennedy, L.G., Baxter, K., Donovan, J., Wilkinson, M. and Bevan, G. (1998), 'Effectveness of Hip Prostheses in Primary Total Hip Replacement: A critical review of evidence and an economic model', *Health Technology Assessment*, 2 (6), pp. 1–146.

Fiol, C.M. (1996), 'Squeezing Harder Doesn't Always Work: Continuing the search for consistency in innovation research', *Academy of Management Review*, 21(4), pp. 1012–21.

Freeman, R.E. and Liedtka, J. (1997), 'Stakeholder Capitalism and the Value Chain', *European Journal of Management*, 15(3), pp. 237–96.

Gaus, C. and Fraser, I. (1996), 'Shifting Paradigms and the Role of Research' *Health Affairs*, 15(2), pp. 235–40.

Gilmartin, M.J. (1998), 'The Nursing Organization and the Transformation of Health Care for the 21st Century', *Nursing Administration Quarterly*, 22(2), pp. 70–86.

Greer, A.L. (1977), 'Advances in the Study of the Diffusion of Innovation in Health Care Organisations', *Milbank Memorial Fund Quarterly*, 55 (3), pp. 505–20.

Haines, A. and Iliffe, S. (1995), 'Innovations in Services and the Application of Science', *British Medical Journal*, 310 (1 April), pp. 815–16.

Hobbs, F.D.R., Delaney, B.C., Fitzmaurice, D.A., Wilson, S. et al. (1997), 'A Review of Near Patient Testing in Primary Care', *Health Technology Assessment*, 1 (5), pp. 1–244.

Huff, E.D., Sandy, L.G., Shojania, K. et al. (2000), 'Unreliability of Physician Report Cards to Assess Cost and Quality of Care' *Journal of the American Medical Association*, 283, pp. 51–61.

Knight, K.E. (1967), 'A Descriptive Model of Intra-firm Innovation Process', *Journal of Business*, 40, pp. 478–96.

Leonard-Barton, D. (1995), *Wellsprings of Knowledge: Building and sustaining the sources of innovation*, Harvard Business School Press, Cambridge, Mass.

Melzer, D. (1998), 'Patent Protection for Medical Technologies: Why some and not others?', *Lancet*, 315 (14 February), pp. 518–19.

Meyer, A.D. and Goes, J.B. (1998), 'Organisational Assimilation of Innovations: A multilevel contextual analysis', *Academy of Management Journal*, 31, pp. 897–923.

Mills, P.K. and Moberg, D.J. (1982), 'Perspectives on the Technology of Service Operations', *Academy of Management Review*, 7, pp. 467–78.

Nelson, R. and Winter, S. (1982), *An Evolutionary Theory of Economic Change*, Belknap Press, Cambridge, Mass.

Neumann, P.J. and Sandberg, E.A. (1998), 'Trends in Health Care R&D and Technology Innovation', *Health Affairs*, 17(6), pp. 111–19.

Nicholl, J., Hughes, S., Dixon, S., Turner, J. and Yates, D. (1998), 'The Cost and Benefits of Paramedic Skills in Pre-hospital Trauma Care', *Health Technology Assessment*, 2 (17), pp. 1–84.

O'Connor, S.J. and Lanning, J.A. (1992), 'The End of Autonomy? Reflections on the Post-professional Physician', *Health Care Management Review*, 17(1), pp. 63–72.

Pasmore, W.A. (1989), *Designing Effective Organisational: The socio-technical systems perspective*, Wiley, New York.

Quinn, J.B. (1992), *The Intelligent Enterprise: A knowledge and service based paradigm for industry*, The Free Press, Simon and Schuster, New York.

Reed, R.R. and Evans, D. (1987), 'The Deprofessionalization of Medicine: Causes, effects and responses', *Journal of the American Medical Association*, 258 (22), pp. 3279–82.

Romano, C.A. (1990), 'Diffusion of Technology Innovation', *Advances in Nursing Science*, 13(2), pp. 11–21.

Root-Bernstein, R.S. (1995), 'The Development and Dissemination of Non-patentable Therapies (NPTs)', *Perspectives in Biology and Medicine*, 31(1), pp. 110–17.

Sandelowski, M. (1996), 'Tools of the Trade: Analysing technology as object in nursing', *Scholarly Inquiry in Nursing Practice*, Spring 10(1), pp. 5–16.

Stevens, A., Miline, R., Lilford, R. and Gabbay, J. (1999), ' Keeping Pace with New Technologies: Systems needed to identify and evaluate them', *British Medical Journal*, 319 (13 November), pp. 1291–9.

Stevens, R.M. (1989), *In Sickness and in Wealth: American hospitals in the twentieth century*, Basic Books, New York.

Tanne, J.H. (1997), 'U.S. Clinical Research under Threat', *British Medical Journal*, 315 (19 July), p. 143.

Verran, J.A. and Reid, P.J. (1987), 'Replicated Testing of the Nursing Technology Model', *Nursing Research*, 36(3), p. 190–4.

Weisbrod, B.A. and La May, C.L. (1999), 'Mixed Signals: Public policy and the future of health care R&D', *Health Affairs*, 18(2), pp. 112–25.

SECTION TWO
BRINGING ABOUT QUALITY
IMPROVEMENT

Chapter Three

Challenges on the Road to Clinical Governance: The United Kingdom's Strategy for Health Care Quality Improvement

Andrew B. Bindman

Introduction

For more than two decades numerous studies have documented variations in health care service delivery across small areas (Folland and Stano, 1990). Although these studies have rarely controlled for underlying differences in patients' health care needs or treatment preferences, the prevailing explanation for small area variation in health care utilisation is that this represents inappropriate variation in physician decision-making. This hypothesis is supported by studies that have found that the greatest variation in service occurs when there is a lack of consensus on the best approach (Wennberg, Barnes and Zubkoff, 1982). Even when there are clear professional practice norms, many patients do not receive appropriate care (Shuster, 1998).

While small area variation in health care utilisation has long been recognised, it is only recently that health planners and policy makers have formally sought to address it. The increased interest in this issue is related to the financial stress associated with the growth of health care costs. Policy makers and planners have promoted the concept that the elimination of variation in health care utilisation will reduce unnecessary care and thereby result in cost savings. This policy is predicated on the assumption that variation in utilisation is more of a sign of unnecessary overuse of services rather than inappropriate underuse of services.

The US and the UK have chosen somewhat different strategies for addressing physician behaviour and practice variation. Contrasting the

Quality in Health Care: Strategic Issues in Health Care Management, H.T.O. Davies, M. Tavakoli and M. Malek (eds), Ashgate Publishing Ltd, 2001.

approaches and results in the two countries could provide an important learning opportunity.

US-managed Care

In the US, much of the activity focused on changing physicians' behaviour is being led by managed care organisations (prepaid health insurance plans with an integrated network of providers), which are developing and implementing a series of mainly top-down management strategies to control physicians' practice patterns. Prior to the emergence of managed care plans, the majority of physicians in the US were free to practice as they saw fit with minimal interference from the patient's health plan. In many cases, physicians benefited financially under a fee-for-service system when they utilised greater amounts of services for their patients. Managed care plans have attempted to rein in physicians' practice patterns by:

1   using primary care physicians as gatekeepers;
2   scrutinising physicians' decision-making with utilisation management tools;
3   profiling physicians' performance on cost and quality measures; and
4   linking physicians' practice patterns with financial incentives.

In managed care, much of this activity has been focused on primary care providers. Managed care organisations have expanded the primary care provider's role beyond clinical functions to include responsibility for controlling patients' costs. Borrowing from a practice that has been present in the UK's National Health Service (NHS) for more than 50 years, managed care plans use primary care physicians as gatekeepers who must authorise patients' referrals to specialists for high cost tests and procedures and for hospitalisation. Prior to the introduction of gatekeeping, many American patients with fee-for-service insurance would self-refer to specialists without first consulting a primary care provider. Managed care plans opted to deploy primary care physicians as gatekeepers because research suggested that this could reduce health care costs (Martin et al., 1989).

In addition to using primary care providers as gatekeepers, most managed care plans use health care utilisation management tools to control physician practices. Utilisation review enables the managed care organisation to alter the clinical plan developed between a physician and patient. Typically, these strategies require physicians to obtain the authorisation of a nurse or other health care professional working on behalf of the plan prior to obtaining expensive diagnostic tests, therapeutic procedures, or hospitalisations. Utilisation review procedures are associated with a decrease in service use. The insertion of the health plan into clinical decisions has not been viewed favourably by patients or providers. However, utilisation review strategies do reduce health care costs. It appears that the requirement for health plan permission in and of itself has a powerful moderating effect on physicians' practice patterns. A randomised trial of utilisation review comparing sham utilisation review procedures in which no services were actually denied versus actual utilisation review procedures found a reduction in service use in both groups over time but that there was no significant difference between the two groups (Rosenberg et al., 1995).

Managed care plans also profile the utilisation patterns of their providers. An individual provider's actual use of services in various categories such as laboratory tests, radiology and specialist referrals, is aggregated over a time period and is compared against the average use in these categories during this same time period by other physicians in the medical group or health plan (Salem-Schatz et al., 1994). Profiling has also been extended to include measures of physicians' quality of care and their patients' ratings of satisfaction with their care. In most cases, these data are used internally within a managed care plan or medical group, but there has also been public reporting of these data so as to inform consumers and to create pressure on the providers to respond to the results (Epstein, 1995). Most of the public reporting is aggregated to an entire managed care plan or medical group, but there has been public reporting of individual physician performance as well.

Managed care plans have also used financial incentives as a means to increase physicians' awareness of their practice patterns and performance. Physician incentives have been linked to a variety of measures including overall use of services, use of specific services such as laboratory tests and radiology, referral rates, patient volume (productivity), rates of performing recommended preventive care and patients' ratings of satisfaction. These bonuses are based on an individual provider's practice or performance, the practice or performance of a provider's medical group, or a combination of the two.

The decline in the growth rate of health care costs and the increased focus on quality with the expansion of managed care in the 1990s has suggested that these various strategies are working. While managed care has been associated with decreased health care utilisation, it remains to be shown whether the decline in service use is related to the attempts to change physician behaviour and whether this decreased activity reflects fewer necessary or unnecessary activities, or both. Managed care advocates point to literature reviews that suggest that managed care organisations do as well if not better than fee-for-service plans for many patients (Miller and Luft, 1994). However, the literature rarely addresses how well these systems do in managing sicker patient populations and there is even less information on which managed care strategies in isolation or together are most effective in changing physician practice.

A growing public backlash against managed care and the perceived wedge it drives between physicians and patients may limit or alter the kinds of strategies that can be used in the US to change physician behaviour in the future. Patients are distrustful of providers who are financially rewarded for limiting their access to services (Grumbach et al., 1999) and many physicians believe that these incentives undermine quality of care (Grumbach et al., 1998). Recognising that dissatisfaction with access to specialists is among the most important reasons patients cite for leaving a health plan (Kerr et al., 1998), several managed care organisations have responded by eliminating the primary care gatekeeping functions and returning patients' ability to self-refer to many specialists.

The public has not responded as negatively to publicly reported physician performance measures. However, developing valid measures of an individual provider's practice and performance has proven to be challenging. Many physicians do not perform enough of any one activity to enable reliable estimates of performance. Furthermore, it is difficult to account for differences in the underlying characteristics of patients when forming judgments about providers. Even if the methodological challenges can be resolved, a recent review of the US experience with public reporting of provider performance suggests that this strategy has had relatively little impact on changing physicians' practice (Marshall et al., 2000).

United Kingdom's Clinical Governance

In the UK, the NHS has long been regarded as a highly centralised top down health care delivery system. Thus, it is striking that recent reforms in the NHS emphasise physician networking and increased professional account-ability rather than top down strategies as a means to changing physicians' behaviour. These changes are most apparent in primary care where the formation of Primary Care Groups (PCGs) has created a networking structure for all primary care physicians in a geographic area to communicate about and to become accountable for the clinical and financial issues associated with their area's population. Each PCG has clinical governance responsibilities which make physicians responsible for participating with one another in the establishment and compliance with group norms for practice (Allen, 2000).

Clinical governance is just getting underway in most PCGs but some common strategies are emerging. In many PCGs, clinical governance is reshaping continuing (postgraduate) medical education from an individual physician-centred activity to a PCG-centred one. Prior to PCGs, many primary care physicians would attend postgraduate conferences on a topic of their choosing as a means to maintain and update their knowledge. There was no expectation that this educational experience would be used by the primary care physician who attended the meeting to educate other practitioners more broadly in their work environment. Because a physician would typically obtain this education in isolation from practice colleagues, there was little opportunity to reflect on the new material with clinical colleagues. Recognising some of the shortcomings of the traditional continuing educational experience, some PCGs have attempted to extend the learning potential of these lectures by providing an incentive for primary care physicians within a PCG to attend training sessions together which are focused on PCG-specific quality improvement. Much of the clinical content is drawn from newly-established evidence-based NHS framework guidelines that are being supplied by the Department of Health. In addition, some of the more ambitious PCGs have succeeded in taking the additional step of creating audit and feedback (profiling) tools linked to the educational experience that highlight variation in practice across general practices within a PCG. Differences in practice patterns among general practices were discussed among the primary care physicians with the goal of aiding outlier practices to move over time toward the group average.

While there is a growing willingness for UK providers to share their clinical experiences, for many PCGs there are only a limited number of areas in which there are data in common across their general practice sites. The most commonly available data are on pharmaceutical prescribing. For example, many PCGs use these data to profile practices' use of generic drugs and antibiotics. These data have the potential to become even more useful when PCGs are able to move beyond global use at the practice level and to link the information back to individual patients so that quality of care judgments can be made about the use of pharmaceuticals in association with specific clinical conditions. In addition to pharmaceutical profiling, many PCGs are actively developing chronic disease registries across general practices which again can facilitate assessments of the variation in the quality of managing sick patients across general practices.

While the commitment to an organisational change in the NHS to improve quality is quite promising, the pace of development has been impeded by several factors. For example, the necessary information system infrastructure has been slow to develop because of limited financial investment and the need to convert in real time several disparate existing information systems. Second, although practitioners are encouraged to participate in clinical governance activities, in fact, it is not clear that they have all the necessary skills to direct improvements in health care systems. Furthermore, it has proved difficult to free doctors from clinical responsibilities with individual patients so that they can participate in the establishment of systems to improve care. Third, doctors remain somewhat leery of the process. They have concerns about the validity of quality improvement measures and whether the government will undermine their attempts to develop skills to manage themselves by reasserting top down management strategies.

Organisational changes in the NHS are occurring in the context of declining public confidence in the health system and, by extension, the government. The public's discontent may push the British government to pressure physicians to accelerate their development of clinical governance activities. Some policy analysts have advocated a more rapid introduction of US-managed care strategies into PCGs and clinical governance as a means to accelerate change in the NHS. For example, Enthoven (2000) argues that the NHS needs to provide financial incentives to reward higher performing practitioners. The UK is also actively considering broadening its efforts to collect and publicly disseminate provider performance measures as has been the trend in the US.

As an alternative to these marketplace strategies the UK could consider building upon the health care professional networking components of PCGs and clinical governance with evidence-based knowledge of how to change physicians' behaviour. Investigators in the UK are already recognised as world leaders in developing and evaluating the evidence on how to most effectively change physician practice. Studies to date suggest that continuing medical education lectures and performance audits with feedback, the strategies most commonly deployed by PCGs to change physician practice, are less successful than some other approaches (Bero et al., 1998). For example, the use of reminders (either paper or computer-based) at the time that a provider is seeing a patient has been demonstrated to be a more powerful change strategy.

The UK could move forward on its clinical governance agenda by encouraging more research on the topic of physician behaviour change and by effectively translating these research findings into practice. The NHS is moving rapidly toward getting all of its providers onto a single computerised network which will enable access to patients' electronic medical records. With this technology in place, the NHS could implement electronic reminders to providers of appropriate prevention and treatment practices targeted to the needs of patients at the time they are seeing their provider. Patient reminders and information could also be generated to encourage patients to stimulate their providers to perform appropriate services. If this approach works as well in practice as it has in research settings then clinical governance activities could be expected to not only change physician utilisation but also to improve quality.

Conclusion

The US and the UK are both eager to influence physician practice with the aim of reducing unnecessary variation and improving quality. It is unclear whether the UK's clinical governance networking and educational approach will prove to be any more successful at changing physicians' behaviour than the top down approach adopted by US-managed care plans. Both countries are engaged in large national experiments with little aid of a control group. Therefore, international comparisons could take on increasing importance in forming conclusions about the relative merits of each approach. By including physicians in the process of change through clinical governance, the NHS may have a more acceptable, sustainable and effective change strategy than that adopted by US-managed care plans. The UK began their process later than the US and its clinical governance networking approach will probably take longer to develop than US-managed care strategies. If managed care continues to be associated with controlling health care costs in the US, there will be increasing pressure within the NHS to import managed care strategies to change physician behaviour. However, rising health care costs within managed care may give the NHS's clinical governance activities some breathing room to develop further, in which case the UK may discover that it has important lessons about changing physician behaviour to share with the rest of the world.

Acknowledgement

Funding for Dr Bindman's time in the United Kingdom was supported by the British Council and a Fogarty Center (US Public Health Service) Senior Investigator Fellowship.

References

Allen, P. (2000), 'Accountability for Clinical Governance: Developing collective responsibility for quality in primary care', *British Medical Journal*, 321, pp. 608–11.

Bero, L.A., Grilli, R., Grimshaw, J.M., Harvey, E., Oxman, A.D. and Thomson, M.A. (1998), 'Closing the Gap between Research and Practice: An overview of systematic reviews of interventions to promote the implementation of research findings', *British Medical Journal*, 317, pp. 465–8.

Enthoven, A.C. (2000), 'A Promising Start, but Fundamental Reform is Needed', *British Medical Journal*, 320, pp. 1329–31.

Epstein, A. (1995), 'Performance Reports on Quality – Prototypes, Problems, and Prospects', *New England Journal of Medicine*, 333(1), pp. 57–61.

Folland, S., Stano, M. (1990), 'Small Area Variations: A critical review of propositions, methods, and evidence', *Medical Care Review*, 47(4), pp. 419–65.

Grumbach, K., Osmond, D., Vranizan, K., Jaffe, D. and Bindman, A.B. (1998), 'Primary Care Physicians' Experience of Financial Incentives in Managed-care Systems, *New England Journal of Medicine*, 339(21), pp. 516–21.

Grumbach, K., Selby, J., Damberg, C., Bindman, A.B., Quesenberry, C., Truman, A. and Uratsu, C. (1999), 'Resolving the Gatekeeper Conundrum: What patients value in primary care and referrals to specialists', *Journal of the American Medical Association*, 282(3), pp. 261–6.

Kerr, E.A., Hays, R.D., Lee, M.L. and Siu, A.L. (1998), 'Does Dissatisfaction with Access to Specialists Affect the Desire to Leave a Managed Care Plan?', *Medical Care Research and Review*, 55(1), pp. 59–77.

Martin, D., Diehr, P., Price, K. and Richardson, W. (1989), 'Effect of a Gatekeeper Plan on Health Services Use and Charges: A randomized trial', *American Journal of Public Health*, (79), pp. 1628–32.

Marshall, M.N., Shekelle, P.G., Leatherman, S. and Brook, R.H. (2000), 'The Public Release of Performance Data: What do we expect to gain? A review of the evidence', *Journal of the American Medical Association*, 283(14), pp. 1866–74.

Miller, R.H. and Luft, H.S. (1994), 'Managed Care Plan Performance Since 1980: A literature analysis', *Journal of the American Medical Association*, 271(19), pp. 1512–19.

Rosenberg, S.N., Allen, D.R., Handte, J.S., Jackson, T.C., Leto, L., Rodstein, B.M., Stratton, S.D., Westfall, G. and Yasser, R. (1995), 'Effect of Utilization Review in a Fee-for-service Health insurance Plan, *New England Journal of Medicine*, 333(20), pp. 1326–30.

Salem-Schatz, S., Moore, G., Rucker, M. and Pearson, S. (1994), 'The Case for Case-mix Adjustment in Practice Profiling', *Journal of the American Medical Association*, 272, pp. 871–4.

Shuster, M.A., McGlynn, E.A. and Brook, R.H. (1998), 'How Good is the Quality of Health Care in the United States?', *Millbank Quarterly*, 76(4), pp. 517–63.

Wennberg, J.E., Barnes, B.A. and Zubkoff, M. (1982), 'Professional Uncertainty and the Problem of Supplier-induced Demand', *Social Science and Medicine*, 16(7). pp. 811–24.

Chapter Four

Health Reforms and Quality of Care: Lessons Learnt from Ghana and Central America

Victoria Doyle and David Haran

Introduction

In industrialised countries, quality of care is widely debated in the context of health care reform (Williamson, 1994), and increasingly this is also becoming the case in middle- and low-income countries. The Alma Ata Declaration had a direct influence in developing countries in focusing efforts to improve access to health services at primary health care (PHC) level. However, with public health resources becoming so stretched the quality of services declined markedly such as was the case in Ghana (Offei, 1995). Policy makers have realised that health services of inferior quality do not promote equity or maximise health gain (World Bank, 1995).

Low utilisation of PHC services has been to a large extent due to consumer perceptions of poor quality (Adogboba et al., 2000). As a result of this, the public has been voting with their feet by being attracted more to private providers than to public health clinics and hospitals. For many reasons, such as low staff morale and reduced income, this has led to further declines in the quality and efficiency of public sector health services.

Whilst the issues for improving quality of care are global, the differences in the availability and allocation of resources (human, financial and material) is vast between high- and low-income countries. It remains a challenge to find innovative approaches that improve the quality of health service delivery. National quality assessment (QA) programmes are one way to improve standards, but strategies to implement QA at district and subdistrict level are sometimes ill-conceived or may not exist at all. This is surprising in view of

Quality in Health Care: Strategic Issues in Health Care Management, H.T.O. Davies, M. Tavakoli and M. Malek (eds), Ashgate Publishing Ltd, 2001.

the fact that health sector reform policies usually include quality as an explicit priority. Whilst greater decentralisation of responsibility and resources might allow enthusiastic districts to remedy this situation, staff need models of good practice to bolster morale and, indeed, improve their quality of care.

Several characteristics of the QA approach, such as its focus on improving processes within current resource constraints, its team based approach and use of routine data (Reerink and Sauerbourn, 1996), make it very appropriate for developing countries. This chapter proposes quality assurance as an approach that governments and health managers should consider in their attempts to systematically monitor and improve service delivery. We ask:

1 what is quality assurance;
2 what kind of QA policy is needed to ensure good quality of care;
3 can governments introduce an 'off the shelf' QA package;
4 how can a QA policy be put into practice?

The answers we provide are based on experiences and results from QA programmes in Ghana, Honduras, Costa Rica and Panama, although we accept that these answers do not apply equally to all situations (Doyle et al., 1995; Doyle, 1998).

What is QA in Health Care?

Definition: *quality assurance (QA) is a planned and systematic approach to monitoring, assessing and improving the quality of health services on a continuous basis within the existing resources.*

QA comes in many guises and may be known as total quality management, clinical audit, quality circles or continuous quality improvement.

Quality of care has different meanings to different stakeholders, for example, doctors and patients. All QA systems should encompass three perspectives on quality:

• clinical standards;
• performance management;
• client satisfaction.

Hence there are usually several elements within the QA system, such as clinical audit, quality control of laboratory services, risk management and client satisfaction surveys. These components do not have to be introduced simultaneously, but can be introduced as distinct packages.

What Kind of QA Policy Ensures Good Quality of Care?

It has become fashionable for government health policies around the world to include statements on the quality of their health services. Such QA statements usually reflect a concern for ensuring that health services are both cost effective and responsive to public needs.

These statements seek to promote quality of care in general terms, and this recognition at a central level is important. But such statements are fairly nebulous and if they merely reflect government lip service to an ideal, they are meaningless. Quality statements that apply to particular aspects of health service delivery are much more manageable and specific quality objectives are far more useful. Here are two examples:

- targets for waiting time for acute hospital services: '80 per cent of inpatient admissions to be within 6 months of diagnosis';
- targets for compliance for TB control programmes: '90 per cent of patients receiving TB treatment complete the full treatment'.

In addition to setting specific objectives for policy statements, outline strategies for implementation should be made clear at central level. Detailed implementation plans are best left to service providers at the local level.

Budget implications of policy statements need to be assessed at an early stage so that implementation activities can be programmed into annual work plans of regions and districts. Successful policy implementation requires continuity of resourcing and will not be sustainable on the basis of special funding or one-off budget allocations.

Is There a 'Universal QA Package'?

Is there a model QA programme that will secure quality improvements in all countries and settings? Agencies involved in the development of quality of care models offer a variety of blueprints which governments of developing countries might find attractive in providing a 'quick fix' solution to improve health service quality. However, experience shows that changes in health service *culture* are a prerequisite for achieving quality improvements (Whittaker et al., 1998). Ownership of the QA programme by the health personnel themselves is part and parcel of this culture change. This would argue against the notion of a universal QA package. Adopting an off-the-shelf package might be evidence of a government's response to public demand for better services. But improving quality of services demands a response from the service providers themselves. This is unlikely to happen with the top down imposition of a bolt-on system for quality improvement.

QA systems developed by facility-based staff are more likely to respond to local priorities and are far more likely to bring about the kind of quality improvements that service users themselves will appreciate. If there is no genuine commitment from the top, QA initiatives can develop in a piecemeal way. It can either be introduced on a small scale at the district or local level, or as a regional programme. Different geographical areas may develop at a different rate and they may use different approaches; however, this can fragment the drive for quality.

In Ghana, the Ministry of Health has been concerned about quality of care for most of the last decade, but improvements in quality have been slow to emerge (Adogboba et al., 2000). This is partly because quality improvement activities have received insufficient priority. Now, with the development of practical strategies for introducing QA, the government has put greater effort into implementing its policies. Even so, stronger leadership is needed from the national and regional offices of the ministry to turn rhetoric into institutionalised programmes that attend systematically to quality of care and lead to quality improvements. A countrywide QA review (Adogboba et al., 2000) highlighted that QA systems have been established in only 56 per cent of regional hospitals, 8.5 per cent of health centres and 39 per cent of private not-for-profit hospitals.

A more systematic approach to QA development has been taken in a project in Central America. Development of a regional QA system in Costa Rica, Panama and Honduras involved four different stages. A recent evaluation of this project (Haran, 1999) showed that improvements were reported in:

1   medical attention;
2   efficiency;
3   variation in quality of service delivery;
4   dissemination of survey results and service performance;
5   staff attitude and a culture of quality;
6   QA capacity building.

Regional QA teams reported that variation in quality between facilities had been reduced, mainly by the very weak facilities with poor performance improving towards the levels of quality demonstrated by the better facilities.

How Can a QA Policy be put into Practice?

Implementing QA systems is as much a 'people' issue as a 'technical' one. Providers implementing QA should guard against over-ambition. They may wish to start by focusing on a single issue then, as a quality culture develops in the health service, add additional elements to the QA programme.

Districts should be encouraged to develop their own QA initiatives as part of the annual work plan with their own budgets. Care should be taken to ensure that these initiatives are guided by national policies with nationally-agreed standards and indicators of quality of care. Menus of practical options for QA strategies should be collected centrally and actively promoted to support weaker districts where QA development is not taking place. However, ownership by local service providers remains the secret to success in turning policy on quality of care into practice.

Interdisciplinary QA teams represent the best mechanism for driving the QA process and at least some of the team members should have managerial responsibility to take decisions that can directly influence service quality. However, for long-term sustainability QA must be integrated into the existing roles and responsibilities of all staff.

QA must be driven from both the bottom and top of the health system if it is become an integral part of the health delivery system. Resource people are required at national, regional and district level to support the QA process. External technical assistance can act as a catalyst for getting things started, especially if there is limited country expertise.

The role of *national level* is to advocate the importance of quality improvements strategies, and facilitate them locally by:

- providing resources;
- coordinating training;
- coordinating standards of care.

A national QA committee would be an appropriate body to have this responsibility. The committee could also support district development by requiring quality of care to be included in the training curriculum of all health service workers, so that a culture of quality is fostered in the health service community, both public and private.

At *regional level* a quality strategy group should monitor quality and provide supportive supervision to districts. A regional training programme should reflect the national strategy with quality indicators and standards based on regional priorities.

At *district level* a quality steering team should support facility-level quality improvements. To support consistent goals for quality across the district, this quality steering team should facilitate effective communications between primary and secondary level facilities.

At *facility level* an interdisciplinary QA team should be responsible for continuously monitoring, assessing and improving quality. Each facility should have targets for its services in line with regional standards. Teams should be able to reallocate resources according to priorities and planned interventions.

Conclusions

Quality assurance provides an approach with a great deal of potential for middle- and low-income countries and evidence from Central America and Ghana has demonstrated that it is possible to improve quality within existing resource constraints. However, it is vital that each country adapts QA to their own context, taking into account cultural norms, values and expectations of both providers and the communities they serve. QA must be driven from both the bottom and top of the health system if it is become an integral part of the health delivery system with clear policy statements explicitly signalling government commitment to achieving better quality and defined roles and responsibilities for each level of the health system.

Acknowledgements

This work was supported by the European Union, and the Department for International Development, UK. We would like to recognise the contributions of all the QA Project staff and health service staff in Ghana, Costa Rica, Panama and Honduras to the successful completion of this project. The views expressed are those of the authors and not necessarily those of the funding agencies.

References

Adogboba, K., Offei, A., Tweneboa, N., Acquah, S., Arvorke, G., Ankrah, V. (2000), *Towards a Unified QA Strategy for Ghana: Quality assurance review 98*, Ministry of Health, Ghana in collaboration with Liverpool School of Tropical Medicine.

Doyle, V. (1998), *Putting Quality into Health Care in Central America: Project advances and synthesis of knowledge generated*, Liverpool School of Tropical Medicine.

Doyle, V., Haran, D., Weakliam, D., Offei, A. and Dovlo, D. (1995), *Quality of Care Programme: A patient-focused approach*, Summary Report, Eastern Region, Ghana.

Ghana Ministry of Health (1995), *The Medium Term Health Strategy.*

Haran, D. (1999), *Evaluation of the Third Year of Proyecto Salud con Calidad*, Consultancy Report, ICAS, Costa Rica.

Honduras Ministry of Health (1998), *The New Health Agenda.*

Offei, A. (1995), 'Ensuring the Quality of Care', *Africa Health*, 17(5), pp. 18–19.

Reerink, I. and Sauerborn, R. (1996), 'Quality of Primary Health Care in Developing Countries: Recent experiences and future directions', *International Journal for Quality in Health Care*, 8(2), pp 131–9.

Whittaker, S., Burns, D., Doyle, V. and Lynam, P. (1998), 'Introducing Quality Assurance to Health Service Delivery: Some approaches from South Africa, Ghana and Kenya', *International Journal for Quality in Health Care*, 10(3), pp. 263–67.

Williamson, J.W. (1994), 'Issues and Challenges in Quality Assurance of Health Care', *International Journal for Quality in Health Care*, 6, pp. 5–15.

World Bank (1995), *Development in Practice. Better Health in Africa: Experience and lessons learnt*, World Bank, Washington DC.

Chapter Five

Life Cycles *in Vivo*: Views from the Front Line in the Implementation of a Performance Management System

Peter Buckley and James Watkin

In Vivo Implementation of a Balanced Scorecard

This chapter explores the pitfall and lessons to be learnt from the implementation of a balanced scorecard performance management system.

While loosely based on the Kaplan and Norton balanced scorecard framework, the 'performing indicators' were developed through comprehensive dialogue with clinical and non-clinical colleagues throughout all areas of St Andrew's Hospital, Northampton, and the system brought the following key benefits:

- wider understanding throughout the organisation of what drives success – both clinical and business;
- greater ownership of indicators through involvement in design and implementation;
- enhanced reflective practice throughout the hospital;
- greater commitment to continued 'business improvement' in all aspects of our service.

Of the many lessons learnt throughout this programme, the following are salient pointers to anyone considering a similar exercise:

- clarity of purpose necessary;
- senior management commitment from the start paramount;
- leaders, lead by example;

Quality in Health Care: Strategic Issues in Health Care Management, H.T.O. Davies, M. Tavakoli and M. Malek (eds), Ashgate Publishing Ltd, 2001.

- process mapping necessary to ensure relevant indicators selected;
- involve front-line staff.

Communicate, communicate and communicate.

Introduction

Performance management literature emphasises the importance of an organisation's developing balanced and effective performance management systems to help 'translate its strategy into action' (Kaplan and Norton, 1996). Writers have stressed the potential pitfalls of overemphasising traditional short-term financial measures of performance, such as return on capital employed and earnings per share, arguing that organisations should develop measurement systems that provide a balanced picture of organisational performance. Appropriate key performance indicators (KPIs) that link to the strategy of organisations in areas such as human resources, product and service quality and operational efficiency and effectiveness should be routinely measured and considered alongside financial performance.

Management accounting literature has led the way in reviewing performance measurement systems. It is argued that the objectives of management accounting are to '... assist managers and to influence their behaviour' (Anthony, 1989, p. 3). However, the traditional focus of management accounting on financial performance has failed to recognise the complex set of interrelated activities that combine to determine the performance of an organisation. The maxim 'what gets measured, done well and rewarded is what gets done' (Collier, 1994, p. 201) helps to explain the concern of overemphasising financial performance measures.

An 'integrated approach' to performance measurement (Nanni et al., 1992) is required which is focused on 'measurement for continual improvement in strategic advantage rather than measurement against past or budgeted financial performance' (ibid., p. 14). Performance measures do influence behaviour and therefore managers need to ensure that the KPIs adopted will help to motivate and guide their employees to achieving the organisation's strategic aims. In this way strategic measurement systems should help managers identify good performance, make explicit the trade off between profit and investment, provide employees with challenging strategic targets and ensure that corporate management knows when to intervene because of poor performance (Bungay and Goold, 1991).

A number of frameworks of performance measurement have been developed in the 1990s including, the 'balanced scorecard' (Kaplan and Norton, 1992), the 'performance pyramid' (Lynch and Cross, 1991), 'integrated performance measurement' (Nanni et al., 1992) and 'performance measurement in service businesses' (Fitzgerald et al., 1991). These models outline the importance of balancing the organisations measurements of performance and selecting measures that will determine future performance, as well as those that report past performance.

Mental Health Industry Background

Government policy on mental health services shifted during the 1990s from a predominant concern with patient's rights to an overriding concern for public safety, following incidents where members of the public were harmed and in some cases murdered (e.g. the murder of Jonathan Zito by Christopher Clunis in 1992). This policy shift was encapsulated in the White Paper 'Modernising Mental Health Services' (Department of Health, 1998) subtitled, 'Safe, sound and supportive'. The White Paper stated, '… services should be safe, to protect the public and provide effective care for those with mental illness at the time they need it' (p. 2). This policy shift was famously articulated by the then Secretary of State for Health Frank Dobson's statement that the policy of closing down large psychiatric hospitals and treating people in the community had failed.

The government's 'third way' for mental health services presents a dichotomy for mental health professionals between encouraging people's independence on the one hand and moving towards institutional, secure care on the other. With this comes the additional service concept of Intermediary Care, emphasising a more assertive approach to maintaining patients in the community.

Other key developments include the renewed concentration on clinical and cost effectiveness in treatments and particularly evidence-based treatments. The National Institute of Clinical Excellence (NICE) has been established to develop clear standards for the delivery of health care which will be policed by the Commission for Health Improvement (CHI). The development of NICE is complemented by the introduction of 'clinical governance' which requires practitioners to accept responsibility for developing and maintaining standards within their organisation. Clinical governance can be defined as the means by which organisations ensure provision of quality clinical care by making individuals accountable for setting, maintaining and monitoring performance standards.

Commissioning arrangements for health services is also undergoing a period of change. Of particular relevance to the St Andrew's Group of Hospitals (SAGH) is the move towards regionally based commissioning of specialist health services such as medium secure psychiatric services and services for those with eating disorders. The majority of commissioning for SAGH has been based on individual case spot purchases by health authority, with a few longer term arrangements with high volume purchasers.

Another significant issue for independent sector providers of mental health care (who provide one-third of the country's medium secure beds) is the government ideology towards non-NHS health care provision. The government is currently committed to providing all health care services within the NHS. As such, opportunities for partnerships and true joint working between statutory sector and independent sector organisations are limited.

St Andrew's Group of Hospitals Background

St Andrew's Group of Hospitals (SAGH) is a charitable trust, operating in the independent health care market, providing specialist mental health and brain injury services in niche markets serving a national catchment area in the United Kingdom. More than 80 per cent of its revenue comes from service agreements with National Health Service (NHS) Health Authorities, trusts and primary care groups, with the remainder being made up of private medical insurance and private self-funding.

Whilst SAGH has to consider the needs of many stakeholders when developing its strategy, the three key groups are; patients and their carers, the doctors who refer patients to the service and the purchasing agencies who pay for the service. The hospital must also ensure that it complies with the standards proposed by the Mental Health Act Commission and, as a registered nursing home, the Nursing Homes Inspectorate.

Performance Management at SAGH

Despite SAGH's aim of meeting the challenge of psychiatric illness, developmental disability and acquired brain injury in a 'highly skilled and therapeutic environment' and commitment to quality, staff development, training and research, the hospital's performance monitoring system had traditionally been focused on bed occupancy and budgetary performance. Measures of staff sickness/absence, turnover and vacancies were only routinely produced since the second half of 1999. As such, the hospital did not yet have a performance measurement system that was entirely linked to achieving its strategic aims.

While a proforma provided by the Chief Executive did give some guidelines as to reporting by divisions, in the main, most reports were actually the result of the individual clinical directors' discretion. Such a lack of structure allows scope for dysfunctional practices to occur, such as those identified by Smith (1995), and include 'gaming', 'myopia' and 'convergence'.

Establishing a Performance Management Framework

Recognising these deficiencies, the Director of Service Development and Agreements (DSDA) wrote a paper to the Board in December 1997 arguing that:

> the Board of Directors have at their disposal a series of paper Board reports ... which at times appear overwhelming, confusing and possibly not focusing on the core business ... If we are to clearly lead the Hospital forward to the next century with a direction that the Board and all staff working at St Andrew's can understand, we need to re-focus these reports in a more user-friendly format, ensure the indicators we are choosing clearly reflect the overall strategy of St Andrew's for the next five years and beyond while also bearing in mind the core remit of our business (Buckley, 1997).

In response to this prompting, a project management structure was put in place to develop a performance management framework for the hospital. The Project Board (PB) included nine directors, Quality Assurance Co-ordinator, Information Manager and Business Manager (Project Manager).

The PB appointed a project development team (PDT) to coordinate the work to develop and produce a balanced scorecard. Working closely with the PDT were seven working groups appointed to work on developing the KPIs in each of the seven selected performance dimensions.

The 'balanced scorecard' approach (Kaplan and Norton, 1992) was adapted to the organisational context of St Andrew's Hospital. It was decided to develop KPIs at both the macro (board of directors) and micro (divisional/departmental) levels. Initial efforts were focused on developing a balanced scorecard for the SAGH Board of Directors.

Figure 5.1 demonstrates a research framework around which a contextual framework evolved for developing a performance management system / KPIs in mental health care – this outlines the environmental factors that impact on the development and implementation of such a performance management system.

The PDT firstly determined the appropriate dimensions of performance before selecting the key performance indicators for SAGH. Initially, the methodology for selecting KPIs was rightly criticised for failing to analyse the organisation in order to highlight the critical points of the systems that required measurement and thus indicate where action was required to ensure effective and efficient progress towards the hospital's strategic aims. As a consequence of this intervention, the PDT undertook a macro level process mapping exercise to identify the key areas for measurement. However, this analytical approach was balanced with a pragmatic agreement amongst the project board members of the necessity to minimising the delay to the project and the delivery of a pilot scorecard as soon as practicable. It was accepted that the pilot scorecard would need to be used carefully at first and subjected to rigorous evaluation.

An initial 'pilot' scorecard was developed comprising twenty-two KPIs, grouped into seven categories (clinical, risk management, human resources, staff education, facilities, reputation, and demand and finance). This pilot scorecard was developed for the BoD to trial and evaluate between April and September 2000.

The development process was led from the top down, but involved a range of staff in developing the actual KPIs in the individual categories. In addition, the PB, in conjunction with the appropriate directors, selected two divisions to trial the implementation of 'micro' KPIs at divisional and departmental level.

A number of software options for producing the scorecard were evaluated in order to identify the model that integrated with the SAGH systems most effectively. The issues associated with data gathering and production of the scorecard were overseen by the hospital's Information Officer who enthusiastically embraced these practical aspects of the project. A stand alone licence of the chosen software package was purchased in the first instance for the pilot scorecard phase.

SAGH, although with charitable objectives, has to be run as a business, and as a health care provider it needs to prioritise patient care. These possibly conflicting objectives can create tensions as to the primary or prioritised KPIs for the organisation.

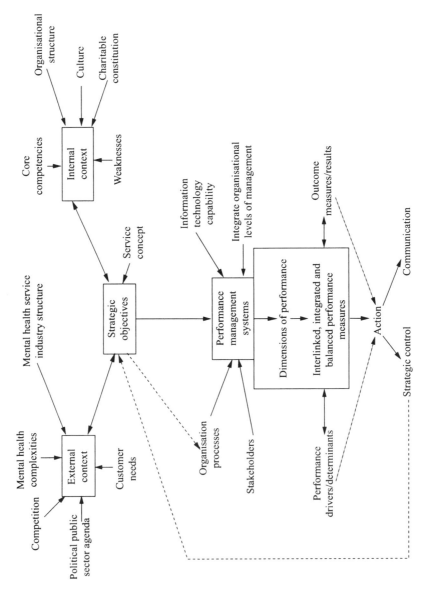

Figure 5.1   Contextual framework for developing performance indicators in the mental health care sector

These differences were examined for their validity and relative priority by exploring the perceptions of different stakeholders in the organisation towards the perceived validity of the 22 KPIs selected to constitute the pilot scorecard. These stakeholders included the Board of Governors (responsible to the Charity Commissioners for running the Charity), the Board of Directors (BoD) (subdivided into executive and Clinical Directors) responsible for running the business, clinical staff responsible for delivering the clinical service, support service and administrative employees. This survey of stakeholders opinions was undertaken during January 2000 at the time when the pilot scorecard was being launched to the BoD.

Summary of Survey Findings

The results of the survey were used to analyse the relative perceptions of the clinical and non-clinical groups within the organisation. The main findings are listed below.

Five Most Important KPIs (Ranked)

Overall, the five most important KPIs identified from the complete survey group were as follows:

1 purchaser/referrer satisfaction (N=38);
2 patient's progress (N=29);
3 financial result (N=27);
4 staff turnover (N=25);
5 compliance with the Care Programme Approach (N=22).

Clinical staff's five most important indicators were:

1 purchaser/referrer satisfaction (N=25);
2 compliance with the CPA progress (N=17);
3 patient's progress (N=17);
4 staff turnover (N=17);
5 training (N=14).

Non-clinical staff's most important indicators were:

1 financial result (N=14);
2 purchaser/referrer satisfaction (N=13);
3 patient's progress (N=12);
4 staff turnover (N=8);
5 patient satisfaction (N=7);

The results demonstrate a degree of correlation between clinical and non-clinical staff regarding the relative usefulness of the 22 KPIs selected for the pilot scorecard, but one notable exception was the complete lack of any financial indicators within the 'top 5s' selected by staff.

The Purchasers' Perspective

Informal interviews were conducted with three of St Andrew's major service purchasers in order to ascertain their main service expectations. A summary of the purchasers' service priorities are shown in Figure 5.2.

The purchasers questioned indicated that they struggle to identify useful clinical outcome measures for mental health services generally, this certainly points the way to future work.

Service priorities
Clear outcome measures
Effective clinical reviews and reports
Clearer indication of lengths of stay – to help planning
Staff to patient ratios
Ability to secure a bed at short notice
Good communication/relationships
Environment/atmosphere on wards/clinical areas
Incidence of serious untoward incidents/complaints
Information on planned and actual clinical inputs

Notes

1 Listing of purchasers' main service expectations and priorities.
2 Results derived from informal interviews conducted with three of St Andrew's major service purchasers.

Figure 5.2 Purchasers' expectations

The Referrers' Perspective

Referrers to the service are another important group of stakeholders. As part of a recent market research exercise, a number of actual and potential referrers to St Andrew's were interviewed and amongst other questions were asked about their expectations of the service. The most important issues are summarised in Figure 5.3.

Service priorities
Ease of access to senior clinicians
Relevant clinical reports/reviews
Fast, responsive service
Length of stay
Clear communication about admissions process and timescales
Experienced multi-disciplinary clinical teams
Effective discharge procedures

Notes

1   Listing of referrers' main service expectations and priorities.
2   Results derived from informal interviews conducted as part of a market research exercise with a number of actual and potential referrers to St Andrew's.

Figure 5.3   Referrers' expectations

Discussion

The Performance Management System

Aware that its performance management approach was dominated by regular reports indicating financial and bed occupancy performance, SAGH decided to develop a performance measurement system that introduced greater balance into its board reports. The organisation decided to develop a measurement system based on the balanced scorecard approach. The decision to adopt the balanced scorecard was largely influenced by one director who was responsible for emphasising the need to improve the hospital's performance management system.

The balanced scorecard approach certainly helped SAGH to think more broadly about its performance management strategy and to consider dimensions of performance other than finance and activity. Furthermore, the 'key performance indicators' initiative within the hospital helped to generate ideas and debate about how the organisation could generally improve its information intelligence, which was a very positive by-product of the project.

The hospital would have also benefited from considering other frameworks and particularly that developed by Fitzgerald and colleagues (Fitzgerald et al., 1991) which was designed specifically for service sector industries. The Fitzgerald model specifically considered the complexities of introducing a performance management system into a service organisation with its specific characteristics such as, intangibility, heterogeneity, simultaneity and perishability.

SAGH is a complex health care organisation which had to adapt the performance management system to its unique set of characteristics and circumstances. Operating in the public sector and particularly within the mental health field presented a further set of challenges in addition to the generic characteristics of service industry businesses when developing and implementing a performance measurement system. The key difficulty with mental health care organisations is developing measures that effectively indicate the effectiveness of treatment interventions. This problem was experienced with the SAGH project.

Strategic Objectives

Kaplan and Norton suggest that periodic financial statements must play an essential role in reminding executives that improved quality, new products and so on are the means to an end and not the end in itself, which is improved sales, reduced operating expenses or higher asset utilisation (Kaplan and Norton, 1996). The authors argue that the ultimate rationale for a more balanced approach to performance measurement is improved financial performance.

The absence of such a simplistic ultimate strategy means that public sector managers have to define tightly what the organisation's strategic objectives are in order to provide staff with a clear unambiguous goal. However, this is not a simple exercise and there is much debate about what should constitute an acceptable strategy. The strategy within health care organisations is to improve the health of patients. The difficulty comes when one considers how to define improved health and whose definition should be accepted as the 'right' one. Heterogeneity is the key to this debate, as perceptions regarding whether health has been improved in any one case will vary between the different stakeholders involved, including the clinical staff, the patient, their carers, the managers, community health council representative and so on.

The difficulty in definition is magnified in the field of mental health care, where perceptions regarding whether or not a patient's health has been improved following the interventions of health care professionals can vary widely. However, defining what is an acceptable outcome of treatment is fundamental and has to be agreed before useful consideration can be given to how to measure whether or not the service is performing well or if corrective actions are required. Such difficulties in determining organisational strategy can lead to the development of strategies that say everything and nothing in order to satisfy the 'needs' of all key stakeholders such that everyone is happy with the words on the page. Such strategies end up being a fudge and do not help staff focus on priorities for action. It is also very difficult to develop a performance management system in such circumstances that provides KPIs that are useful to managers in helping to steer the organisation towards what is/are ill conceived and ambiguous strategic goals.

The corporate strategic objectives of an organisation should directly influence the development of its performance management system in order to ensure that the KPIs implemented help the organisation achieve its objectives. The framework shown in Figure 5.1 highlights additional factors which have an impact upon the development of the performance measurement system including, the organisation's processes and systems, the needs of stakeholders, information technology requirements and integrating all levels of the organisation.

As of August 2000, the pilot is nearing completion, and although the CEO and Project Director referred to previously have both left St. Andrew's Hospital, the new CEO is absolutely committed to using a balanced scorecard and is actively sponsoring the project. In addition, continuity has been maintained with the project manager promoted to the role of project director.

While there is still a tendency towards an emphasis on the financial KPIs, clinical commitment to the development and implementation of non-financial measures continues. However, it is proving difficult to develop reliable indicators of clinical effectiveness.

While the board is coming to terms with the balanced scorecard, and 'trusting' the information, the information is beginning to be used by the board to help manage the organisation even before the end of the pilot! In addition, the wider effects on organisational behaviour are already being felt, as staff adapt working practice to ensure 'good' scores.

Conclusions

Selection of a performance system should encompass the dimensions or categories of performance that so often are not considered important by short-term, financially focused Boards. The literature highlights a number of dimensions such as finance, customer perspective, service development and so on. Within each of the categories of performance individual KPIs should be selected to provide measures of performance in the key areas that will identify where action or further investigation is required to ensure that the organisation's strategic objectives are achieved. These KPIs should provide a balanced and integrated picture of an organisation's performance indicating past performance as well as providing measures of factors that determine future performance. Furthermore, the selected KPIs should be linked in a series of cause and effect relationships critical to the success of the business.

Routine monitoring of the KPIs should indicate where action and adjustments are required to steer the organisation towards attainment of its strategic objectives. The measures should also help to communicate the organisation's progress to its stakeholders in addition to providing information for planning and business deliberations about an organisation's future strategy.

While difficult to implement, the journey is truly worthwhile for the benefits resulting from the programme within SAGH included:

- wider understanding throughout the organisation of what drives success – both clinical and business;
- greater ownership of indicators through involvement in design and implementation;
- enhanced reflective practice throughout the Group;
- greater commitment to continued 'business improvement' in all aspects of our service.

Of the many lessons learnt throughout this programme, the following are salient pointers to anyone considering a similar exercise:

- clarity of purpose necessary;
- senior management commitment from the start paramount;
- walk-the-talk;
- process mapping necessary to ensure relevant indicators selected;
- involve front-line staff;
- communicate, communicate and communicate;

- ensure that the KPIs lead to management action to improve performance;
- ensure that the KPIs selected link to achieving the organisation's strategic objectives.

Acknowledgement

This paper is based on an MBA dissertation carried out by James Watkins at Warwick Business School with support from Paul Walley, Course Lecturer.

References

Anthony, R.N. (1989), 'Reminiscences about Management Accounting', *Journal of Management Accounting Research* (Fall), Vol. 1, No. 1.

Buckley, P. (Director of Contracting and Service Development) (1997), 'Performance Indicators and Instrument Panel; St Andrew's Hospital towards the 21st Century', December.

Bungay, S. and Goold, M. (1991), 'Creating a Strategic Control System', *Long range Planning*, 24, 3.

Collier, D.A. (1994), *The Service/Quality Solution – Using Service Management to Gain Competitive Advantage*, Irwin, New York.

Department of Health (1998), 'Modernising Mental Health Services, Safe Sound and Supportive', Department of Health, London.

Fitzgerald, L., Johnston, R., Brignall, S., Silvestro, R. and Voss, C. (1991), *Performance Measurement in Service Businesses*, CIMA.

Kaplan, R.S. and Norton, D.P. (1996), *The Balanced Scorecard: Translating Strategy into Action*, Harvard Business School Press, Boston (first published in 1992).

Nanni, A.J. et al. (1992), 'Integrated Performance Management: Management accounting to support the new Manufacturing Realities', *Journal of Management Accounting Research*, 4, Fall, pp. 1–19.

Smith, P. (1995), 'On the Unintended Consequences of Publishing Performance Data in the Public Sector', *International Journal of Public Administration*, 18 (2&3), pp. 227–310.

Chapter Six

Benchmarking Bed Management:
the State of the Art?
An Exploration of Best Practice
in Bed Management

Ruth Boaden, Paul Haywood, John Turner and Mary Massey

Introduction

The hospital bed has traditionally been considered a major 'unit of currency' within the NHS, in that the status of consultants was often perceived to be related to the number of beds that they could each claim to control (Audit Commission, 1992). Finding beds for patients was an administrative function carried out under the direction of consultants. However, this system broke down when staff found they were spending increasing amounts of time searching for beds and arguing about their relative 'rights' to admit patients to them (Green and Armstrong, 1994). Recent years have seen a major change in this 'ownership' rationale, spurred on by a profound change in political thinking. Beds are now seen as a dynamic and flexible resource to be managed locally in response to contracted patient workload (Audit Commission, 1992). This has put the onus on hospital management to develop new and innovative ways of bed capacity planning. Such a requirement has become increasingly pressing as hospitals are faced with the problem of relatively high waiting lists (National Audit Office (NAO), 2000) – a consequence of the significant increase in numbers of both elective (i.e. pre-booked) and non-elective (i.e. emergency) in-patient admissions. Around 50,000 patients each year are having their operations cancelled at the last minute (ibid.).

However, there has also been a marked change in the way that acute hospital beds are being used; patients are now being treated and discharged much more rapidly than in the recent past. There was a 60 per cent increase in

Quality in Health Care: Strategic Issues in Health Care Management, H.T.O. Davies, M. Tavakoli and M. Malek (eds), Ashgate Publishing Ltd, 2001.

the average number of in-patients being treated in each acute hospital bed period between 1977 and 1988 (Audit Commission, 1992). It was also predicted that the reduction of perceived inefficiencies in bed usage would result in a reduction in the need for in-patient beds nationwide by almost one third (ibid.). Such a reduction in numbers has been achieved but is now being reviewed (Department of Health, 2000) due to frequent crises in bed availability across the UK.

This chapter describes research into the process of bed management at three NHS Trusts. The main focus of the work was on University Hospitals Aintree Trust (AHNT) in Liverpool, and it is this hospital's bed management system that is analysed in depth. Another two hospitals were also studied – Salford Royal Hospitals NHS Trust (SRHNT) and South Manchester University Hospitals Trust (SMUHNT), both of which are in Greater Manchester, and their bed management systems are benchmarked against those at AHNT. The objective of the study was to document practice, compare it with other Trusts and identify elements of best practice.

Background

In 1992 the Audit Commission produced a report entitled *Lying in Wait* (Audit Commission, 1992) which provided NHS Trusts with considerable background into the concept of bed management and also offered them broad guidelines regarding what hospitals should consider in order to implement and operate an effective bed management system. Previous to this there was very little literature on bed management, but subsequently a number of other reports, papers and documents have been written by various health-related agencies discussing bed management systems, although there is little if any documentation of best practice in terms of case studies.

Lying in Wait (Audit Commission, 1992) examined in detail both the 'flow' of patients through a hospital and how beds should be managed and allocated, and regarded the efficient use of hospitals beds as being achieved by good practice in five key interrelated areas (Figure 6.1):

- admission – how patients are referred and admitted to hospital;
- placement – how patients are allocated to a bed and under which consultant;
- stay – how the patients' time in hospital is organised and controlled;
- discharge – how and when arrangements are made for patients to leave hospital.

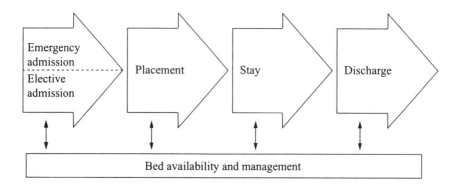

Figure 6.1   The elements of bed management

Source: Audit Commission, 1992.

*   bed availability and management – how hospital beds are matched to the patient workload.

The report then considered each element in depth, looking at the practices and problems that militated against optimal bed use and suggesting ways that these obstacles could be overcome.

The National Audit Office study (NAO, 2000), which looks at the practices and performance of hospital admission and bed management, was published in February 2000. It acted as authoritative evidence for the drawing of conclusions and recommendations, presented for consideration by the Committee of Public Accounts (a committee of Members of Parliament). It also contained specific examples of successful practice and good performance in bed management. At the time of writing no formal recommendations have yet been published but this study is the most up to date and comprehensive presentation of the state of bed management to have been produced.

This chapter describes the benchmarking of the bed management process. Benchmarking is 'the search for industry best practices, which lead to superior performance' (Cross and Leonard, 1994, p. 56). There are three main categories of benchmarking activity: internal, competitive and functional/generic (ibid., p. 58). Internal benchmarking is where one department in a organisation benchmarks a similar activity with one or more other internal departments. Competitive benchmarking involves comparing organisational performance with direct competition and functional/generic benchmarking compares specific functions in an organisation with the best in industry. The work described in this chapter was of the functional/generic type as it was a comparison of a specific function. However, this could not be done 'with the best in industry' (ibid.), as this standard has not yet been defined. The benchmarking was therefore performed with two comparable bed management systems in terms of the quantity of allocable hospital beds, patient admission numbers and the length of time the bed management function had been operating as a 24-hour activity. In this research, only the planning and analysis (ibid.) phases were undertaken, with the integration and action phases left to the management of the Trusts concerned after the end of this stage of research.

Methodology

The methodology used for this research was 'phenomenological' (primarily qualitative) in that it was concerned with understanding human behaviour from the author's own frame of reference (Hussey and Hussey, 1997). The work had all the features of this paradigm in that it:

- produced more qualitative data than quantitative data;
- was based on a small sample (three hospitals);
- was undertaken within a natural location;
- generated theories;
- sought to understand what happens in a situation.

The prime means of gathering information was through interviewing. Most of the interviews were undertaken by use of an 'interview guide' which required a semi-structured but informal style (Gilbert, 1993). This allowed for the possibility of nondirective interviewing in which the interviewee's replies determined the course of the interview.

The interviews were largely undertaken with the General Manager – Medical Services (GMMS), the Admission and Discharge Co-ordinator (A&D Co-ord.) and some Bed Managers at AHNT. However other shorter and more ad-hoc interviews were also required with the appropriate managers and clinicians from other directorates and with social workers and related staffs from departments external to the hospital. Interviews were carried out with several Bed Managers at the two Manchester hospitals, and with these hospitals' Discharge Co-ordinators and social workers. The interview guide technique offered useful insights into how the staff worked and the methods they used, and offered useful anecdotes that brought issues and problems to the fore.

The data from the interviews was translated into a series of flowcharts to describe the process of bed management. It is not possible to reproduce the level of detail from the original research here (Haywood, 1999), but standard flowchart notation was used. A variation on standard notation was developed specifically for this work to illustrate a very high-level process summary. It has been termed a summary chart, but is designed, as is a standard flowchart, to act as a device in the study of processes and to provide a visual representation.

Each summary chart gives a one page précis of one complete process and illustrates the most common movements of patients and information, without showing some of the more unusual movements. It begins with a 'start' from where a patient first enters the process. The patient then flows through the process via the sub-processes, which are illustrated as fine-lined boxes and referenced with the sub-processes' name and number. The arrows indicate the direction of patient flow during their transformation depending on the type of patient and their specific circumstances. Arrows also indicate how the sub-processes interrelate with other sub-processes, and how sub-processes feed inputs into other processes (shown as thick-lined, round-cornered boxes containing the process name and number). Clear arrows and boxes indicate physical patient movement, whereas arrows with dotted lines and hatched boxes indicate the movement of patient information. The summary chart also illustrates process buffers (in broken-lined ovals) and external influences (in dotted hexagons). Patients who have moved through the complete hospital transformation process leave ('end') the processing.

Results

Background to the Trusts Studied

Prior to 1996, AHNT provided a bed management service whereby one full-time Bed Manager ('F' grade nurse) allocated patients to hospital beds between 9.00 am and 5.00 pm each day. She collected information frequently each day regarding the location of empty beds throughout the hospital and then used her clinical knowledge to arrange patient placement into a bed on the most appropriate ward for the patient's condition. Out of regular working hours the junior doctors and nursing staff in AED took on the role of Bed Manager.

In 1996 the senior management at AHNT acknowledged that its part-time bed management system was both inefficient and anything but 'customer focused' (that is, it failed to put the patient first). They therefore authorised the extension of the bed management role to cover 24-hour working in line with best practice, thereby raising the profile of the process within the Trust. In 1997 the Trust's Chief Executive nominated the GMMS to take responsibility for overseeing and improving the bed management task for the acute beds within the hospital. A fundamental review led to some key changes, which included:

- establishing an IT database for the input of hospital admission and discharge statistical data to allow trend analysis and to underpin future planning and forecasting of bed demand;
- agreeing a series of performance indicators against which standards for bed management could be measured;
- designing a forecasting tool which would enable appropriate action to be taken in response to pressures and to maximise elective work;
- introducing a hospital-wide bed management team to provide clinical leadership and high level management input.

The result of the review was that a rota of staff was established to work continuously on the hospital's bed management activity (see Table 6.1). Subsequently a Low Dependency Unit (LDU) Liaison Officer was appointed to supervise patient discharge into the LDU – a building with 60 en-suite bedrooms on the AHNT estate, privately owned and managed by Swallow Hotels. Hospital statistics gathered over the following year showed that:

- the practice of cancelling elective procedures on the day of operation, due to lack of bed availability, had been virtually eliminated within the Trust;
- patterns of daily admissions into and discharges from the hospital could be estimated with a 95 per cent confidence interval, thereby enabling the anticipation of demand and thus enhancing capacity planning.

The current structure of the bed management function is shown in Table 6.1, which compares AHNT with SRHNT and SMUHNT.

AHNT has a total of 1,200 beds, with 310 beds dedicated to maternity, neurological and mental health units and controlled by their own bed resource managers, leaving 890 controlled by the bed management function. Patients largely come from three social service areas: Liverpool (40 per cent); Sefton (40 per cent); and Knowsley (20 per cent). Sefton and Liverpool social services have social workers permanently on site; Sefton social services social workers are responsible for three wards each and Liverpool for six wards.

Table 6.1   Structure of the bed management function at the three Trusts

	AHNT	SRHNT	SMUHNT
Senior staff	Admission and Discharge Co-ordinator (G grade)	Senior Bed Manager (H grade)	Senior Bed Manager (management grade)
Day staff	4 Bed Managers (F grade) LDU Liaison officer (F grade)	5 Bed Managers (F grade)	4 f/t, 12 p/t staff (F grade) (=10 FTEs total)
Night coverage	3 permanent night staff (do other duties too)	Night Managers	Night Managers
Discharge co-ordination	A&D Co-ordinator (see Senior Staff)	OT: not part of team	G grade nurse: reports to Senior Bed Manager
Uniform	Worn by Discharge Co-ordinators but not Bed Managers	Worn by all bed management team and considered to be important for liaison and communication	Worn by Discharge Co-ordinators but not Bed Managers

Full-time bed management at SRHNT has been established for the past two years (see Table 6.1). The Discharge Co-ordinator is located in a different part of the hospital. There are plans for daily meetings with the bed management team, to move the office nearer to the bed management team and eventually to integrate her as part of the team. SRHNT only has Salford social services to deal with – their social workers are ward based, with one per ward.

SMUHNT is currently comprised of Wythenshawe Hospital and Withington Hospital, both located in south Manchester, four miles apart. Bed management started at SMUHNT in 1995 with a senior Bed Manager and two assistants, one for each site. In 1997, a full time shift system was started. The current structure is shown in Table 6.1. At SMUHNT the vast majority of patients are from the Manchester social services area (90 per cent) and the social workers are ward based.

The two sites together have 1,215 beds, with Withington being the bigger by only 70 beds. The Bed Managers control 939 beds (464 at Withington and 475 at Wythenshawe), not including psychiatric, paediatric and maternity wards. However, due to staffing difficulties 100 of the Trusts beds are long-term closed.

The two Manchester hospitals utilise the Greater Manchester Bed Management System (GMBMS) system, which was established in 1997 following collaborative work between 14 Greater Manchester hospital trusts, their respective Health Authorities and the Greater Manchester Ambulance Service (GMAS) who provided the technical infrastructure and ongoing technical support. It was introduced with the aim of assisting in the rapid transfer of emergency patients requiring hospital admission from a hospital which had a severe short-term bed shortage to another hospital with no current bed shortage (Boaden et al., 1998).

Each of the 14 participating hospitals is linked to the GMBMS system and Bed Managers regularly update the central database via their terminal to inform the other participating hospitals of their current bed status. A simple colour-coding indicator is used where each hospital is coded as Red (a hospital is full and can only 'treat and transfer' emergency patients), Amber (the hospital has reached its agreed minimum of beds and will therefore only assess and admit GP referred patients from its own catchment area plus patients transferred from a Red hospital) or Green (the hospital has available beds).

Statistical Comparative Summary of the Trusts

Table 6.2 presents a summary of the key comparative data between the three hospitals.

Process Flow Charts

The main charts outlining the processes involved in the admission/placement/ stay/discharge stages (Audit Commission, 1992) for any patient at AHNT are shown in Figures 6.2–6.5. The details of how these compare with the other two Trusts in the study are discussed below.

Discussion

The similarities and differences between the methods of working within each of the sub-process procedures for the benchmark hospitals when compared to AHNT are summarised in Table 6.3. The term 'different' is used to indicate major differences in methods, not minor matters such as alternative methods

Table 6.2   Comparison of key statistics for the three Trusts in the study

Description (all admission figures are quoted at the 4 year average)	AHNT	SRHNT		SMUHNT	
No of beds (allocable by Bed Managers)	890	804*		939*	
Day-time bed management staff (by site)	4	5	1	5^	5^
Beds/bed management staff (by site)	222	112	244	92	95
Average total patient admissions per day/ bed management staff	41.8	23.5		21.7	
No of Discharge Co-ordinators	1	1		1	
Bed occupancy level (estimated)	97%	97%		97%	
Total emergencies via AED	23,033	11,645		15,198	
Average emergencies via AED/day	63	32		42	
Total 'other' emergencies	8,300	13,673		17,165	
Average 'other' emergencies/day	23	37		47	
Total emergencies	31,333	25,319		32,363	
Average emergencies/day	86	69		89	
Total electives	11,752	8,527		21,038	
Average electives/day	32	23		58	
Total day cases	18,158	17,794		25,980	
Average day cases/day	50	49		71	
Total admissions	61,093	51,639		79,340	
Average total admissions/day	167	141		217	

Notes

*   Does not include closed beds.
^   Estimates for part time staff.

of data collection, doing things at different times, or small differences in times for various activities.

The key differences are discussed below:

Admission Process (Process 1)

Sub-Process 1.2 – Elective Patient Summoning Procedure

Patient classification: medical elective patient At AHNT, medical elective patients are called in by the bed management team, which enables AHNT to balance the level of medical elective work with the demand from emergency

Process summary

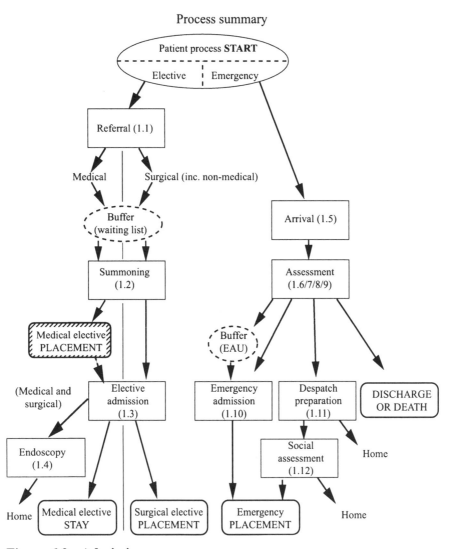

Figure 6.2   Admission process

patients. However this is not the case at the two benchmark Trusts. The medical waiting list at SRHNT is kept, updated and controlled by the appropriate specialty which, on the Bed Manager's authority, arranges for patient admission. At SMUHNT there is only a five-day medical ward – consultants draw up the lists of patients to come in, and they are summoned by the ward nursing staff without any bed management authority or intervention.

Process summary

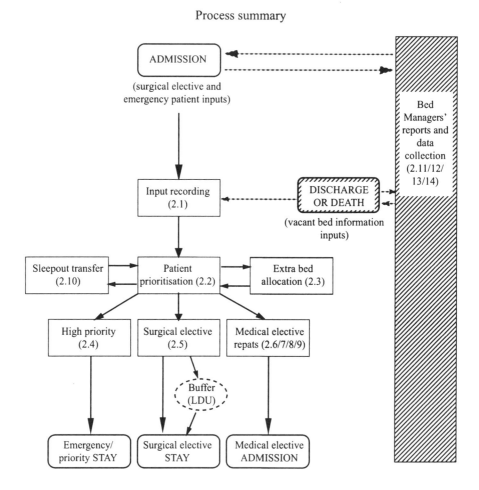

Figure 6.3   Placement process

Patient classification: surgery/non-medical elective patients Like AHNT, surgery and non-medical elective patients at both hospitals are called forward by consultants and the Bed Managers have no influence on their summoning. Also like AHNT, the consultants have no knowledge of the expected bed availability, and the Bed Managers have no knowledge of expected length of patient stay. However, at SRHNT the Bed Managers are given several weeks notice of who is coming in depending on the specialty, but – similarly to AHNT – this information is only used as a general planning aid.

Process summary

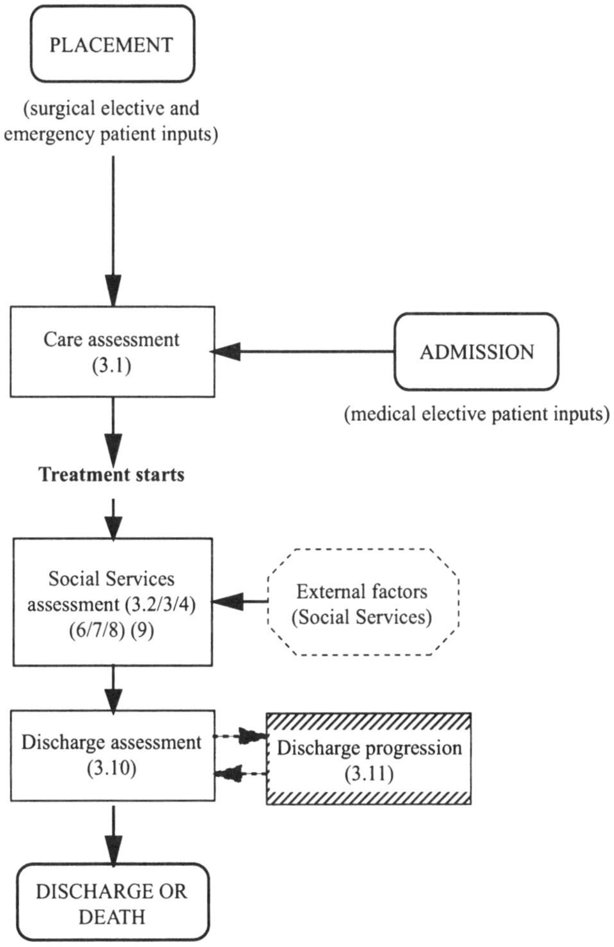

Figure 6.4   Stay process

Sub-Process 1.5 – Emergency Patient Categorisation and Registration Procedure

Emergency patient capacity Both the benchmark hospitals can employ GMAS to move emergency patients to other hospitals after initial AED treatment if their beds are full. AHNT have no such information system informing them of capacity available at other hospitals. Whilst it is very unusual for SRHNT

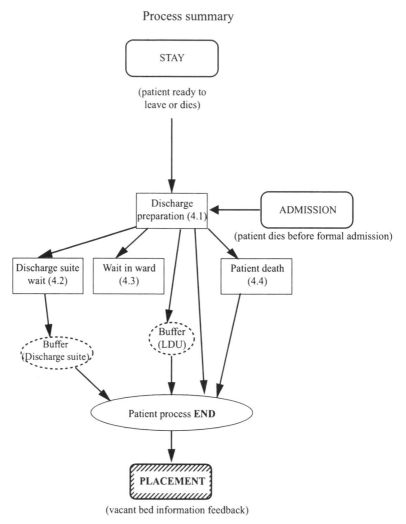

Process summary

Figure 6.5   **Discharge or death**

to transfer patients in this way, it is very common at SMUHNT who, in the first six months of 1999, have treated and transferred 172 patients to other hospitals.

Sub-Process 1.8 – Moving and Assessing EAU Patient Procedure

Input buffering SRHNT has an input buffer ward called the Medical Assessment Ward (A3) into which it moves its GP referrals and appropriate

Table 6.3   Comparison of hospital ways of working by sub-process

Process		Sub-process		Ways of working	
No.	*Name*	*No.*	*Name of procedure*	*SRHNT*	*SMUHNT*
1	Admission	1.1	Elective patient referral	Same	Same
		1.2	Elective patient summoning	Different	Different
		1.3	Elective patient admission	Same	Same
		1.4	Elective patient endoscopy	Same	Same
		1.5	Emergency patient categorisation and Registration	Different	Different
		1.6	Moving and assessing critical care patient	Different	Different
		1.7	Moving and assessing high urgency patient	Same	Same
		1.8	Moving and assessing EAU patient	Same	Different
		1.9	Moving and assessing lower urgency patient	Same	Same
		1.10	Emergency patient admission	Same	Same
		1.11	Emergency patient hospital despatch	Same	Same
		1.12	Emergency patient OT/social assessment	Different	Different
2	Placement	2.1	Pre-placement patient recording	Same	Same
		2.2	Initial consideration factors prior to placement	Same	Same
		2.3	Extra bed allocation	Different	Different
		2.4	Placement of non-elective and LDU patients	Same	Same
		2.5	Elective surgery placement	Different	Different
		2.6	Initial tasks prior to placement of high priority elective patients	Same	Same
		2.7	Initial tasks prior to placement of routine elective patients	Different	Different
		2.8	Placement for medical elective patients	Same	Same
		2.9	Repatriation	Same	Same
		2.10	Sleepout transfer	Different	Different
		2.11	Bed Managers' A shift duties	Same	Same
		2.12	Bed Managers' B shift duties	Same	Same
		2.13	Bed Managers' C shift duties	Same	Same
		2.14	Shift ward walk-around	Different	Different
3	Stay	3.1	Initial patient care requirement	Same	Same
		3.2–3.8	Social Services referral	Different	Different
		3.9	Residence selection	Same	Same
		3.10	Patient discharge assessment	Same	Same
		3.11	A&D Co-ord.'s discharge progression	Different	Different
4	Discharge or death	4.1	Initial patient discharge	Same	Same
		4.2	Discharge suite	Different	Different
		4.3	Ward discharge	Same	Same
		4.4	Patient death	Same	Same

Triage Category 3 patients from AED without needing to refer to the Bed Managers. This is similar to the AHNT Emergency Admissions Unit (EAU), where the patient receives non-specialist care, prior to a doctor assessing them and either admitting or despatching them. SMUHNT also has a Medical Assessment Unit (MAU) where general medical patients are moved directly from AED, assessed and those suitable for discharge filtered out with the remainder being admitted usually within 24 hours.

Sub-Process 1.12 – Emergency Patient Occupational Therapist (OT)/Social Assessment Procedure

AED social assessment At AHNT, patients over 75 years old or any patients who report social problems to the AED staff must be assessed by the AED OT or AED social worker (who work 9.00 am–5.00 pm). Outside of these hours, any patient that a doctor in AED considers has OT or social problems must be admitted into the hospital until they can be professionally assessed. SRHNT has an AED social worker plus an OT, a physiotherapist, a charity worker from Age Concern, a Community Psychiatric Nurse (CPN) and an alcohol liaison officer all working 9.00 am–5.00 pm (except the CPN who work in shifts up to midnight). There is also 24-hour access to a social worker. At SMUHNT social workers, physiotherapists and district nurses are attached to each AED from 9.00 am–5.00 pm (but they have no OT presence). There is also 24-hour access to a social worker. Once patients go to the acute wards from either hospital they fall under the ward social worker jurisdiction and must be referred to them by the standard procedure, which like AHNT can take up to three days.

Placement Process (Process 2)

Sub-Process 2.5 – Elective Surgery Placement Procedure

LDU input buffering Neither hospital has an elective patient input buffer such as a Patient Hotel. Instead, the benchmark hospitals instruct elective patients to phone the specialty wards on their morning of admission, and the patient is informed whether a bed is available.

Sub-Process 2.10 – Outliers Transfer Procedure

Internal prioritising Unlike AHNT, both SRHNT and SMUHNT routinely move their medical and surgical outliers back into the appropriate ward as soon as a bed is available.

Sub-Process 2.14 – Shift Ward Walk-Around Procedure

Communications and liaison The SRHNT Bed Managers walk around all the wards at 8.30 am and at 5.00 pm. They also ring round all wards for information at 10.00 am and 1.00 pm. SMUHNT Bed Managers walk around the hospital four times a day at each site. They also update their Admission Department at midnight on the bed state. Unlike AHNT, which places patients immediately on notification of a free bed during the walk-around, both hospitals usually collect all the data on all empty beds around all the wards before acting upon that information and placing emergency patients or permitting wards to call in elective patients.

Management information collection The benchmark hospitals have a similar system of data collection, recording and dissemination. However, neither hospital collects as much data as AHNT, and neither routinely send data summaries to their executive officers apart from SMUHNT which sends the Director of Strategy and Development its daily bed state statistics. The benchmark hospitals send statistics each week to the Greater Manchester Emergency Admission Project Manager regarding AED admissions and associated data.

Stay Process (Process 3)

Sub-Processes 3.2 to 3.8 – Social Services Procedures

Case recording At AHNT there are different procedures for each of the three social services involved. SRHNT carries out two kinds of discharge assessment; a Joint Assessment for Discharge (JAD) and the 'standard' assessment (SA) (the author's term as the hospital has none). JAD is used to assess acute medical patients and general surgery elective patients, who tend to be simpler assessments and so only involve a small team of assessors. However, unlike AHNT the social services documentation used during assessment is the same for the vast majority of patients since most are Salford referrals. SMUHNT are currently using a system similar to the SA system at SRHNT, but they are changing in September 1999 to a new system of screening, based on an identical multi-disciplinary assessment plan much like the SRHNT JAD.

Case screening At AHNT, most social services will contact the ward within two days of a patient's referral to confirm the patient's discharge date. Patients are screened for a full assessment of need only once the clinicians have finished both treatment and any rehabilitation, and social services may take up to seven days to complete this. Patients at SRHNT are visited and screened within 48 hours of their referral if they are on a JAD referral. Unlike AHNT however, the SA patients at SRHNT are often screened and assessed on a partial basis before clinically fit. SMUHNT currently work on a similar system to the SA, where patients are seen within 24 hours of referral. The new SMUHNT Discharge/Assessment Plan screening scheme intends to make assessing even more rapid and responsive.

Case Problems At SRHNT, multidisciplinary meetings are called each week by most wards to discuss patients, and case conferences are called by the Discharge Co-ordinator for specific problem patients in order to brainstorm a solution. SMUHNT too has weekly based multidisciplinary meetings of some wards for updates on delayed discharges, and case conferences are called as required by the appropriate ward social workers.

Sub-Process 3.11 – Admission and A&D Co-ord.'s Discharge Progression Procedure

Patient discharge hastening and progressing Each week the SRHNT Discharge Co-ordinator phones each ward to monitor delayed patients and their problems with discharge. At SMUHNT the Discharge Co-ordinator walks around the Trust on one day every week and collates information on delayed discharge for a weekly report. A comparison of patient discharge figures between the three Trusts is shown in Table 6.3. The SRHNT data is taken from a four month average from May–July 1999, whilst the SMUHNT data is from one week in July 1999 which was stated to be typical.

Discharge or Death Process (Process 4)

Sub-Process 4.2 – Discharge Suite Procedure

Discharge suite output buffer SRHNT does not have a Discharge Suite that could operate as an output buffer. SMUHNT has one at the Wythenshawe site in an area adjoined to the MAU, but largely because of staff supervision problems in this ward its use is not encouraged and hence it is unused.

Table 6.4   Comparison of delayed discharge patients at three hospitals

	Delayed patients	Total days bed blocked	Average days bed blocking/ patient	% hospital beds blocked (no of beds)
Trust (SS)				
AHNT (Sefton)	19	687	36}	}
AHNT (Liverpool)	34	1,265	37} 38	} 6.85% (890)
AHNT (Knowsley)	8	355	44}	}
SRHNT (Salford)	29	400	14	3.60% (804) *
SMUHNT (Manchester)	5	153	31} 63	} 1.19% (839)
SMUHNT (others)	5	475	95}	}

*   Does not include closed beds.

Conclusions

Recognised Best Practice

All the hospitals in the study operated a centralised bed management model under the supervision of a designed officer, which was described by the HSA (1997) as best practice. Moreover, all operated 24 hours, 365 days-a-year systems (HSA, 1997).

Patient buffers are good practice in bed management to reduce pressure points and bottlenecks in AED and the wards (LHEC, 1996); but only AHNT operates a wide range of input and output buffers. The different procedures for managing placement of elective patients at the benchmark hospitals meant that they had less need of such buffers, and so it is not clear what could be regarded as best practice in this area.

The best bed management systems should involve regular dialogue, feedback and reviews with the CE or senior management (ibid.), but only AHNT undertakes this routinely. This may be related to the position in the organisation of the person with key responsibility for the bed management function.

Hospitals should not accept outlying as a fact of life (ibid.), but this is largely accepted by all Trusts in this study, although only done after much consideration. This may relate to the overall high levels of bed occupancy which, it is proposed, will lead to such problems (Bagust, 1999).

It is important that discharge issues are addressed as early as possible in the stay process (NAO, 2000). AHNT appears to be the tardiest of the three hospitals at starting at least a cursory assessment of patients' discharge issues, with almost no pre-assessment interviews and practically no social services involvement with a patient until their treatment is completed.

Potential Best Practice

This study did not aim to assess whether the discharge procedures at SRHNT or SMUHNT were necessarily better than AHNT as insufficient time was available to fully study these systems and compare them analytically. What is clear is that SRHNT and SMUHNT both have far fewer clinically well patients bed blocking, and their delayed discharge rates are very small in comparison with that at AHNT (Table 6.4). This is believed to be largely a result of SRHNT and SMUHNT each only having one main social services involved with patient discharge, giving more ward-based social workers and a more unified way of working across each hospital. Also, their Health Authorities currently have fewer funding issues, which means that the inbuilt delays caused by patients having their funding cases considered at social services panel meetings each period just do not occur. It is interesting to speculate whether the development of funding problems at the benchmark hospitals would result in bed blocking rates increasing to those seen at AHNT, or whether the Manchester hospitals have sufficiently robust and flexible procedures to still keep their patient discharge delays significantly lower. There is little literature to support this hypothesis at present, although the use of Care Co-ordinators has been shown to improve the speed of patient discharge (Bridges, 1999).

There is no accepted best practice in size or structure of the bed management function. Whilst the Bed Managers at AHNT have only one site to manage, its 'bed:bed management staff' ratio is higher than that of the main Hope site at SRHNT or either site at SMUHNT, and its 'total daily average patient admission:bed management staff' ratio is much higher than the other two hospitals. These ratios imply that AHNT utilises its staff resources very effectively. All the hospitals operate their Bed Manager teams in a similar way, but the Discharge Co-ordinators functioned very differently between the three hospitals.

AHNT were more sophisticated than the other hospitals in the data that they recorded about the bed management function and the way in which they used it. They had developed a forecasting system that enabled them to monitor availability and demand against forecast, based on moving average and data trends for over a year. This could be considered to be best practice. However, none of the hospitals used the same computer systems – each uses different types of PC programs to record data about bed management, although all are working towards a 'live' bed state system on their respective PAS. Future developments in this area will depend largely on the way in which suppliers develop PAS systems, and should be the subject of future research.

There is no agreement on the optimum location for the bed management function – AHNT and SMUHNT bed management offices were located separately to the other hospital departments, whereas the SRHNT bed management team was co-located with the Admission Department. Theoretically improved IT should make the location irrelevant.

At AHNT the close working relationship between senior clinicians from the Medical Directorate and the bed management team was observed. Although this was not the main focus of this study, and was not therefore investigated in detail at the other benchmark hospitals, it was clearly important in establishing and maintaining the status of bed management at AHNT. This aspect is to be the subject of further research.

The Way Forward

The benchmark exercise has shown that of the 35 separate sub-processes identified from the summary charts, 12 sub-processes at SRHNT and 13 at SMUHNT were operated differently to AHNT. This proportion of difference demonstrates how the task of bed management has evolved over time in the absence of either a clear framework on working practices or a guide to best practice. It also raises questions about how best practice is to be judged, and the performance measures that might be appropriate for the bed management function. This is to be the subject of further research. However, there are examples of good practice and other areas where good practice guidelines could be developed, which contribute to theory in this area and also provide practical evidence for other hospitals to assess and utilise.

Acknowledgement

The authors would like to thank all those who took part in this research, including staff at Aintree Hospitals NHS Trust, Salford Royal Hospitals NHS Trust and South Manchester University Hospitals NHS Trust.

References

Audit Commission (1992), *Lying in Wait: The use of medical beds in acute hospitals*, HMSO, London.

Bagust, A, Place, M. and Posnett, J.W. (1999), 'Dynamics of Bed Use in Accommodating Emergency Admissions: Stochastic simulation model', *British Medical Journal*, 319, pp. 155–8.

Boaden, R., Proudlove, N. and Wilson, M. (1998), *Evaluation of the 'Managing Emergency Delivery' Project – Report on Stage 2 Bed Management*, UMIST, May.

Bridges, J. (1999), 'Smooth Passage', *Health Service Journal*, 17 June, pp. 19–20.

Cross, R. and Leonard, P. (1994), 'Benchmarking: A strategic and tactical perspective', in B.G. Dale (ed.), *Managing Quality* (2nd edn), Prentice Hall, Hemel Hempstead.

Department of Health (2000), *Shaping the Future NHS: long-term planning for hospitals and related services – Consultation Document on the findings of the National Beds Inquiry*, Department of Health, London. Also available at www.doh.gov.uk/nationalbeds.htm.

Gilbert, N. (1993), 'Research, Theory and Method', in N. Gilbert (ed.), *Researching Social Life*, Sage Publications, London.

Green, J. and Armstrong, D. (1994), 'The views of service providers', in D.C. Morrell, J. Green, D. Armstrong, J. Bartholomew, F. Gelder, C. Jenkins, R. Jankowski, S. Mandalia, N. Britten, A. Shaw and R. Savill (eds), *Five Essays on Emergency Pathways*, Kings Fund Institute, for the King's Fund Commission on the Future of Acute Admissions to London Hospitals, King's Fund, London.

Haywood, P. (1999), *An Analytical and Comparative Study of Bed Management*, dissertation submitted in partial fulfilment for the degree of MSc, Manchester School of Management, UMIST, Manchester.

Health Services Accreditation (1997), *Service Standards for Emergency Medical Admissions*, HSA, Battle.

Hussey, J. and Hussey, R. (1997), *Business Research*, Macmillan Business Press, Basingstoke.

London Health Economics Consortium (LHEC) (1996), *Stocktake of Good Practice – the management of emergency admissions and beds*, LHEC, London.

National Audit Office (NAO) (2000), *Inpatient Admissions and Bed Management in NHS Acute Hospitals*, NAO, London.

Chapter Seven

Quality of Care: Should we Legislate or Educate? The Nursing Home Scenario as a Case Study

Carmel M. Hughes

Introduction

The impact of an ageing population on health resources has been widely discussed and debated within a number of different forums: government, academia, various health care settings, e.g. hospital and community. The debate has focused on the economic and social implications of an ageing population, and in 1997, some 100 major medical journals each devoted an issue to ageing (Greengross et al., 1997). The aim of this concerted strategy was to alert interested parties to the radical changes which were occurring due to the ageing population and to contribute to research and information on this important topic.

Despite the growing recognition that the ageing population represents a major challenge in health care, there has been no major government policy initiative on this topic. However, it is timely that a Royal Commission was established in the UK to consider the funding of long-term care for elderly people. The Commission, which reported in March, 1999, had been instructed to consider a number of issues, including: 'the expectations of elderly people for dignity and security in the way in which their long-term needs are met' (Royal Commission, 1999, p. 1).

Although the Commission focused on funding, it was implicit within the above statement that quality of care should also be considered and in fact, the Commission recommended a more systematic approach to the delivery and assessment of care. This is something that has long been a topic of debate in the United States, where long-term care has undergone dramatic changes in the past 10 years.

Quality in Health Care: Strategic Issues in Health Care Management, H.T.O. Davies, M. Tavakoli and M. Malek (eds), Ashgate Publishing Ltd, 2001.

Changes in the delivery of care in the USA have been largely brought about through legislation and regulation, both at the federal and state level. One particular facet of care which was a feature of this legislation was the prescribing of psychoactive medication and the appropriateness of such prescribing. Such drugs, i.e. antipsychotics, hypnotics, anxiolytics, antidepressants, have been described as 'chemical restraints', used to control problem behaviour (Institute of Medicine, 1986). It would seem from a number of studies, particularly those conducted in the USA, that this was an appropriate description of the way in which medication was being used in these institutions.

This chapter seeks to describe the background to this legislation, its implementation in the nursing home environment, its influence on nursing home care delivery, and possible lessons for the UK.

Institute of Medicine Report

In 1983, the US Congress asked the Institute of Medicine to make recommendations for improving the quality of care in nursing homes (Stoudemire and Smith, 1996). A report was published in 1986, highlighting that many studies from the early 1970s had revealed substantial evidence of appallingly bad care in many parts of the USA. Further studies in the 1980s reported that problems continued to exist in some facilities. Neglect and abuse leading to premature death, permanent injury, increased disability and unnecessary fear and suffering on the part of the residents had all been documented (Institute of Medicine, 1986). One of the key recommendations from the report was that 'each resident is to receive high-quality care to meet individual physical, mental and psychosocial needs. The care should be designed to maintain or improve the residents' physical, mental, and emotional well-being' (ibid., p. 4).

The Omnibus Budget Reconciliation Act of 1987 (OBRA 87)

Following this report, legislation was passed within the USA to improve care in nursing homes – the Nursing Home Reform Act which was embedded in the Omnibus Budget Reconciliation Act of 1987 (OBRA 87) – and was implemented in October 1991 (Elon and Pawlson, 1992; Stoudemire and Smith, 1996). This law applied to all residents of Medicare/Medicaid certified facilities regardless of residents' actual source of payment (Eichmann et al., 1992).

To implement this law, Congress directed the Health Care Financing Administration (HCFA; this federal agency is responsible for setting nursing home standards) to develop a set of regulations, outlining all aspects of nursing home operation; these regulations are further supplemented by interpretive guidelines which are used by surveyors (inspectors) who inspect the nursing home facilities (Elon and Pawlson, 1992; Streim, 1995; Llorente et al., 1998). The interpretive guidelines have generated controversy as to whether they go beyond the intent of the law, whether specific aspects of the guidelines are strictly enforceable and what the costs of implementation have been. Although the legislation, regulations and interpretive guidelines have attempted to specify and standardise the survey process nationally, individual surveyors still have to apply a degree of personal judgement in assessing deviation from the regulations. All regulations and interpretive guidelines are contained within State Operations manuals (HCFA, 1995), which detail pre-survey preparation, survey team workload, guidance on the composition of the survey team and how surveys should be conducted (they are often conducted unannounced).

If a nursing home facility is deemed not be attaining the required standard, a number of sanctions (termed 'remedies' in the documentation) are available as shown in Table 7.1.

Table 7.1   Available enforcement remedies which may be applied following survey of nursing homes

Available enforcement remedies

- Termination of the provider agreement
- Temporary management
- Denial of payment for all Medicare and/or Medicaid residents by HCFA
- Denial of payment for all new Medicare and/or Medicaid admissions
- Civil money penalty
- State monitoring
- Transfer of residents
- Transfer of residents with closure of facility
- Directed plan of correction
- Directed in-service training
- Alternative or additional state remedies approved by HCFA

Source: HCFA, 1995.

When selecting the appropriate remedy, the seriousness of the deficiency must be assessed, as specific levels of seriousness are correlated with specific categories of enforcement responses. A seriousness rating system has been developed and the factors which must be considered are as follows:

- no actual harm with a potential for minimal harm;
- no actual harm with a potential for more than minimal harm, but not immediate jeopardy;
- actual harm that is not immediate jeopardy;
- immediate jeopardy to resident health or safety.

Additionally, consideration must be given as to whether deficiencies are isolated, constitute a pattern or are widespread (HCFA, 1995).

OBRA has focused on a number of issues within long-term care, with regulations pertaining to the following key areas:

- quality of care and resident rights;
- resident assessment and care planning;
- use of physical restraints;
- drug therapy guidelines.

As a means to assist in standardisation of care, it was necessary to develop an instrument which could be used in the collection of patient data. The Resident Assessment Instrument (RAI) was produced by a research consortium in conjunction with HCFA (Morris et al., 1990) and which has since been updated to Version 2.0 (Morris et al., 1997). It includes a set of central assessment items known as the Minimum Data Set (MDS) and 18 Resident Assessment Protocols (RAPs); the latter guide the assessor through the best practice of care planning for common problems experienced in the elderly e.g. falls, cognitive loss/dementia. Items within the MDS which indicate that the resident is having a particular problem, act as a trigger to the implementation of a specific RAP for that problem (Fries et al., 1997). MDS data can be linked to Medicare information, enabling resident assessment to be related to health services use. In the vast majority of cases, it has been the nursing staff who have been responsible for the collection of this information (Marek et al., 1996).

Outcomes from OBRA

This comprehensive data collection and care planning strategy has generated a huge administrative burden for nursing homes, but receipt of Medicare and Medicaid payments and continued accreditation are reliant on this system. Perhaps more importantly, with this level of regulation, inspection and sanction, the outcomes from this legislation have been eagerly awaited. At this stage, the literature is suggesting that quality of care has improved at a process level, but in terms of patient-related outcomes, this is much more difficult to ascertain. Marek et al. (1996) reported the perspectives of a broad group of nursing home employees, regulators, advocates and professional associations on whether the legislation had produced positive change for residents. The general consensus was that quality of nursing care had improved, although some respondents perceived that physician practice had not changed markedly after the introduction of OBRA.

Resident Assessment and Care Planning

As previously discussed, the MDS/RAI has been the main means by which resident assessment and care planning are organised and implemented. Work has been emanating from some research groups on the clinical outcomes in patients.

Hawes et al. (1997) reported that through the implementation of the RAI, the process of care had improved in a number of aspects. The accuracy of information in residents' medical records increased substantially as did the completeness and comprehensiveness of care plans. Specific aspects of care which improved included a decline in the use of physical restraints and in-dwelling catheters. Examples of good practice were also more evident after the implementation of the RAI with the presence of advance directives, participation in activities, and the use of toileting procedures for residents with bowel incontinence. Phillips et al. (1997) evaluated the impact of the RAI in over 2,000 nursing home residents in changes in nine outcomes which broadly covered functional status, cognitive status and psychosocial well-being. There was a reduction in the rate of decline in seven of the nine outcomes under consideration. However, reductions in improvements were also observed in all outcomes. It was suggested that the RAI had focused staff's attention on the needs and requirements of specific sub-populations of residents e.g. staff may have directed their attention to those residents who were the most impaired. Fries et al. (1997) examined the effect of the implementation of the

RAI on dehydration, falls, decubitus ulcers, vision problems, stasis ulcers, pain, dental status and malnutrition in 268 nursing homes in 10 states. Dehydration and stasis ulcers had significantly lower prevalence after the implementation of the instrument, although there was an increase in the prevalence of pain. The combined eight conditions showed reductions in the rates of both decline and improvement. Finally, hospitalisation rates amongst cohorts of nursing home residents were compared before and after the implementation of the RAI (Mor et al., 1997). It was noted that there were substantial declines in hospitalisation rates in these patients which was attributed to improved assessment information through the use of the RAI.

Use of Physical Restraints

Schnelle et al. (1992) evaluated a management system to improve staff adherence to OBRA regulations in relation to patient restraint. The percentage of residents restrained over two hours was significantly reduced during the intervention phase. Further reports in the literature have documented educational interventions which have decreased restraint use, without the need to increase staff, psychoactive drugs, or serious fall-related injuries (Evans et al., 1997; Siegler et al., 1997).

Drug Therapy Guidelines

Prescribing behaviour in US nursing homes has changed, and in fact, changes were observed prior to the formal implementation of the regulations i.e. anticipatory changes. Approximately a 33 per cent reduction in prescriptions for antipsychotics was realized after the Nursing Home Reform Act (Rovner et al., 1992; Semla et al., 1994; Shorr et al., 1994). Substitution of other psychotropic drugs was not apparent as the reductions in use were accompanied by a small increase in antidepressant use and no increase in sedatives/hypnotics (Rovner et al., 1992). Patients with documented symptoms appropriate for the use of an antipsychotic, pre-legislation, were less likely to have their antipsychotic stopped (Semla et al., 1994). It appeared that the reductions observed were due to a decrease in new users (Shorr et al., 1994).

More recent work would suggest that it is difficult to discern the impact of OBRA in terms of patient outcomes. Hughes et al. (2000a) quantified the impact of this legislation on nursing home residents, psychotropic drug use and the occurrence of falls in the USA compared to five other countries without equivalent legislation. Prevalence of psychotropic drug use varied substantially across countries, with the USA demonstrating much lower prevalence rates compared to Denmark, Iceland, Italy, Japan and Sweden. In Denmark, Italy and Sweden, residents were twice as likely to receive these drugs, while in Iceland, the risk was increased to over six times. However, elderly nursing home residents were less likely to fall in Italy, Iceland and Japan compared to the USA, despite more extensive use of psychotropic medication, while residents in Sweden and Denmark were more likely to fall. Clearly, these findings must be interpreted with some caution as multiple factors such as other medical and environmental causes have been implicated in falls. It should also be borne in mind that internal factors are also at work in terms of influencing prescribing within nursing homes. Hughes et al. (2000b) examined the effect of facility and resident characteristics on the use of antipsychotic drugs in almost 15,000 US nursing homes. For-profit facilities and the presence of mental health professionals were associated with higher antipsychotic drug use, while increasing home size, being part of a chain and higher occupancy rate were associated with decreased use of anti-psychotics. Increasing percentages of residents covered by Medicaid insurance, with dementia and mental retardation were also predictive of increased drug use. It is difficult to differentiate between the impact of internal facility characteristics and the external legislation force in terms of quality of care and recognition of both factors must be considered in determining a strategy for better care.

Nursing Home Regulation in the UK

Regulation of nursing homes (and residential facilities) is also governed by legislation in the form of the Registered Homes Act (1984) and accompanying regulations in England and Wales, and equivalent legislation in Northern Ireland and Scotland. This legislation is largely concerned with registration of homes with local authorities and this process applies to all homes whether they are privately run or managed by local bodies.

However, in contrast to OBRA 1987, there are no explicit criteria or standards laid down in relation to the quality of care, the use of restraints or the prescribing of psychoactive medication. For example, in relation to drug use, the regulations state that 'the person registered shall, having regard to the size of the home and the number, age, sex and condition of residents ... make adequate arrangements for the recording, safe-keeping, handling and disposal of drugs' (Registered Homes Act, 1984, p. 5). Some of the reports from UK studies on drug use in UK nursing homes would suggest that prescribing is not always optimal and when the OBRA regulations are applied, the decisions are considered to be in contravention of the legislation (McGrath et al., 1996; Oborne et al., 1998).

Policy Implications for the UK

There is certainly evidence that the utilisation of the care planning and assessment instrument, the MDS/RAI appears to improve the quality of care and a number of important outcomes through a more structured and systematic approach to patient assessment and treatment (Fries et al., 1997; Hawes et al., 1997; Mor et al., 1997; Phillips et al., 1997). In the UK, it is currently being evaluated in home care settings to assess its potential as a means of structuring and standardising care with hopefully, improved outcomes (Challis et al., 1996). Indeed, recent publications have highlighted that the quality and quantity of data on health needs of patients in UK long stay facilities is poor and research is needed to effectively monitor these aspects; additionally, it has been suggested that clear patient assessment and review, in association with research into effective interventions should be considered as strategies to improve patient care in the nursing home setting (Turrell et al., 1998; Hughes et al., 1999).

However, the issue of legislation governing a more structured, systematic approach to nursing home care has not been debated. The use of the MDS/ RAI is mandatory in the USA; it is currently being evaluated in Japan, Iceland, Sweden, the Netherlands, Switzerland, Italy and France. Participation by homes in Iceland in this evaluation is mandatory (Bernabei et al., 1997). The implementation has also required a significant training investment for staff and clearly this has resource implications. If the MDS/RAI were to be adopted nationally within the UK, which approach would be best: implementation through legislation or education?

It has been strongly suggested that a contributing factor to poor nursing home care is the inadequate training in geriatric medicine which many physicians receive; this is particularly so in the field of geriatric drug therapy (Avorn, 1990; Smith, 1990; Stoudemire and Smith, 1996). Kane and Garrard (1994) argued that regulation was not the best way to control prescribing choices and advocated the option of education through targeted, personalized approaches. Such programmes have proved to be successful in altering prescribing patterns and the long-term benefits for physicians, other health care professionals and patients are much greater (Avorn et al., 1992; Ray et al., 1993). This option is also much more acceptable and familiar to the UK physician, as medical and pharmaceutical advisors have used such educational means to improve prescribing within general practice. Educational interventions have also been successful in reducing the use of restraints in nursing homes (Evans et al., 1997; Siegler et al., 1997).

It should also be recognised that legislation may be seen as adversarial by some health care providers and indeed, recent evidence from the US has demonstrated that despite the presence of this legislative framework, nursing home care still leaves much to be desired. Importantly, variation in the enforceability of the OBRA regulations in US nursing homes has led to continued reports of serious deficiencies in the provision of care. This was highlighted by a report from the US General Accounting Office (GAO) to Congress in March, 1999 (GAO, 1999). More than a quarter of homes had deficiencies that caused actual harm to residents or placed them at risk of death or serious injury. Sanctions initiated by HCFA were never implemented in the majority of cases and generally did not ensure that the homes maintained compliance with standards. The report concluded that enforcement of penalties should be pursued and better management information systems were required to record, track and monitor enforcement actions.

Facility characteristics should also be considered as factors influencing quality of care. In US nursing home environments in which there is more demand on increasing profits, findings suggest that there may be inappropriate use of antipsychotic drugs (Hughes et al., 2000b). Such facility-dominated demand does not bode well for the quality of care for nursing home residents. This may be accentuated by the recent introduction of a prospective payment system for drugs in American nursing homes, with additional pressures to contain expenditures. Drug use in nursing homes may become an area of care where residents will be denied certain medications because of cost and inappropriate drugs may be used to substitute for more appropriate care, again, because of cost. At present, there are no published data in the UK to indicate if nursing home residents have been denied treatment because of cost; however, recent proposed changes in the funding of long-term care in the UK should be critically examined in this respect (Pollock, 2000).

Interdisciplinary working should be a component of any new model of nursing home care. In the USA, health professionals e.g. nurse practitioners, consultant pharmacists, behavioural psychologists, social workers, nursing staff, working together within assessment teams has been advocated as a way of improving the overall care of patients, through improved communication and a more comprehensive assessment of the individual

(Stoudemire and Smith, 1996). Perhaps the combination of the implementation of the MDS/RAI, educational intervention and greater interdisciplinary working represents the ideal package for improved care in nursing homes and is the impetus for a more holistic approach to care in the elderly. It is doubtful if we can legislate to improve care *per se*, but through using imaginative and innovative approaches, it may be possible to move some way towards this goal.

Acknowledgements

Part of this work was carried out while Dr Hughes was a Harkness Fellow in Healthcare Policy 1998–99. Fellowship funding for Dr Hughes was provided by The Commonwealth Fund, a New York City-based private independent foundation. The views presented here are those of the author and not necessarily those of The Commonwealth Fund, its directors, officers or staff.

References

Avorn, J.L. (1990), 'The Elderly and Drug Policy: Coming of age', *Health Affairs*, 9, pp. 6–19.
Avorn, J., Soumerai, S.B., Everitt, D.E., Ross-Degnan, D., Beers, M.H., Sherman, D., Salem-Schatz, S.R. and Fields, D. (1992), 'A Randomized Trial of a Program to Reduce the Use of Psychoactive Drugs in Nursing Homes', *New England Journal of Medicine*, 327, pp. 168–73.
Bernabei, R., Murphy, K., Frijters, D., DuPaquier, J.-N. and Gardent, H. (1997), 'Variation in Training Programmes for Resident Assessment Instrument implementation', *Age and Ageing*, 26, pp. 31–7.
Challis, D., Carpenter, I. and Traske, K. (1996), *Assessment in Continuing Care Homes: Towards a national standard instrument*, Personal Social Services Research Unit, University of Kent at Canterbury.
Elon, R. and Pawlson, L.G. (1992), 'The Impact of OBRA on Medical Practices within Nursing Facilities', *Journal of the American Geriatrics Society*, 40, pp. 958–63.
Eichmann, M.A., Griffin, B.P., Lyons, J.S., Larson, D.B. and Finkel, S. (1992), 'An Estimation of the Impact of OBRA-87 on Nursing Home Care in the United States', *Hospital and Community Psychiatry*, 43, pp. 781–9.
Evans, L.K., Strumpf, N.E., Allen-Taylor, L., Capezuti, E., Maislin, G. and Jacobsen, B. (1997), 'A Clinical Trial to Reduce Restraints in Nursing Homes', *Journal of the American Geriatrics Society*, 45, pp. 675–81.
Fries, B.E., Hawes, C., Morris, J.N., Phillips, C.D., Mor, V. and Park, P.S. (1997), 'Effect of the National Resident Assessment Instrument on Selected Health Conditions and Problems', *Journal of the American Geriatrics Society*, 45, pp. 994–1001.

General Accounting Office (1999), *Nursing Homes: Additional steps needed to strengthen enforcement of federal quality standards*, Report to Congressional Requesters, Washington DC, March.

Greengross, S., Murphy, E., Quam, L., Rochon, P. and Smith, R. (1997), 'Aging: A subject that must be at the top of world's agendas', *British Medical Journal*, 315, pp. 1029–1030.

Hawes, C., Mor, V., Phillips, C.D., Fries, B.E., Morris, J.N., Steele-Friedlob, E., Greene, A.M. and Nennestiel, M. (1997), 'The OBRA-87 Nursing Home Regulations and Implementation of the Resident Assessment Instrument: Effects on Process Quality', *Journal of the American Geriatrics Society*, 45, pp. 977–85.

Health Care Financing Administration (HCFA) (1995), *State Operations Manual*.

Hughes, C.M., Lapane, K.L. and Mor, V. (1999) 'Impact of Legislation on Nursing Home Care in the United States: Lessons for the United Kingdom', *British Medical Journal*, 319, pp. 1060–63.

Hughes, C.M., Lapane, K.L., Mor, V., Ikegami, N., Jonsson, P.V., Ljunggren, G. and Sgadari, A. (2000a), 'The Impact of Legislation on Psychotropic Drug Use in Nursing Homes: A cross-national perspective', *Journal of the American Geriatrics Society*, 48, pp. 931–37.

Hughes, C.M., Lapane, K.L. and Mor, V. (2000b), 'The Influence of Facility Characteristics on Anti-psychotic Drug Prescribing in Nursing Homes', *Medical Care*, in press.

Institute of Medicine (1986), *Improving the Quality of Care in Nursing Homes*, National Academy Press, Washington DC.

Kane, R.L and Garrard, J. (1994), 'Changing Physician Prescribing Practices', *Journal of the American Medical Association*, 271, pp. 393–4.

Llorente, M.D., Olsen, E.J., Leyva, O., Silverman, M.A., Lewis, J.E. and Rivero, J. (1998), 'Use of Antipsychotic Drugs in Nursing Homes: Current compliance with OBRA regulations', *Journal of the American Geriatrics Society*, 46, pp. 198–201.

McGrath, A.M. and Jackson, G.A. (1996), 'Survey of Neuroleptic Prescribing in Residents of Nursing Homes in Glasgow', *British Medical Journal*, 312, pp. 611–12.

Marek, K.D., Rantz, M.J., Fagin, C.M. and Krejci, J.W. (1996), 'OBRA '87: Has it resulted in positive change in nursing homes?', *Journal of Gerontological Nursing*, 22, pp. 32–40.

Mor, V., Intrator, O., Fries, B.E., Phillips, C.D., Teno, J., Hiris, J., Hawes, C. and Morris, J. (1997), 'Changes in Hospitalization Associated with Introducing the Resident Assessment Instrument', *Journal of the American Geriatrics Society*, 45, pp. 1002–10.

Morris, J., Hawes, C., Fries, B.E., Phillips, C., Mor, V. and Katz, S. (1990), 'Designing the National Resident Assessment System for Nursing Homes', *Gerontologist*, 30, pp. 293–307.

Morris, J.N., Nonemaker, S., Murphy, K., Hawes, C., Fries, B.E., Mor, V. and Phillips, C. (1997), 'A Commitment to Change: Revision of HCFA's RAI', *Journal of the American Geriatrics Society*, 45, pp. 1011–16.

Oborne, C.A., Li, K.C. and Jackson, S.H.D. (1998), 'How Appropriate is Neuroleptic Prescribing in UK Nursing Homes', *Pharmaceutical Journal*, 261, R59.

Phillips, C.D., Morris, J.N., Hawes, C., Fries, B.E., Mor, V., Nennstiel, M. and Iannacchione, V. (1997), 'Association of the Resident Assessment Instrument (RAI) with Changes in Function, Cognition and Psychosocial Dtatus', *Journal of the American Geriatrics Society*, 45, pp. 986–93.

Pollock, A.M. (2000), 'Will Intermediate Care be the Undoing of the NHS?', *British Medical Journal*, 321, pp. 393–4.

Ray, W.A., Taylor, J.A., Meador, K.G., Lichtenstein, M.J., Griffin, M.R., Fought, R., Adams, M.L. and Blazer, D.G. (1993), 'Reducing Antipsychotic Drug Use in Nursing Homes. A Controlled Trial of Provider Education', *Archives of Internal Medicine*, 153, pp. 713–21.

Registered Homes Act (1994), London, HMSO.

Rovner, B.W., Edelman, B.A., Cox, M.P. and Schmuely, Y. (1992), 'The Impact of Antipsychotic Drug Regulations on Psychotropic Prescribing Practices in Nursing Homes', *American Journal of Psychiatry*, 149, pp. 1390–92.

Royal Commission (1999), *With Respect to Old Age: Long term care-rights and responsibilities*, a report by The Royal Commission on Long Term Care, The Stationery Office, London, March.

Schnelle, J.F., Newman, D.R., White, M., Volner, T.R., Burnett, J., Cronqvist, A. and Ory, M. (1992), 'Reducing and Managing Restraints in Long-term Care Facilities', *Journal of the American Geriatrics Society*, 40, pp. 727–8.

Semla, T.P., Palla, K., Poddig, B. and Brauner, D.J. (1994), 'Effect of the Omnibus Reconciliation Act 1987 on Antipsychotic Prescribing in Nursing Home Residents', *Journal of the American Geriatrics Society*, 42, pp. 648–52.

Shorr, R.I., Fought, R.L. and Ray, W.A. (1994), 'Changes in Antipsychotic Drug Use in Nursing Homes During Implementation of the OBRA-87 Regulations', *Journal of the American Medical Association*, 271, pp. 358–62.

Siegler, E.L., Capezuti, E., Maislin, G., Baumgarten, M., Evans, L. and Strumpf, N. (1997), 'Effects of a Restraint Reduction Intervention and OBRA '87 Regulations on Psychoactive Drug Use in Nursing Homes', *Journal of the American Geriatrics Society*, 45, pp. 791–6.

Smith, D.A. (1990), 'New Rules for Prescribing Pscychotropics in Nursing Homes', *Geriatrics*, 45, pp. 44–56.

Stoudemire, A. and Smith, D.A. (1996), 'OBRA Regulations and the Use of Psychotropic Drugs in Long-term Care Facilities. Impact and Implications for Geropsychiatric Care', *General Hospital Psychiatry*, 18, pp. 77–94.

Streim, J. (1995), 'OBRA Regulations and Psychiatric Care in the Nursing Home', *Psychiatric Annals*, 25, pp. 413–18.

Turrell, A.R., Castleden, C.M. and Freestone, B. (1998), 'Long Stay Care and the NHS: Discontinuities between policy and practice', *British Medical Journal*, 317, pp. 942–4.

Chapter Eight

Transformational Change in Health Care Quality: Systemic Reorientation – Not Magic Bullets

Huw Talfryn Oakley Davies

Introduction

Health care quality is high on the agenda in most developed nations and many developing ones (Secretary of State for Health, 1998; The President's Advisory Commission on Consumer Protection and Quality in the Health Care Industry, 1998; and see Doyle and Haran, this volume). Whether this is because of a genuine public policy concern with quality, a more hard-nosed view that quality variations reflect service inefficiencies, or a desire to address manifest public concerns remains moot. Whatever the reasons, recent years have seen unprecedented policy activity aimed at improving health care quality. This chapter explores some of the factors behind this activity and enumerates the key strategies deployed in pursuit of change. It concludes by exploring the need to create more coherent and comprehensive strategies aimed at quality improvement which meld and build on burgeoning previous experience.

Driving the Quality Agenda

A significant success of health services research has been in documenting variations in health care quality (Wennberg and Gittelsohn, 1973; McPherson et al., 1982; Chassin et al., 1986; Anderson, 1990). Several consistent findings have now emerged from over two decades of careful study. First, quality of care – or at least significant aspects of it – can indeed be measured and assessed

Quality in Health Care: Strategic Issues in Health Care Management, H.T.O. Davies, M. Tavakoli and M. Malek (eds), Ashgate Publishing Ltd, 2001.

(Brook, Kamberg and McGlynn, 1996; Davies, 2001). Although much work remains to be done to improve the metric properties of quality measures, their meaningfulness and their risk adjustment, many aspects of structure, process and outcome are undoubtedly now amenable to quantitative study.

Second, comparison of quality measures between individuals, teams, provider organisations, areas or countries almost always shows marked variation – sometimes many fold (Anderson, 1990; Epstein, 1990; also various authors, this volume). Although such variation can often be explained by sociodemographic factors – in particular, deprivation and social disadvantage – much remains unexplained. Thus the (probably well-founded) suspicion remains that at least some of the residual reflects real differences in the quality of care.

Third, for all that some providers (a term used loosely to cover individual practitioners, teams or institutions) may demonstrate excellent performance, the wide variation seen is variation about a relatively poor mean. Studies of health care quality and appropriateness that use objective benchmarks almost always reveal disappointingly low attainment (Frater, 1992; Brook, 1997; Chassin, 1998; Chassin and Galvin, 1998; Schuster, McGlynn and Brook, 1998; The President's Advisory Commission on Consumer Protection and Quality in the Health Care Industry, 1998).

Finally, the experience of the last decade of intensive activity in quality improvement (widely defined) suggests that bringing about significant change will be far from easy (Chassin, 1996; Hopkins, 1996). The rest of this paper explores the strategies employed and their (relative) lack of success, before suggesting how we can build on this experience to develop more coherent approaches to quality improvement.

Strategies for Promoting Quality Improvement

Since the late nineteenth century (for example, the seminal work of both Florence Nightingale (Crombie et al., 1993) and Ernest Codman (Neuhauser, 1990)) but more especially over the past two decades, a wide variety of approaches have been developed aimed at quality improvement in health care:

- regulatory oversight;
- professional self-regulation;
- project-based quality improvement;
- continuous quality improvement/total quality management;

- performance measurement and management;
- public release of performance data;
- evidence-based practice;
- individual and organisational learning;
- change management strategies;
- market-based strategies.

In detailing these separately it is not intended to imply that they are always so distinct in practice, or that there is no interplay between them. Nonetheless it is useful to distinguish between the various separate strands before assessing how they may be better interwoven.

Regulatory Oversight

Michael Power (1997) has written of living in an 'audit society' – and with the subtitle 'rituals of verification' one can surmise that his analysis disputes the instrumentality of the approach. Nonetheless, many countries (most notably the US with its *Joint Commission on the Accreditation of Healthcare Organisations*, and the UK with the newly founded *Commission for Health improvement*) have increased the level of external oversight placed on health care organisations. While such an approach may have merit in placing bare-minimum floors under quality levels (Brennan, 1998), the widespread evidence of quality deficiencies in the face of overwhelming success in gaining accreditation suggests that the approach is a blunt tool indeed for promoting excellence. Further evidence for this view can be seen in the chapter by Hughes (this volume).

Professional Self-regulation

Health care professionals claim special knowledge about what works in health care and consequently have always claimed rights to professional self-regulation. By this model, the profession attends to quality both by restricting entry to those suitably qualified (licensure), and dealing with those found in breach of professional standards (malpractice enquiries). Over-reliance on this approach has received sustained critique in the 1990s, not least in response to a series of health care scandals (Klein, 1998; Smith, 1998; Davies and Shields, 1999). These have revealed serious shortcomings in the ability of professional self-regulation to respond in a systematic and timely manner to broader questions of competence as opposed to simpler questions of malpractice. That is not to suggest that professional self-regulation has been superseded (Irvine, 1999). It has instead been revitalised with a broader remit – for example, to begin to address competence and performance through such schemes as revalidation.

Project-based Quality Improvement

The private study of personal case-series has long been a part of the professional doctor's practice (Anonymous, 1990). Although frequently such study was aimed more at research questions (on epidemiology or clinical epidemiology) rather than health care quality, nonetheless such reflection on empirical evidence is nothing very new. However, through the 1980s and 1990s, significant policy efforts were made in many countries to formalise such activity. Called medial or clinical audit in the UK and elsewhere (Department of Health, 1989; Amouretti, Beraud and Saint-Martin, 1992), or the PDSA cycle (Plan–Do–Study–Act) in the US (Berwick, 1996), efforts were made to encourage more systematic collection and analysis of data on personal clinical practice. Such locally-organised, professionally-owned, confidential and project-based approaches to quality improvement have however seen only sporadic success (Maynard, 1991; Hopkins, 1996; Miles et al., 1996; Robinson, 1996). Although individual projects may indeed bring significant benefits, professional buy-in has been limited, progress has been halting and the effects uneven (Johnston et al., 1998, 1999).

Continuous Quality Improvement/Total Quality Management

More holistic than project-based quality investigations is the philosophy of continuous quality improvement (CQI) or total quality management (TQM) (Neave, 1987; Berwick, Enthoven and Bunker, 1992a, 1992b). Building on such ideas as statistical process control, the approach favours the reduction of variation as an essential goal for quality improvement. Although these ideas have been much taken up in health care (and developed in various guises, such as the 'health care collaboratives' run through the Institute for Healthcare Improvement (www.ihi.org)), there is again little hard evidence that the strategy has had widespread impact (Gerowitz, 1998; Shortell, Bennett and Byck, 1998; Shortell et al., 2000). Nonetheless, much has been learned along the way about how to engage doctors and other health care professionals in systematic quality improvement activity. Even if the approach itself has delivered incremental improvements rather than transformation, there is still much to learn from an examination of the implementation process (Grol and Grimshaw, 1999; Solberg et al., 2000).

Performance Measurement and Management

The growing realisation that clinical performance can, at least in part, be measured has lead to increased interest in performance measurement and management in health care (Bloomberg et al., 1993; Davies and Lampel, 1998; McKee and Sheldon, 1998; Davies and Marshall, 1999; Marshall et al., 2000). Utilisation review and physician profiling look hard at individual physician decisions and compare patterns of practice between physicians as a means of identifying targets for change. Other approaches, such as the balanced scorecard (Kaplan and Norton, 1992; Buckley and Watkins, this volume), take a broader perspective aiming to incorporate financial, organisational and other stakeholders' goals. Of course, such approaches are often as much concerned with financial performance as clinical performance and thus may be more focused on cost containment/reduction than quality improvement.

Public Release of Performance Data

Whereas many approaches to quality improvement emphasise confidentiality of the data (e.g. clinical audit) or limited release within selected professional groups (e.g. bench-marking), the 1990s saw an explosion of schemes aimed at releasing comparative data into the public arena (Gordon, 1995; Chassin, Hannan and DeBuono, 1996; Lansky, 1998; Davies and Marshall, 1999; Marshall et al., 2000). The rationales for this were varied, ranging from a public 'right to know' and notions of accountability, through informing the market (to allow purchasing on quality as well as cost), and stimulating change in errant providers (naming and shaming). Initially treated with indifference, disdain or even outrage, this flood of public data has now become a largely-accepted part of the new health care environment.

Public release has undoubtedly stimulated a greater intensity of effort aimed at improving the quality, quantity and meaningfulness of the data available. However, problems remain in several key areas. First, the data information content is often poor with only limited risk adjustment (Davies and Crombie, 1997; Iezzoni, 1997). Second, patients and other stakeholders have manifest difficulties in making sense of the data (Hibbard and Jewett, 1997; Hibbard et al., 1998). They thus spend little time seeking it out or using it in key decisions. This is as true for large purchasers and referring physicians as it is for individual patients (Hibbard et al., 1997; Schneider and Epstein, 1998). Third, concerns remain that the ready availability of such data may induce dysfunctional consequences and thus distort institutional efforts to provide high-quality, efficient and equitable care (Smith, 1995; Smith, 1995). Counterbalancing these concerns however, is the hopeful sign that at least some public release schemes may help promote beneficial quality improvement activities among some providers (Marshall et al., 2000; Marshall, this volume).

Evidence-based Practice

Much of health service research and clinical epidemiology has been aimed at identifying what works in clinical practice (Davies and Nutley, 1999). The development of randomised controlled clinical trials in the post war period and, more recently, systematic review and meta-analysis, has made available a growing and increasingly reliable body of evidence. Serious concerns have remained however about the ability of health care professionals to respond to this body of evidence, and change clinical practice. Several seminal studies from a decade ago showed that clinical practice often lags robust evidence by 10 years in terms of either implementing effective remedies or abandoning useless (or sometimes harmful) therapies (Antman et al., 1992; Lau et al., 1992; Ketley and Woods, 1993).

The response to these deficiencies has been threefold (Davies and Nutley, 1999). First, a massive research effort aimed at answering priority questions of clinical effectiveness. Second, a concomitant effort to search, appraise and synthesise best evidence, and disseminate the resulting guidance in digestible form (e.g. guidelines, protocols or care pathways). Third, has been the inculcation of the skills of 'evidence based practice' (EBP) amongst the current and upcoming generation of doctors and other health care professionals. Such skills include: searching for evidence; appraisal of evidence; and integration of robust evidence with patient preferences. As a result, studies of centres with a committed interest to evidence-based practice do often show that a large proportion of first-line decisions are now evidence-based (Ellis et al., 1995; Gill et al., 1996; Summers and Kehoe, 1996), and the skills and values underlying evidence-based practice have now permeated many parts of health systems across the globe. Yet evidence-based practice remains only a partial (although certainly crucial) approach to high quality health care.

Individual and Organisational Learning

Central to evidence-based practice is the capacity for ongoing individual learning – not just of facts, but also of skills, for example, in literature searching, or in problem definition and solution (Nutley and Davies, 2001). Despite the effort devoted to continuing medical education (CME), the evidence is that such strategies, unless very carefully designed to promote active involvement, are largely ineffective (Davis et al., 1992; Bero et al., 1998). Moreover, learning is not just about the capabilities of individuals: a second major concern lies with the ability of those organisations within which health care practitioners are embedded to develop, retain and deploy learning (Argyris and Schön, 1978, 1996; Davies and Nutley, 2000). Such ideas, although well articulated in a number of popularising books (e.g. Senge, 1994), remain underdeveloped – although of great potential – in health care.

Change Management Strategies

Whereas a rich literature on organisational development and change management exists in both the private and public sector, this literature is only rarely drawn on for work in the health care arena (Flood, 1994; Garside, 1998; Koeck, 1998; Moss, Garside and Dawson, 1998). Although specific change management models are occasionally seized upon and upheld as exemplars (e.g. Business Process Re-engineering (Browns and McNulty, 1999)), more usual is muddling through change. The fact that greater awareness of lessons learned from previous change experience is gradually filtering through to health care, together with a concomitant research strategy in this area is however to be welcomed (e.g. the new 'Service Delivery and Organisation' research funding stream in the UK NHS).

Market-based Strategies

All of the above strategies have been used in diverse health care systems, whether publicly or privately financed, publicly or privately provided, or every possible hybrid. However, especially worthy of attention are the attempts that have been made to link progress on quality to financial rewards – either at the individual practitioner level or at some organisational level. Such strategies have reached their apotheosis under the banner 'managed care'. Here the evidence does suggest that attaching financial rewards to, for example, performance indicators may be helpful – especially where the intention is simply to increase activity (or constrain costs). The downside however is that the introduction of powerful incentives may also distort behaviour in less then desirable ways – perhaps even introducing perverse incentives that militate against some measures of quality whilst simultaneously encouraging progress on others.

Bringing it Together: The Need for Organisation-wide Strategies

Each of the activities and strategies outlined above has contributed not just greater insight and knowledge but also, in part, to a cultural reorientation of health care services and health care professionals. Some of the major changes seen are:

- a growing awareness of the extent of quality problems and a willingness to address these at a policy level and with managerial action;
- acceptance of measurement of clinical performance and (more reluctantly) agreement that such comparative measures will be made public;
- an emerging balance between examining health outcomes as indicators of quality, and reporting process measures as more readily identifiable targets for change (Davies and Crombie, 1995, 1997; Crombie and Davies, 1998);
- gradual understanding of the importance of taking a 'systems' view of quality problems – most notably in the area of medical errors (Kohn, Corrigan and Donaldson, 1999). What goes with this is the eschewing of a blame culture and recognition of the severe limitations of simple exhortation as a means to quality improvement;
- realisation that there are no 'magic bullets' in bringing about quality improvement. Current evidence suggests that almost all of the strategies aimed at physician behaviour change are successful some of the time, but none are successful all of the time (Bero et al., 1998; Effective Health Care Bulletin, 1999). Thus multifaceted approaches have more chances of success, and this is enhanced further if a proper 'diagnostic analysis' of the underlying problems is carried out;
- it follows from this that, in implementing any of the above strategies for quality improvement, the context of implementation is seen as being of prime importance (Halladay and Bero, 2000; Nutley, Davies and Tilley, 2000);
- finally, recent years have seen greater cognisance that attempts to leverage quality improvement may also result in unintended and unwanted responses

as well as benefits (Smith, 1995). Thus strategies for quality improvement are more explicitly seen as balancing acts rather than sure-fire bets.

This analysis suggests the need for more joined up thinking about quality improvement that seeks to exploit the favourable factors within each of the various strategies. That is, building on our emerging understanding of complex social/technological systems to provide coherent, interlocking, mutually reinforcing strategies – not magic bullets working in isolation. Such an approach emphasises wholesale organisational change and cultural transformation over the application of simple interventions (Davies, Nutley and Mannion, 2000).

Concluding Remarks

The past two decades have seen the development of a rich variety of approaches to quality improvement in health care. Contained within each separate strand are diverse ideas, many meritorious with much potential, others potentially more mixed in effect. These diverse approaches should not necessarily be seen as being in opposition – many are complementary, albeit with a need to deal with conflicts and friction, and to create better coherence. The developing conceptual and empirical base to these strategies does however provide great opportunities for more sophisticated policy stances and more effective management styles.

Effective health care policy is that which sets an environment which encourages the emergence of self-governing organisations dedicated to clinical excellence, innovation and learning – within given cost constraints. There is thus a need for enhanced policy frameworks that encourage organisation-wide strategies, and remove crosscutting incentives. Moving away from a problem conceptualisation of 'what levers?' to one of 'what systems and cultures' is just the beginning of this process.

References

Amouretti, M., Beraud, C. and Saint-Martin, E. (1992), 'Medical Audit in France: From ideal to reality', *British Medical Journal*, 304, pp. 428–30.
Anderson, T.F. (1990), *The Challenges of Medical Practice Variations*, Basingstoke, Macmillan.
Anonymous (1990), 'Should we Case-control?', editorial, *Lancet* 335, pp. 1127–8.

Antman, E.M., Lau, J., Kupelnick, B. and Chalmers, T.C. (1992), 'A Comparison of Results of Meta-analyses of Randomized Control Trials and Recommendations of Clinical Experts', *Journal of the American Medical Association*, 268, pp. 240–8.

Argyris, C. and Schön, D.A. (1978), *Organizational Learning*, London, Addison-Wesley.

Argyris, C. and Schön, D.A. (1996), *Organizational Learning II*, Reading, Mass., Addison-Wesley.

Bero, L.A., Grilli, R., Grimshaw, J.M., Harvey, E., Oxman, A.D. and Thomson, M.A. (1998), 'Closing the gap between research and practice: an overview of systematic reviews of interventions to promote the implementation of research findings', *British Medical Journal*, 317, pp. 465–8.

Berwick, D.M. (1996), 'Primer on Leading Improvement of Systems', *British Medical Journal*, 312, p. 619.

Berwick, D.M., Enthoven, A. and Bunker, J.P. (1992a), 'Quality Management in the NHS: The doctor's role – I', *British Medical Journal*, 304, pp. 235–9.

Berwick, D.M., Enthoven, A. and Bunker, J.P. (1992b), 'Quality Management in the NHS: The doctor's role – II', *British Medical Journal*, 304, pp. 304–8.

Bloomberg, M.A., Jordan, H.S., Angel, K.O., Bailit, M.H., Goonan, K.J. and Straus, J. (1993), 'Development of Clinical Indicators for Performance Measurement and Improvement: An HMO/purchaser collaborative effort', *The Joint Commission Journal on Quality Improvement*, 19, pp. 587–95.

Brennan, T.A. (1998), 'The Role of Regulation in Quality Improvement', *Milbank Quarterly*, 76(4), pp. 709–31.

Brook, R.H. (1997), 'Managed Care is not the Problem, Quality is', *Journal of the American Medical Association*, 278(19), pp. 1612–4.

Brook, R.H., Kamberg, C.J. and McGlynn, E.A. (1996), 'Health System Reform and Quality', *Journal of the American Medical Association*, 276, pp. 476–80.

Browns, I.R. and McNulty, T. (1999), 'Re-engineering Leicester Royal Infirmary: An Independent Evaluation of Implementation and Impact', Sheffield, School of Health and Related Research (ScHaRR), University of Sheffield.

Chassin, M.R. (1996), 'Quality of Health Care Part 3: Improving the quality of care', *New England Journal of Medicine*, 335, pp. 1060–63.

Chassin, M.R. (1998), 'Is Health Care Ready for Six Sigma Quality?', *Milbank Quarterly*, 76, pp. 565–91.

Chassin, M.R., Brook, R.H., Park, R.E. et al. (1986), 'Variations in the Use of Medical and Surgical Services by the Medicare Population', *New England Journal of Medicine*, 314, pp. 285–90.

Chassin, M.R. and Galvin, R.W. (1998), 'The Urgent Need to Improve Health Care Quality. Institute of Medicine National Roundtable on Health Care Quality', *Journal of the American Medical Association* 280(11), pp. 1000–5.

Chassin, M.R., Hannan, E.L. and DeBuono, B.A. (1996), 'Benefits and Hazards of Reporting Medical Outcomes Publicly', *New England Journal of Medicine*, 334(6), pp. 394–8.

Crombie, I.K. and Davies, H.T.O. (1998), 'Beyond Health Outcomes: The advantages of measuring process', *Journal of Evaluation in Clinical Practice*, 4, pp. 31–8.

Crombie, I.K., Davies, H.T.O., Abraham, S.C.S. and Florey, C.d.V. (1993), *The Audit Handbook: Improving health care through clinical audit*, Chichester, John Wiley & Sons.

Davies, H.T.O. (2001), 'Exploring the Pathology of Quality Failings. Measuring Quality isn't the Problem – Changing it is', *Journal of Evaluation in Clinical Practice*, in press.

Davies, H.T.O. and Crombie, I.K. (1995), 'Assessing the Quality of Care: Measuring well supported processes may be more enlightening than monitoring outcomes', *British Medical Journal*, 311, p. 766.

Davies, H.T.O. and Crombie, I.K. (1997), 'Interpreting Health Outcomes', *Journal of Evaluation in Clinical Practice*, 3(3), pp. 187–200.

Davies, H.T.O. and Lampel, J. (1998), 'Trust in Performance Indicators', *Quality in Health Care* 7, pp. 159–62.

Davies, H.T.O. and Marshall, M.N. (1999), 'Public Disclosure of Performance Data. Does the Public Get What the Public Wants?', *Lancet*, 353, pp. 1639–40.

Davies, H.T.O. and Nutley, S.M. (1999), 'The Rise and Rise of Evidence in Health Care', *Public Money and Management*, 19, pp. 9–16.

Davies, H.T.O. and Nutley, S.M. (2000), 'Developing Learning Organisations in the New NHS', *British Medical Journal*, 320, pp. 998–1001.

Davies, H.T.O., Nutley, S.M. and Mannion, R. (2000), 'Organisational Culture and Quality of Health Care', *Quality in Health Care*, 9, pp. 111–19.

Davies, H.T.O. and Shields, A. (1999), 'Public Trust, and Accountability for Clinical Performance: Lessons from the media reporting of the Bristol enquiry', *Journal of Evaluation in Clinical Practice*, 5, pp. 335–42.

Davis, D.A., Thomson, M.A., Oxman, A.D. and Haynes, R.B. (1992), 'Evidence for the Effectiveness of CME. A Review of 50 Randomized Controlled Trials', *Journal of the American Medical Association*, 268(9), pp. 1111–17.

Department of Health (1989), *Medical Audit: Working Paper 6*, London, HMSO.

Effective Health Care Bulletin (1999), 'Getting Evidence into Practice', NHS Centre for Reviews and Dissemination, York.

Ellis, J., Mulligan, I., Rowe, J. and Sackett, D.L. (1995), 'Inpatient General Medicine is Evidence Based', *Lancet*, 346, pp. 407–10.

Epstein, A.M. (1990), 'The Outcomes Movement – Will it Get us Where we Want to Go?', *New England Journal of Medicine*, 323, pp. 266–9.

Flood, A.B. (1994), 'The Impact or Organizational and Managerial Factors on the Quality of Care in Health Care Organizations', *Medical Care Review*, 51, pp. 381–428.

Frater, A. (1992), 'Health Outcomes: A challenge to the status quo', *Quality in Health Care*, 1, pp. 87–8.

Garside, P. (1998), 'Organisational Context for Quality: Lessons from the fields of organisational development and change management', *Quality in Health Care*, 7 (Suppl.), S8–S15.

Gerowitz, M.B. (1998), 'Do TQM Interventions Change Management Culture? Findings and Implications', *Quality Management in Health Care*, 6, pp. 1–11.

Gill, P., Dowell, A.C., Neal, R.D., Smith, N., Heywood, P. and Wilson, A.E. (1996), 'Evidence-based General Practice: A retrospective study of interventions in one training practice', *British Medical Journal*, 312, pp. 819–21.

Gordon, N.P. (1995), 'Surveillance of Health, Functional Status, and Satisfaction of Health Plan Members by Mailed Survey: Potential sources of bias', *American Public Health Association Abstract*, p. 303.

Grol, R. and Grimshaw, J. (1999), 'Evidence-based Implementation of Evidence-based Medicine', *Joint Commission Journal on Quality Improvement*, 25, pp. 503–13.

Halladay, M. and Bero, L. (2000), 'Implementing Evidence-based Practice in Health Care', *Public Money AND Management*, 20, pp. 43–50.

Hibbard, J.H. and Jewett, J.J. (1997), 'Will Quality Report Cards Help Consumers?', *Health Affairs*, 16, pp. 218–28.

Hibbard, J.H., Jewett, J.J., Engelmann, S. and Tusler, M. (1998), 'Can Medicare Beneficiaries Make Informed Choices?', *Health Affairs*, 17, pp. 181–93.

Hibbard, J.H., Jewett, J.J., Legnini, M.W. and Tusler, M. (1997), 'Choosing a Health Plan: Do large employers use the data?', *Health Affairs*, 16, pp. 172–80.

Hopkins, A. (1996), 'Clinical Audit: Time for a reappraisal?', *Journal of the Royal College of Physicians of London*, 30(5), pp. 415–25.

Iezzoni, L.I. (1997), 'The Risks of Risk Adjustment', *Journal of the American Medical Association*, 278(19), pp. 1600–7.

Irvine, D. (1999), 'The Performance of Doctors: The new professionalism', *Lancet*, 353, pp. 1174–7.

Johnston, G., Crombie, I.K., Davies, H.T.O., Alder, E.M. and Millard, A. (1998), 'Barriers to Successful Audit: What are they and how can they be overcome?', Clinical Resource and Audit Group, The Scottish Office, Edinburgh.

Johnston, G., Davies, H.T.O., Crombie, I.K., Alder, E.M. and Millard, A. (1999), 'Managing Clionical Audit: Diagnosing the problems and designing solutions', in H.T.O. Davies, M. Tavakoli, M. Malek and A.R. Neilson (eds), *Managing Quality: Strategic issues in health care management*, Aldershot, Ashgate, pp. 89–102.

Kaplan, R. and Norton, D. (1992), 'The Balanced Scorecard – Measures that Drive Performance', *Harvard Business Review*, 70(1), pp. 71–9.

Ketley, D. and Woods, K.L. (1993), 'Impact of Clinical Trials on Clinical Practice: Example of thrombolysis for acute myocardial infarction', *Lancet*, 342, pp. 891–4.

Klein, R. (1998), 'Competence, Professional Self Regulation, and the Public Interest', *British Medical Journal*, 316, pp. 1740–2.

Koeck, C. (1998), 'Time for Organisational Development in Healthcare Organisations', *British Medical Journal*, 317, pp. 1267–8.

Kohn, L.T., Corrigan, J.M. and Donaldson, M. (1999), 'To Err Is Human: Building a safer health system', Institute of Medicine, Washington DC.

Lansky, D. (1998), 'Measuring what Matters to the Public', *Health Affairs*, 17, pp. 40–41.

Lau, J., Antman, E.M., Jimenez-Silva, J., Kupelnick, B., Mosteller, F. and Chalmers, T.C. (1992), 'Cumulative Meta-analysis of Therapeutic Trials for Myocardial Infarction', *New England Journal of Medicine*, 327, pp. 248–54.

Marshall, M.N., Shekelle, P.G., Leatherman, S. and Brook, R.H. (2000), 'The Public Release of Performance Data. What do we Expect to Gain? A Review of the Evidence', *Journal of the American Medical Association*, 283, pp. 1866–74.

Maynard, A. (1991), 'Case for Auditing Audit', *Health Service Journal* (18 July), p. 26.

McKee, M. and Sheldon, T. (1998), 'Measuring Performance in the NHS', *British Medical Journal*, 316, p. 322.

McPherson, K., Wennberg, J.E., Hovind, O.B. and Clifford, P. (1982), 'Small-area Variations in the Use of Common Surgical Procedures: An international comparison of New England, England, and Norway', *New England Journal of Medicine*, 307(21), pp. 1310–14.

Miles, A., Bentley, P., Polychronis, A., Price, N. and Grey, J. (1996), 'Clinical Audit in the National Health Service: Fact or fiction?', *Journal of Evaluation in Clinical Practice*, 2, pp. 29–35.

Moss, F., Garside, P. and Dawson, S. (1998), 'Organisational Change: The key to quality improvement', *Quality in Health Care*, 7 (Suppl.), S1–S2.

Neave, H.R. (1987), 'Deming's 14 Points for Management: Framework for success', *Statistician*, 36, pp. 561–70.

Neuhauser, D. (1990), 'Ernest Amory Codman, M.D., and End Results of Medical Care', *International Journal of Technology Assessment in Health Care*, 6, pp. 307–25.

Nutley, S.M. and Davies, H.T.O. (2001), 'Developing Organisational Learning in the NHS', *Medical Education* (in press).

Nutley, S.M., Davies, H.T.O. and Tilley, N. (2000), 'Getting Research into Practice', *Public Money and Management*, 20, pp. 3–6.

Power, M. (1997), *The Audit Society: Rituals of verification*, Oxford University Press, Oxford.

Robinson, S. (1996), 'Evaluating the Progress of Clinical Audit', *The International Journal of Theory, Research and Practice*, 2, pp. 373–92.

Schneider, E.C. and Epstein, A.M. (1998), 'Use of Public Performance Reports: A survey of patients undergoing cardiac surgery', *Journal of the American Medical Association*, 279, pp. 1638–42.

Schuster, M.A., McGlynn, E.A. and Brook, R.H. (1998), 'How Good is the Quality of Health Care in the United States?', *Milbank Quarterly*, 76, pp. 517–63.

Secretary of State for Health (1998), *A First Class Service: Quality in the new NHS*, Department of Health, London.

Senge, P.M. (1994), *The Fifth Discipline: The art and practice of the learning organisation*, Currency Doubleday, New York.

Shortell, S., Jones, R., Rademaker, A. et al. (2000), 'Assessing the Impact of Total Quality Management and Organizational Culture on Multiple Outcomes of Care for Coronary Artery Bypass Graft Surgery patients', *Medical Care*, 38(2), pp. 201–17.

Shortell, S.M., Bennett, C.L. and Byck, G.R. (1998), 'Assessing the Impact of Continuous Quality Improvement on Clinical Practice: What it will take to accelerate progress', *Milbank Quarterly* 76(4), pp. 593–624.

Smith, P. (1995), 'On the Unintended Consequences of Publishing Performance Data in the Public Sector', *International Journal of Public Administration*, 18, pp. 277–310.

Smith, P. (1995), 'Outcome-related Performance Indicators and Organizational Control in the Public Sector', in J. Holloway, J. Lewis and G. Mallory (eds), *Performance Measurement and Evaluation*, Sage, London, pp. 192–216.

Smith, R. (1998), 'Repositioning Self Regulation', *British Medical Journal*, 317, p. 964.

Solberg, L.I., Brekke, M.L., Fazio, C.J. et al. (2000), 'Lessons from Experienced Guidelines Implementers: Attend to many factors and use multiple strategies', *The Joint Commission Journal on Quality Improvement*, 26, pp. 171–88.

Summers, A. and Kehoe, R.F. (1996), 'Is Psychiatric Treatment Evidence-based?', *Lancet*, 347, pp. 409–10.

The President's Advisory Commission on Consumer Protection and Quality in the Health Care Industry (1998), *Quality First: Better Health Care for all Americans*, US Government Printing Office, Washington DC.

Wennberg, J. and Gittelsohn, A. (1973), 'Small Area Variations in Health Care Delivery', *Science*, 182, pp. 1102–8.

SECTION THREE
VARIATIONS IN HEALTH CARE

Chapter Nine

Variance in Practice Emergency Medical Admission Rates: Is it Due to Patients, Doctors or Society?

Rebecca Duffy and Harry Staines

Introduction

Hospital admission is a significant and potentially costly event for both patients and the health service. Hospital admission can be a traumatic adverse life event, particularly for the elderly. Emergency admissions have even greater impact than arranged admissions because of their unplanned and unpredictable nature. The bed crisis and cancellation of waiting list surgery provoked by the flu outbreak in the winter of 2000 vividly illustrated (Abbasi, 2000) the effect of unplanned emergency medical admissions on other services (Hanratty and Robinson, 1999).

Variance in medical practice has been observed in virtually all areas studied and provokes concern as to its implications for quality of care and efficient use of resources. Wide variations in general practitioner non-emergency referral rates to hospital have been reported, up to 20-fold at the extremes (Crombie and Fleming, 1988; Morrell, Gage and Robinson, 1971; Noone et al., 1989; Secretaries of State for Social Services, 1987; Wilkin and Smith, 1987a). Although this variation has been extensively investigated, it remains largely unexplained. Differences in patient characteristics, practice structure and doctor characteristics have failed to explain more than a fraction of the variation (Wilkin, 1992; Wilkin and Smith, 1987b). It has also been argued that a substantial proportion of the variation in reported referral rates is due to chance because of the small numbers in many studies (Moore and Roland, 1989). There has been little work reported on general practitioners emergency referral rates although emergency referrals account for 19 per cent of GP referrals (Anonymous, 1992). This is probably due to the difficulties of collecting

Quality in Health Care: Strategic Issues in Health Care Management, H.T.O. Davies, M. Tavakoli and M. Malek (eds), Ashgate Publishing Ltd, 2001.

meaningful data in this area. Referral rates reported by individual practices as required by the 1990 contract are likely to have serious flaws because of the difficulties in ensuring completeness of the data (Roland, 1992). Emergency referrals are more likely than non emergency referrals to be made by telephone or handwritten letter and to be made out of hours. The use of routinely collected hospital data for examining practices' or individual general practitioners' referral rates is also fraught with difficulties as patients may be referred to several different hospitals, especially in large metropolitan areas (Coulter, Noone and Goldacre, 1989).

Emergency admission rates have been rising steadily in recent years, with the majority of the increase due to emergency medical admissions (Moore, 1995). Possible causative factors include changing demography, incidence of disease, admission thresholds and multiple admissions or so called 'revolving door patients' and appropriateness of admission (Capewell, 1996; Kendrick, 1996). One factor could be the quality of primary care that patients receive both in preventing disease, effectively managing chronic diseases and appropriateness of referral for admission. If large variations in the quality of such care exist, large variations in emergency medical admission rates between practices could be expected to reflect this.

The aim of this study was to quantify the size of any variation in medical emergency admission rates between practices and to investigate patient and doctor factors that could be associated with this variation. We hoped to test the hypothesis that variation in emergency medical admission rate is determined by the quality of primary care offered by general practitioners.

Method

There are 33 practices in and around the city of Dundee who refer emergency medical admissions to Dundee Teaching Hospitals Trust, serving a registered population of 193,893. At the time of the study (1996/97) emergency medical admissions were also referred from the accident and emergency department of Dundee Royal Infirmary and the emergency unit at Ninewells Hospital. It is possible to use hospital admission data to reliably calculate emergency medical admission rates for Dundee practices because Dundee is served by a single Acute Hospitals Trust with acute medical admissions going to two hospitals only. Although two outlying practices may occasionally admit to Tayside's other acute hospitals these admissions were included. The population of Dundee is stable. Few emergency admissions occur out with the city.

Details of all hospital admissions are recorded via the Scottish Morbidity Record 1 (SMR1), which contains details of all hospital consultant episodes. The practice that a patient is registered with is reliably recorded, whereas the referring doctor (general practitioner or accident and emergency staff) is not recorded. The following data were obtained from Tayside Health Board:

- anonymised SMR1 data for all emergency admissions to medical specialties within Dundee Teaching Hospitals Trust for the period 1 October 1996 to 31 September 1997;
- the total number of patients;
- number aged under 65 years, 65–74 years, over 75 years, attracting high, medium and low rate deprivation payments registered with each practice for the quarter 1 October 1996 to 31 December 1996; and
- the practices' fundholding status.

To reflect the increased workload associated with deprivation, patients who live in areas designated as deprived, based on the Jarman index (Jarman, 1983) attract deprivation payments, at one of three rates; low, medium or high. Information regarding practices' training status was obtained from the Tayside Centre for General Practice and on individual practitioners' possession of membership of the Royal College of General Practitioners (MRCGP) from the East Scotland Faculty of the College. These data were used to calculate individual practices' emergency medical admission rates per 1,000 registered patients. For each practice the number of patients per 1,000 was calculated for the following: aged under 65 years, aged 65 to 74 years, over 75 years and attracting deprivation payments – low, medium and high rates. These ratios were then standardised to an expected value of 100. Other practice variables examined are summarised in Box 9.1.

Forward selection was used to find a suitable multiple regression model to predict each practices' standardised emergency medical admission rate from the variables identified above. The model was subjected to standard diagnostic checks such as verifying the variables in the model were significant, identifying potential outliers and whether the residuals had constant variance and were normally distributed.

Results

During the study period, there were a total of 12,630 emergency medical

Box 9.1   Variables examined

No. of patients aged under 65 years standardised
No. of patients aged 65–74 years standardised
No. of patients aged over 75 years standardised
No. of patients eligible for low rate deprivation payments standardised
No. of patients eligible for medium rate deprivation payments standardised
No. of patients eligible for high rate deprivation payments standardised
List size
Average list per partner
No. of partners (whole time equivalents)
Proportion of partners with MRCGP
Fundholding status
Training status

admissions to Dundee Hospitals, 9,751 from patients registered with the 33 practices in the study, 1,273 from other practices in Tayside (Dundee is a tertiary referral centre), 1,380 from practices in Fife (Dundee being the nearest location of an acute hospital for several Fife practices) and 226 from patients registered with general practitioners out with Tayside or Fife. There were 36 emergency medical admissions to Tayside's other acute hospitals by patients registered with Dundee practices, giving a total of 9,787 emergency medical admissions for the 33 practices. The mean practice emergency medical admission rate per 1,000 per year was 50.2 (standard deviation 10.7); 95 per cent confidence interval 46.4 to 54.2; range 28.8 to 71.4. The ratio of the ninetieth centile (66.0) to the tenth centile (36.3) showed a 1.8-fold difference for crude practice emergency admission rates per 1,000 patients per year. Table 9.1 shows the mean, standard deviation and range for each of the variables examined.

Entering these variables into a forward stepwise regression model resulted in three variables being included in the model: high and low rate deprivation payments and age 65–74. These three variables explained 42 per cent of the variation among practices. The t ratios for the three explanatory variables were 2.00, 2.90 and 2.29 respectively. The model had an R^2 of 42.1 per cent and the test statistic for the overall model was highly significant ($F(3,29) = 7.04; p = 0.001$). The model performed well except for two practices; one practice had a standardised emergency medical admission rate of 76, predicted 111 (standardised residual = -2.15) and another practice whose observed and predicted standardised admission rate values were 88 and 121 respectively (standardised residual = -3.34). Otherwise the model's assumptions were not

Table 9.1   Mean (SD), 95%CI, range and centiles

Factor	Mean (SD); 95%CI	Range	Centiles	
			10th	90th
List size	5876 (2553); 4970 to 6781	1330–11293	2104	9204
No. of partners (WTE)	3.6 (1.5); 3.0 to 4.1	1–7	1.3	5.9
Mean list/partner	1640 (196); 1571 to 1709	1301–1994	1372	1916
No. of patients aged under 65/1000	839.3 (39); 825.5 to 853.2	744–918	780	898
No. of patients aged 65–74/1000	90.6 (19); 84.0 to 97.3	47–132	69	117
No. of patients aged over 75/1000	70.0 (22); 62.2 to 77.8	28–124	38	107
No. of patients attracting high rate deprivation payments/1000	71 (58); 46.6 to 82.5*	0–295	2.6	145
No. of patients attracting medium rate deprivation payments/1000	57 (36); 42.9 to 66.3*	0–150	3.4	111
No. of patients attracting low rate deprivation payments/1000	89 (40); 76.4 to 107.8*	0–141	6.1	131
No. of partners with MRCGP (%)	35.7(32); 24.4 to 47.0	0–100	0	86

Notes

1   No of fundholding practices = 12.
2   No of training practices = 9.
3   * = 95% confidence intervals for the median as not normally distributed.
4   All other variables were approximately normally distributed, using the Anderson-Darling test (each p>0.05).

violated: the standardised residuals were normally distributed and showed no departure from the homoscedascity of variance assumptions. If the latter practice is excluded, the R^2 value increases to 64 per cent and the standardised low rate deprivation payments becomes nonsignificant. This practice had particularly high levels of deprivation among its patients, standardised high rate deprivation payments more than double the practice with next highest rate, it also had a substantially younger population than average and these factors may explains why it did not fit the model. Figure 9.1 shows the correlation between standardised emergency medical admission rates and standardised high rate deprivation payments, the outlier is the latter practice that did not fit the model.

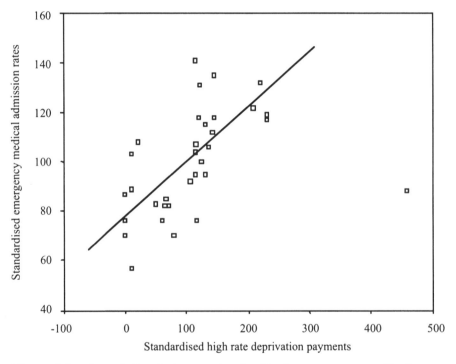

Figure 9.1   Correlation between standardised emergency medical admission rates and standardised high rate deprivation payments

Note

Spearman's rank correlation = 0.674; p>0.0001 (Spearman's rank correlation, excluding outlying practice = 0.737; p>0.0001).

After correcting for age and deprivation there was a 1.22-fold variation between the top and bottom deciles for practice emergency medical admission rates.

Discussion

The 1.8-fold variation in crude emergency medical admission rates between practices was a smaller variation than had been described for non-emergency referrals (Wilkin and Smith, 1987b). The variation was largely explained by socio-demographic factors; the regression model explained 42 per cent of the variance across the 33 practices (64 per cent, excluding one practice). This finding does not support the hypothesis that variations in the quality of primary care influencing prevention of disease, chronic disease management or management of acute exacerbations are reflected in variations in emergency medical admission rates between practices.

The quality of primary care would be expected to influence the outcome of many chronic diseases and while some studies have demonstrated a link between the quality of care for individual chronic diseases such as asthma and diabetes and reduced hospital admission (Griffiths et al., 1996; Farmer and Coulter, 1990), others have not (Durojaiye, Hutchison and Madeley, 1989). However good the quality of primary care a practice offers it cannot be expected to mitigate against the powerful effects on health of deprivation. This study again demonstrates the influence of age and deprivation on health, as these were the most powerful associations with a practice's emergency admission rate, consistent with previous research (Kendrick, 1996; Morrison et al., 1997; Smith, 1995).

Many factors are likely to be involved in influencing whether an emergency admission happens or not. One of these factors will be the 'gatekeeper' doctor, usually either a general practitioner or accident and emergency staff (often junior). In many cases the decision to admit will not be clear cut but influenced by the doctor's perception of risk, knowledge of the patient and their circumstances, the doctor's tolerance of uncertainty, knowledge of and availability of alternatives (Jones, 1992; Newton, Hayes and Hutchinson, 1991). This factor will operate at an individual level but is unlikely to have a significant effect on a practice's overall medical emergency admission rate. Likewise, an individual patient's health care seeking behaviour and expectations are also likely to influence the admission process (Walsh, 1995). A previous study of emergency medical admissions in Dundee has suggested that patients admitted via a general practitioner are more likely to be rated as an appropriate admission than those admitted via a 999 call or self-referral to accident and emergency (Duffy et al., 1998). Further analysis of data from this study suggests that deprived patients are more likely to be admitted via accident and emergency than a general practitioner (unpublished) supporting the hypothesis that patients from different socioeconomic backgrounds access health care differently. So deprivation may work at many different levels to influence its effect on health by affecting the incidence and severity of disease and in patterns of health service use.

Emergency medical admission rates for general medical practices was chosen as the unit of analysis rather than individual general practitioner emergency referral rates for several reasons. Roland has argued convincingly that referral rates for individual practitioners should only be calculated if they can be related to the number of consultations carried out by the individual practitioner. Otherwise referral rates should be calculated for whole practices using list size as the denominator (Roland et al., 1989, 1990; Roland, 1992). In the context of this study it was not possible to determine individual general practitioners' consultation rates, whereas practice list sizes were readily determined. Also, general practitioners are not responsible for referring all emergency medical admissions, at least 40 per cent arriving via a 999 call or self-referral to accident and emergency (Duffy, Bain, Neville and Staines, 1998). Finally, out of hours general practice care was provided by two co-operatives that cover all but two of the practices in the study, so patients were unlikely to see their own general practitioner out of hours and 45 per cent of emergency medical admissions occur out of hours in Dundee (Duffy, 1997).

Our findings are consistent with other reported work. Reid et al. (1999) in their study of general practice hospital admission rates in one London health authority found a 1.9-fold difference between top and bottom deciles in practices' crude emergency admission rates, with sociodemographic factors accounting for 45 per cent of the variation. A study of admission rates for asthma, diabetes and epilepsy across 90 family health service authorities in England (Giuffrida, Gravelle and Roland, 1999) found that at health authority level socioeconomic characteristics, health status and secondary care supply factors explained 45 per cent of the variation in admission rates for asthma, 33 per cent for diabetes and 55 per cent for epilepsy.

Another study in Glasgow (Blatchford et al., 1999) found a 1.9-fold variation in emergency medical admission ratios between the top and bottom practice deciles after correcting for age, sex and deprivation, which is larger than the 1.22-fold variation found in our study. There were differences in methodology in that the Glasgow study used postcodes to assign Carstairs deprivation categories (Carstairs and Morris, 1991) to individual registered patients whereas our study defined deprivation using deprivation payments to practices based on the Jarman index. Both deprivation indices use 1991 census data linked to postcodes but they are not directly comparable. Also in Glasgow there are several large acute hospitals and it is possible that differences in admission policies or cultures between hospitals could have influenced the result. The influence of admitting hospital on general practice admission rates was demonstrated by Reid's study where the percentage of each practice's admissions to the different hospitals added significantly to the explanation of variation. A strength of our study is that admissions were to one acute Trust and the vast majority to one hospital so differences in hospital admission policies or culture are unlikely to have biased the results.

This study suggests that patient factors, particularly age and deprivation, are the biggest determinants in variations between general practices' emergency admission rates. Doctor factors are unlikely to have a significant impact on emergency medical admissions at a population level. Attempts to blame doctors for the rising tide of emergency medical admissions will be fruitless. If admission rates are to be used as performance indicators they must be adjusted for factors outside the control of general practice, such as the age and deprivation of patients and secondary supply factors. Rising admission rates appear to be a function of changes in society, not the health service.

Acknowledgements

Rebecca Duffy was supported by a fellowship from the Scottish Council for Postgraduate Medical and Dental Education. We are grateful to Ingrid Gilray Data Manager Analyst, Information services, Tayside Health Board for her help with extraction of SMR data and to Ron Neville and Professor Martin Roland for helpful comments on the manuscript.

References

Abbasi, K. (2000), 'The Flu News Epidemic', *British Medical Journal*, 320, 7229, p. 258.
Anonymous (1992), 'The European Study of Referrals from Primary to Secondary Care. Concerned Action Committee of Health Services Research for the European Community', *Occasional Paper – Royal College of General Practitioners*, No. 56, pp. 1–75.

Blatchford, O., Capewell, S., Murray, S. and Blatchford, M. (1999), 'Emergency Medical Admissions in Glasgow: General practices vary despite adjustment for age, sex and deprivation', *British Journal of General Practice*, 49, pp. 551–4.

Capewell, S. (1996), 'The Continuing Rise in Emergency Admissions', *British Medical Journal*, 312, 7037, pp. 991–2.

Carstairs, V. and Morris, R. (1991), *Deprivation and Health in Scotland*, Aberdeen University Press, Aberdeen.

Coulter, A., Noone, A. and Goldacre, M. (1989), 'General Practitioners' Referrals to Specialist Outpatient Clinics. II. Locations of Specialist Outpatient Clinics to which General Practitioners Refer Patients', *British Medical Journal*, 299, 6694, pp. 306–8.

Crombie, D.L. and Fleming, D.M. (1988), 'General Practitioner Referrals to Hospital: The financial implications of variability', *Health Trends*, 20, pp. 53–6.

Duffy, R., Bain, J., Neville, R. and Staines, H. (1998), 'Relationship between Route of Referral for Acute Medical Admissions, Patient Characteristics and Appropriateness of Admission', *Health Bulletin*, 56, 6, pp. 863–70.

Duffy, R.J. (1997), *Acute Admissions Study. Report for Tayside Heath Board*, Tayside Centre for General Practice, Dundee.

Durojaiye, L.I., Hutchison, T. and Madeley, R.J. (1989), 'Improved Primary Care Does not Prevent the Admission of Children to Hospital', *Public Health*, 103, 3, pp. 181–8.

Farmer, A. and Coulter, A. (1990), 'Organization of Care for Diabetic Patients in General Practice: Influence on hospital admissions', *British Journal of General Practice*, 40, 331, pp. 56–8.

Giuffrida, A., Gravelle, H. and Roland, M. (1999), 'Measuring Quality of Care with Routine Data: Avoiding confusion between performance indicators and health outcomes', *British Medical Journal*, 319, pp. 94–8.

Griffiths, C., Naish, J., Sturdy, P. and Pereira, F. (1996), 'Prescribing and Hospital Admissions for Asthma in East London', *British Medical Journal*, 312, 7029, pp. 481–2.

Hanratty, B. and Robinson, M. (1999), 'Editorial: Coping with Winter Bed Crises. New Surveillance Systems Might Help', *British Medical Journal*, 319, 7224, pp. 1511–12.

Jarman, B. (1983), 'Identification of Underprivileged Areas', *British Medical Journal*, 286, 6379, pp. 1705–9.

Jones, R. (1992), 'Decision-making and Hospital Referrals', in M.O. Roland and A. Coulter (eds), *Hospital Referrals*, Oxford University Press, Oxford, pp. 92–107.

Kendrick, S. (1996), 'The Pattern of Increase in Emergency Hospital Admissions in Scotland', *Health Bulletin*, 54, 2, pp. 169–83.

Moore, A.T. and Roland, M.O. (1989), 'How Much Variation in Referral Rates among General Practitioners is Due to Chance?', *British Medical Journal*, 298, 6672, pp. 500–2.

Moore, W. (1995), *Emergency Admissions. The Management Challenge*, National Association of Health Authority Trusts Research Paper Number 20.

Morrell, D.C., Gage, H.G. and Robinson, N.A. (1971), 'Referral to Hospital by General Practitioners', *Journal of the Royal College of General Practitioners*, 21, 103, pp. 77–85.

Morrison, C., Woodward, M., Leslie, W. and Tunstall-Pedoe, H. (1997), 'Effect of Socio-economic Group on Incidence of, Management of, and Survival after Myocardial Infarction and Coronary Death: Analysis of community coronary event register', *British Medical Journal*, 314, 7080, pp. 541–6.

Newton, J., Hayes, V. and Hutchinson, A. (1991), 'Factors Influencing General Practitioners' Referral Decisions', *Family Practice*, 8, 4, pp. 308–13.

Noone, A., Goldacre, M., Coulter, A. and Seagroatt, V. (1989), 'Do Referral Rates Vary Widely between Practices and Does Supply of Services Affect Demand? A study in Milton Keynes and the Oxford region', *Journal of the Royal College of General Practitioners*, 39, 327, pp. 404–7.

Reid, F.D.A., Cook, D.G. and Majeed, A. (1999), 'Explaining Variation in Hospital Admission Rates between General Practices: Cross sectional study', *British Medical Journal*, 319, pp. 98–103.

Roland, M.O. (1992), 'Measuring Referral Rates' in M.O. Roland and A. Coulter (eds), *Hospital Referrals*, Oxford University Press, Oxford, pp. 62–75.

Roland, M.O., Bartholomew, J., Morrell, D.C., McDermott, A. and Paul, E. (1990), 'Understanding Hospital Referral Rates: A user's guide', *British Medical Journal*, 301, 6743, pp. 98–102.

Roland, M.O., Middleton, J., Goss, B. and Moore, A.T. (1989), 'Should Performance Indicators in General Practice Relate to Whole Practices or to Individual Doctors?', *Journal of the Royal College of General Practitioners*, 39, 328, pp. 461–2.

Secretaries of State for Social Services (1987), *Promoting Better Health. The Government's Programme for Improving Primary Health Care*, HMSO, London.

Smith, T. (1995), 'Differences between General Practices in Hospital Admission Rates for Self-inflicted Injury and Self-poisoning: Influence of socioeconomic factors', *British Journal of General Practice*, 45, 398, pp. 458–62.

Walsh, M. (1995), 'The Health Belief Model and Use of Accident and Emergency Services by the General Public', *Journal of Advanced Nursing*, 22, 4, pp. 694–9.

Wilkin, D. (1992), 'Patterns of Referral: Explaining variation', in *Hospital Referrals*, in M.O. Roland and A. Coulter (eds), *Hospital Referrals*, Oxford University Press, Oxford, pp. 76–91.

Wilkin, D. and Smith, A.G. (1987a), 'Variation in General Practitioners' Referral Rates to Consultants', *Journal of the Royal College of General Practitioners*, 37, 301, pp. 350–3.

Wilkin, D. and Smith, A. (1987b), 'Explaining Variation in General Practitioner Referrals to Hospital', *Family Practice*, 4, 3, pp. 160–9.

Chapter Ten

Variations in General Practitioner Referral Rates: Are there Lessons in the Literature?

Catherine A. O'Donnell

Introduction

Primary medical care in the UK is based on an encounter system with a general practitioner (GP). The GP is usually the first point of contact with the National Health Service (NHS) and controls access to secondary care via the referral system, acting as a gatekeeper to secondary care. An international comparison of primary care suggested that the gatekeeper system may result in better levels of health and lower costs (Starfield, 1994). However, referral by a GP is not the only mode of entry into secondary care. Other routes include emergency admissions and patient self-referral through accident and emergency departments.

In common with other areas of the NHS, this 'gateway' between primary and secondary care is under increasing scrutiny. In 1998 a consultation document, 'The New NHS, Modern and Dependable: A national framework for assessing performance', proposed a range of performance indicators for primary and secondary care (NHS Executive, 1998). Indicators relevant to the primary-secondary care interface included access to elective surgery; emergency hospital admissions for the over-75s; and admission rates for certain acute and chronic conditions.

Research has demonstrated that admission rates (both elective and emergency) are a poor measure of general practice performance (Blatchford et al., 1999; Giuffrida et al., 1999 ; Reid et al., 1999). Variation in admission rates between practices was largely explained by the sociodemographic profile of the practice population, by patient morbidity and by hospital supply factors.

Quality in Health Care: Strategic Issues in Health Care Management, H.T.O. Davies, M. Tavakoli and M. Malek (eds), Ashgate Publishing Ltd, 2001.

Giuffrida and his colleagues also suggested that a performance indicator should relate to factors that are under the control of the health care professionals to which it is being applied (Giuffrida et al., 1999). If so, then referral rates may be perceived to be a more appropriate performance indicator for general practice than admission rates. Data on referrals are considered easy to collect, even by GPs (Jankowski, 1993). Referrals, along with admissions and prescribing, have been identified as areas of major expenditure for primary care groups in England and Wales (Majeed, 1999; Majeed and Malcolm, 1999). These will also be areas of concern to primary care trusts and local health care cooperatives in Scotland. However, there is widespread variation between individual GPs and between practices in both referrals and prescribing (Wilkin and Smith, 1987a; Coulter, 1998; Greenhalgh, 1998). Indeed, it has been suggested that practices with low referral rates or with efficient prescribing policies may be reluctant to join with practices perceived as less developed (Gillam and Coulter, 1998).

Policy makers and governments have long identified this variation in referral rates as something that must be acted upon and improved and it has been suggested that general practitioners may be able to influence the observed variation (Jankowski, 1999). The 1989 White Paper 'Working for Patients' suggested that there was a 20-fold variation in GP referral rates (Secretaries of State for Health, 1989). The National Institute for Clinical Excellence (NICE), in announcing its referral protocol project, stated they would 'help GPs refer patients to specialists, more efficiently and effectively' (The National Institute for Clinical Excellence, 1999). The Accounts Commission for Scotland suggested that hospitals should identify and deal with GPs whom they suspected were referring 'inappropriately' (Accounts Commission for Scotland, 1998) and the University of Sheffield's report on the poorly performing doctor scheme suggested that referral rates may be one way of assessing quality. Calculation of inpatient admission costs resulting from referral demonstrated a 10-fold difference in hospital costs (at 1981 prices) associated with high and low rates of referral (Crombie and Fleming, 1988). However, the decision to admit a patient is taken in secondary care, not primary care. In addition, at least 50 per cent of emergency admissions result from patient self-referral (Jankowski and Mandalia, 1993; Hobbs, 1995). Thus inpatient admission costs are only indirectly attributable to GPs and GP referrals are only one part of a complicated total system in which primary and secondary care interact. Examining only part of this system may be misleading.

The National Centre for Primary Care Research and Development recommended that referral rates should not be used as a quality indicator unless adjusted for the social, demographic and economic conditions of the practice population (Roland et al., 1998). However, the development of 'referrals advisors' in primary care suggests that referral rates are perceived to be a measurable, and therefore controllable, entity. Is this supported by evidence?

A critical review of the literature on variation in GP referral rates was undertaken, with particular emphasis on the epidemiology of these variations, likely explanatory variables and the effect of GPs' decision-making on the process of referral (submitted to Family Practice). This chapter describes briefly the findings of the review and discusses the implications of this existing research for primary care groups, primary care trusts and local health care cooperatives.

Methodology

Six computerised bibliographic databases were searched: Embase, Medline, Science Citation Index, Social Science Citation Index, International Bibliography of the Social Sciences, and CINAHL. Search terms included 'general practice', 'general practitioner', 'referral' and 'variation'. Searches were also carried out based on the names of grantholders in the list of current projects identified by Wilkin and Dornan in 1990 (Wilkin and Dornan, 1990). Finally, the Cochrane Library, the NHS Centre for Reviews and Dissemination and the National Research Register were searched.

A total of 1,076 papers were identified and the titles and abstracts screened. Papers dealing with GP referral rates, variation in referral rates, possible explanations of those referrals and decision-making in the context of referral were selected. Referral could be to any speciality, for an outpatient or inpatient appointment and for any reason. Papers dealing with referral letters and their contents were not selected as these were considered to be of limited relevance to the issue of variation in referral rates. This identified 287 papers. The abstracts were reviewed and duplicates excluded. This identified 88 relevant papers, which were reviewed by the author.

Variation in Referral Rates: History and Problems

Many studies have reported variation in referral rates, with variation more apparent at the level of individual GPs than practices (Table 10.1). Studies of

Table 10.1 Comparison of referral rates from identified studies, 1970–present

Reference	Number of GPs or practices	Type of referral	Length of data collection	Number of consultations	Number of referrals	Referral rate Mean	Range
Second National Morbidity Survey, 1970–71 (Office of Population Censuses and Surveys et al. 1974)	60 practices	Outpatients and inpatients	Two years	–	–	36.0 per 1,000 consultations p.a.	18.0–76.0
Morrell et al., 1971.	3 GPs in a single practice	Outpatients, inc. specialty breakdown	One year	21,098	529	25.1 per 1,000 consultations p.a	15.4–27.3
Third National Morbidity Survey, 1981–82 (Royal College of General Practitioners et al. 1986)	60 practices	Outpatients and inpatients	Two years	–	–	32.0 per 1,000 consultations p.a.	6.0–55.0
Cummins et al., 1981	4 GPs in a single practice	Outpatients	Five years	65,538	3,545	54.1 per 1,000 consultations p.a.	42.5–66.7
Dowie, 1983	65 GPs	Outpatients	Three months	–	370	3.5 per 1,000 population[a]	0–15.0
Crombie, 1984	39 practices	Outpatients and inpatients	One year	–	–	33 per 1,000 consultations p.a.[a]	19.0–64.0
Gillam, 1985	18 GPs	Outpatients and domiciliary visits	Three months	27,847 patients	898	31.4 per 1,000 consultations	17.8–62.9
Hartley et al., 1987	21 GPs	Outpatients	One year	N/A	–		0.02–0.08 per patient p.a.
Jones, 1987	451 practices	Outpatients, including non-GP referrals	Six weeks	–	–	200 per 1,000 practice population p.a.	137–226
Wilkin and Smith, 1987b	201 GPs	Outpatients and inpatients	20 days	89,030	5,467	66 per 1,000 consultations	0–240

Table 10.1 cont'd

Reference	Number of GPs or practices	Type of referral	Length of data collection	Number of consultations	Number of referrals	Referral rate Mean	Range
Armstrong et al., 1988	122 GPs	Outpatients	5 days	17,445 patients	967	55.4 per 1,000 patients	—
Christensen et al., 1989	141 GPs	Outpatients and inpatients, inc. speciality breakdown	One year	525,554	17,586	70 per 1,000 patients p.a.[a]	52.0–89.0[b]
Noone et al., 1989	25 practices (8 in Milton Keynes; 17 in rest of Oxford region)	Outpatients, inc. speciality breakdown	11 weeks in 1983 / 11 weeks in 1984	—	4,663 / 5,105	Milton Keynes: 101.8[c] / Oxford: 100.6[c] / Milton Keynes: 114.0[c] / Oxford: 104.3[c]	84.0–181.0 / 69.0–164.0 / 67.0–159.0 / 51.0–151.0
Madeley et al., 1990	34 practices	Outpatients, inc. speciality breakdown	3 months	—	3,534	96.0 per 1,000 patients p.a.	28.0–176.0
Rashid and Jagger, 1990	6 practices	Emergencies, outpatients and inpatients	One month	3,875	216	55.7 per 1,000 patients	23.0–105.0
Roland et al., 1990	9 GPs in a single practice	Outpatients and inpatients	Six months	10,553	554	52.9 per 1,000 consultations	26.0–95.0
Reynolds et al., 1991	6 GPs in a single practice	Outpatients	Nine months	21,784	612	28.0 per 1,000 consultations	16.0–39.0
Calman et al., 1992	6 family physicians and 2 family nurse practitioners	Specialists	19 months	35,218	868	24.6 per 1,000 consultations	
Coulter and Bradlow, 1993	16 practices (10 fundholding; 6 non-fundholding)	Outpatients	6 months in both phase 1 and phase 2	—	28,371 over both phases	Fundholders: 107.3 and 111.4 per 1,000 pop. p.a. Non-fundholders: 95.0 and 112.0 per 1,000 pop. p.a.	—

Table 10.1 cont'd

Reference	Number of GPs or practices	Type of referral	Length of data collection	Number of referrals	Number of consultations	Referral rate Mean	Range
Fertig et al., 1993	31 practices	Outpatients	One year	–	–	–	84.0–208.0 per 1,000 patients p.a.
Evans, 1993	19 GPs	Outpatients	One year	112,413	5,028	44.7 per 1,000 consultations p.a.	17.4–71.0
Haikio et al., 1995	29 GPs	Outpatients and inpatients	One month	–	359	45.0 per 1,000 consultations	16.0–100.0
Hungin et al., 1995	128 GPs	Open access gastroscopy	One year	987,880	1,210	1.0 per 1,000 consultations p.a.	0.7–1.3
Surender et al., 1995	16 practices	Outpatients	4 months	–	10,311	Fundholders: 115.4 per 1,000 population p.a. Non-fundholders: 120.3 per 1,000 population p.a.	–
Vehvilainen et al., 1996	851 GPs in 93 health centres	Secondary care	7 days	59,065	2,921	49.7 per 1,000 consultations	By GP: 6.9–114.6 per 1,000 consultations[d] By health centre: 31.6–74.8 per 1,000 consultations[d]
Delnoij and Spreeuwenberg, 1997	161 GPs in 102 practices	Outpatients and inpatients	3 months	387,250	4,803	49.6 per 1,000 consultations p.a.	–
Hippisley-Cox et al., 1997a	183 general practices	Medical and surgical referrals	One year	–	–	215.4 per 1,000 patients p.a.	83.5–533.0
Sturdy et al., 1997	164 practices	Paediatric referrals	One year	–	23,467		

Notes: a) median value; b) lower and upper quartiles; c) per 1,000 population per annum; d) lower and upper quintiles.

individual GP referral rates within a single practice reported variation of two- to threefold (Morrell et al., 1971; Cummins et al., 1981). Larger studies comparing GPs from many practices reported much greater variation, e.g. a 20-fold difference in referral rates between 201 GPs in Manchester (Wilkin and Smith, 1987b). Studies reporting at a practice level found that referral rates generally varied by three- or fourfold (Crombie and Fleming, 1988; Noone et al., 1989; Wilkin, 1992). However, there are difficulties in comparing the data.

The first is the actual number of referrals made within any one study. General practitioners make, on average, about five outpatient referrals per 100 consultations per year (Coulter, 1998). Small numbers of referrals, coupled to short periods of data collection, may result in inaccurate estimates of referral rates. Campbell and Elton suggest that reliable conclusions about the average referral pattern of individual general practitioners require a minimum sample size of 490 consecutive consultations per general practitioner (Campbell and Elton, 1994). The effect of random variation on the number of referrals is generally unaccounted for (Moore and Roland, 1989; Roland et al., 1990; Coulter et al., 1991). In one of the largest studies of GP referral rates, chance accounted for at least 15 per cent of the observed variation (Moore and Roland, 1989). In many studies it is unclear what the referral is for or to which speciality, leading to difficulties in comparing similar referrals across studies. Private referrals are often excluded, but can account for up to half of a practice's referrals (Gillam, 1985; Coulter et al., 1991).

Another issue is the comparison of denominators (Roland et al., 1990; Wilkin and Dornan, 1990; Coulter et al., 1991; Roland, 1992a). Reported denominators have included the practice population, the list size of individual GPs or the number of annual consultations. This leads to confusion when studies are compared and difficulties in standardising referral rates for age and sex.

Many studies quote maximum and minimum referral rates. However, such data presentation reflects outliers and increases with sample size. A clearer picture is obtained by presenting referral rates by centiles or with 95 per cent confidence intervals. In the third national morbidity survey, referral rates ranged from 6–55 per 1,000 consultations, a ninefold difference (Crombie and Fleming, 1988). However, there was only a twofold difference in rates between the 20th and 80th centiles (23–41 per 1,000 consultations). The use of confidence intervals allows a judgement to be made about the precision of the estimated referral rate: studies with a small number of referrals will have large confidence intervals; studies with larger numbers of referrals will have smaller confidence intervals.

Therefore, even before explanations for the observed variation are sought, the problem may not be as great as initially perceived.

Explanations for the Variation in Referral Rates

Attempts to explain the variation in referral rates have concentrated on four areas:

1 patient characteristics;
2 practice characteristics;
3 GP characteristics;
4 access to specialist care.

Patient Characteristics

The age, sex and social class of those consulting the GP had little effect on the observed variation. Adjusting the referral rate for any, or all, of these variables reduced the observed variation by no more than 10 per cent (Table 10.2) (Morrell et al., 1971; Roland et al., 1990). When high and low referring GPs were compared, they saw similar proportions of patients in each age and sex category and in each social class (Wilkin and Smith, 1987b). High referring GPs referred more patients within each group.

Table 10.2   Effect of standardising for age and sex or age, sex and social class of those consulting on variation in referral rates

Reference	Adjustment	Range (no. referrals per 1,000 consultations)
Morrell et al., 1971	Rates unadjusted	15.4–27.3
	Rates adjusted for age and sex	16.0–26.2
	Rates adjusted for social class	15.2–27.1
Cummins et al., 1981	Rates unadjusted	43.0–67.0
	Rates adjusted for age, sex and social class	43.0–64.0
Roland et al., 1990	Rates unadjusted	26.9–95.5
	Rates adjusted for age and sex	25.9–82.3
Fleming et al., 1991	Rates unadjusted	73.0–245.0
	Rates adjusted for age, sex and social class	58.0–191.0

These studies defined the social class of those patients consulting a GP using the Registrar General's Occupational Groups (Office of Population

Censuses and Surveys, 1981). A more recent study examined the relationship between variation in GPs' referral rates and the socioeconomic profile of the whole practice population, rather than those who actually consulted, using the Jarman underprivileged area (UPA(8)) score (Hippisley-Cox et al., 1997a). Practices with high Jarman scores had high total referral rates. Potential explanatory variables for this variation were examined using linear regression. The Jarman score explained 23 per cent of the variation in total referral rates. Multivariate analysis was used to examine the contribution of a number of variables, including Jarman score, age and sex of the practice population, fundholding status, and number of partners on the observed variation. This model explained 29 per cent of the variation in total referral rates, with the Jarman score the strongest predictor of referral rates compared with the other variables used in the model.

One weakness of this study was its use of the Jarman (UPA(8)) score (Scrivener and Lloyd, 1997; Sturdy et al., 1997; Williams et al., 1997). Although often used as a proxy measure for deprivation, the Jarman score was constructed to measure GP workload (Jarman, 1983, 1984). Thus, a score indicating high GP workload could be expected to be associated with higher rates of referral. Criticism prompted the authors to re-analyse their data using the Townsend score, a census-based measure of socioeconomic deprivation (Townsend et al., 1988). This model explained 27 per cent of the variation in total referral rates (Hippisley-Cox et al., 1997b).

The effect of case mix is also unclear. Morrell et al. demonstrated that adjustment for diagnostic case mix reduced variation by approximately 14 per cent (Morrell et al., 1971). A Dutch study of referrals to specialists in internal medicine found that 45 per cent of the variation in new referrals was explained by patient morbidity (Delnoij and Spreeuwenberg, 1997). However, Wilkin and Smith again showed that the case mix of high and low referring GPs was similar, with high referrers referring a greater percentage of patients across all diagnostic categories (Wilkin and Smith, 1987b).

Practice Characteristics

There is conflicting evidence about the relationship between practice size and referral variation. When high and low referring GPs were compared, there were no significant differences in list size or number of partners (ibid.). Madeley et al. found no difference in referral rates between single-handed GPs and those in partnerships in Lincolnshire (Madeley et al., 1990). In contrast, a study in Nottinghamshire found a significant association between single-handed practices and high referral rates (Hippisley-Cox et al., 1997a). A Danish study found no association between referral rates and the number of GPs in the practice, but did find a significant association between referral rate and practice list size, with referral rates falling slightly as the practice size increased (Christensen et al., 1989). Conversely, in the Netherlands, referrals were found to increase as GP list size increased (Delnoij and Spreeuwenberg, 1997).

Fundholding practices were expected to have increased control over their referral rates. This does not appear to be the case. Descriptive studies comparing referral rates before and after fundholding found little difference one year on, although fundholders' referral rates were slightly lower than the comparator non-fundholders after two years (Coulter and Bradlow, 1993; Surender et al., 1995). Hippisley-Cox also found that referral rates were lower for fundholders than for non-fundholders, with fundholding explaining about 5 per cent of the observed variation (Hippisley-Cox et al., 1997a).

The distance of the practice to the hospital may influence referral rates. In Wales, higher rates were associated with shorter distances from the practice to the outpatient clinic (Jones, 1987). A study of referral patterns in 56 practices in Lincolnshire found that GPs classified as rural GPs had significantly lower referral rates than urban GPs (Madeley et al., 1990). However, this may reflect other differences between urban and rural practices. In an urban area, 22 per cent of practices with high referral rates were within one mile of a district general hospital, but 37 per cent of those with low rates were equally close (Wilkin and Smith, 1987b).

GP Characteristics

Two UK studies found no relationship between referral rates and age of GP, years of experience or membership of the RCGP (Cummins et al., 1981; Wilkin and Smith, 1987b). In Finland, higher referral rates were associated with young, relatively inexperienced GPs (Vehvilainen et al., 1996). In the UK, GP trainees referred more patients for emergency admission than their trainers (Rashid and Jagger, 1990). However, it is unclear in both of these studies if less experienced GPs were more willing to refer, or if they saw patients in greater need of referral.

GPs with an interest or training in a particular speciality may have a higher referral rate in that speciality, perhaps due to differences in case mix (Morrell et al., 1971). One study collected data on referral patterns from a practice of five GPs, documenting their specialist interests and consultation case mix

(Reynolds et al., 1991). GPs with a specialist interest in ENT and ophthalmology had high referral rates to these specialities, which persisted after adjusting for case mix. These GPs felt 'more confident than average' in managing these problems, so the high referral rate could not be explained in terms of a lack of confidence in these clinical areas.

Access to Specialist Care

The availability of specialist care appears to affect referral rates. The opening of a district general hospital led to an increase in referral rates for those specialities now providing a local consultant-based service (Noone et al., 1989). A UK-wide study investigated the relationship between outpatient referral rates and the number of consultants per 100,000 population in four specialities: medicine, thoracic medicine, psychiatry and dermatology (Roland and Morris, 1988). They reported that the number of outpatients seen was strongly associated with the provision of consultants. However, how much of the variation in referral rates can be attributed to specialist supply is unknown.

In summary then, variations in referral rates remain largely unexplained. The role of social class is not clear-cut, depending on the measure used to quantify deprivation and on whether the measure is based on the patients actually consulting a GP or on the practice population as a whole. A combination of patient and practice population characteristics and case mix still explains no more than 50 per cent of the observed variation in referral rates. Practice and GP characteristics that have been measured have only minimal influence, accounting for less than 10 per cent of the variation. Hospital supply factors may be important, but there is no information on their contribution to variation.

The lack of strong predictors of variation raises the question of whether such variation is indeed a problem. Instead, it may be more fitting to concentrate attention on the appropriateness of the referrals that are made.

Judging Appropriateness – an Inexact Science

Policy makers tend to regard high levels of referral as inefficient, regarding many of these referrals as inappropriate (Roland, 1992b; Coulter, 1998). However, little is known about what is 'appropriate' and it is not even clear that 'the norm' is appropriate (Marinker et al., 1988; Wilkin et al., 1989). The reason for a referral to outpatients generally falls into one of three categories (Coulter et al. 1989):

- investigation and/or diagnosis;
- treatment;
- advice and reassurance for the patient and/or GP.

Judging appropriateness needs to take account of the different objectives for each of these categories.

Judging Appropriateness

Studies in which the referring GP and/or specialists have retrospectively reviewed a series of referrals have led to mixed results. In some, hospital consultants were critical of GPs' referral behaviour (Samantha and Roy, 1988; Sladden and Graham-Brown, 1989; Helliwell and Wright, 1991). For example, 55 per cent of hospital consultants across a range of specialities felt that the GP could have done more before referring the patient (Grace and Armstrong, 1987). Other studies suggest that GPs do refer appropriately (Emmanuel and Walter, 1989; Bowling and Redfern, 2000). In Cambridge, consultants reviewed 521 GP referrals and judged only 10 per cent to be inappropriate (Fertig et al., 1993). In the same study, GPs reviewed 308 cases for which referral guidelines were available and judged 16 per cent to be inappropriate. GPs also reviewed referrals in Elwyn and Stotts's study and found 34 per cent to be inappropriate, generally due to a lack of resources, knowledge or specialist skills and procedures (Elwyn and Stott, 1994). Using subsequent hospital admission as a proxy for appropriateness, 91 per cent of urgent referrals to general surgery were judged appropriate (Moss et al., 1984). This may be speciality-related, as referral rates to outpatient clinics and subsequent admission are higher for general surgery than for any other speciality (Coulter et al., 1990).

There are methodological problems with these types of study.

1 Research into the appropriateness of referrals often arises from specialities or geographical areas where the specialist perceives there to be a problem and may not be generalisable to other specialities or areas.
2 The referral event is reviewed retrospectively, often after many months. Thus, factors influencing the decision to refer, in particular non-clinical factors, may have been forgotten.

3   Even amongst specialists, there is no consensus as to what is appropriate. Hospital admission rates were as variable as referral rates (Coulter et al., 1990) and patients from high referring practice were as likely to be operated on as those from low referring practices (Roland, 1992b).

4   There is no information on patients with similar symptoms and conditions who were not referred. The importance of including this group of patients in studies of referral outcome has been discussed (Dowie, 1983).

5   Appropriateness can really only be judged if there is subsequent information on outcomes.

6   The judgement of appropriateness generally rests with the subjective view of the clinicians. The patients' view of appropriateness is rarely addressed.

Outcomes

Few studies have examined long-term clinical outcomes following referral (Coulter et al., 1991a, 1991b; Sullivan et al., 1992) and none have explicitly compared high and low referring practices. Coulter followed up referrals for menstrual problems and for back pain five years after the original index referral (Coulter et al., 1991a, 1991b). Investigations and/or treatment had been carried out for the majority of patients (93 per cent of patients with menstrual disorders; 75 per cent of patients with back pain). Of those referred, menstrual symptoms had resolved in 86 per cent of patients and back pain in 67 per cent. For women referred with menstrual disorders, symptoms resolved spontaneously in 4 per cent of cases, whereas hysterectomy (with or without drug treatment) led to resolution of symptoms in 42 per cent of patients. General practice consultation rates for those problems also decreased after referral.

In Sullivan's study, patients were asked whether their symptoms had improved two years after an initial referral to either a rheumatology, vascular surgery or dermatology clinic: 8 per cent felt their condition had been cured; 38 per cent that it had improved; and 46 per cent that it was unchanged (Sullivan et al., 1992). However, there was no clinical verification as to whether the conditions had improved.

The Patient's Perspective

Few studies have examined appropriateness of referral from the patient's perspective. Patients generally perceive their referral to be necessary (Grace and Armstrong, 1987; Bowling and Redfern, 2000). However, there may be conflict between this view and those of clinicians. In comparing the views of patients, referring GPs and specialists, Grace and Armstrong found low levels of agreement between these groups regarding the appropriateness of each referral (Grace and Armstrong, 1987). A recent study found much higher levels of agreement between the three groups (Bowling and Redfern, 2000). However, it is clear that more work is required into the differing perspectives of these groups.

Appropriateness and Variation

There is little evidence to support the contention that inappropriate referrals contribute to the variation in referral. A Dutch study demonstrated that 57 per cent of referrals from high referring GPs and 55 per cent from average referring GPs had clear medical indications for the referral (Knottnerus et al., 1990). These results must be viewed with caution as there were only two GPs in each group. Coulter demonstrated that practices with higher referral rates also had higher admission rates, casting doubt on the idea that high referring practices were referring patients inappropriately (Coulter et al., 1990). In Fertig's study, elimination of all referrals judged inappropriate would have reduced the variation in practice referral rates from 2.5-fold to 2.1-fold. Indeed, the strict application of referral guidelines would have increased the absolute number of patients referred (Fertig et al., 1993).

Under-referral may be a greater problem than over-referral. Indeed, it has been suggested that the real cost to the health service may lie not with the small number of patients who are referred unnecessarily, but with those patients who are referred late or not at all (Marinker et al., 1988; Wilkin et al., 1989). Only one study has addressed this issue (Hippisley-Cox et al., 1997c). In examining whether patients who present late with cancer were from low referring practices, the authors found no association between late presentation and either low or high referral rates.

What is 'Appropriateness'?

Wilkin and colleagues suggest that referral rates tell us nothing about the appropriateness of those referrals. Average referrers may refer as inappropriately as high or low referrers (Wilkin et al., 1989). All consultations with a GP can be classified in terms of the benefit or disbenefit which would be derived from a referral to hospital, with the benefits of referral outweighing the benefits of continuing GP care in only the minority of consultations (Figure 10.1). What is required is to change the shape of the curve, reducing inappropriate

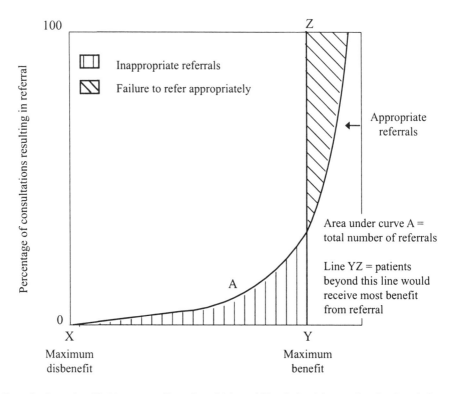

Consultations classified in terms of benefits which could be derived from referral to hospital

Figure 10.1 Theoretical relationship between referral rate and benefits of hospital treatment

Source: Wilkin et al., 1989.

referrals, where there is no benefit, and increasing appropriate referrals, where there is benefit. Simply changing the referral rate itself will not alter the balance between the appropriate and inappropriate, merely pick up more or less of each group. Thus, whether a GP is a high, average or low referrer is less important than the percentage of appropriate referrals made.

The literature shows that it is difficult to assess appropriateness with regard to referrals. Most studies rely on the view of the specialist as to what is and is not appropriate and this view is often in disagreement with the GP and with the patient. A lack of data on outcomes makes it difficult to judge appropriateness. Studies are required which take account of both the GPs' and patients' views and which attempt to identify and track patients who are not referred to determine if they have the same, or different, outcomes. Until such studies are carried out, great care must be taken in passing judgement on practices that are high or low referrers compared to a numerical norm. This is well summarised by Mooney and Andersen (1990, pp. 194–5) who wrote:

> The philosophy of 'cosiness' – all getting together around some common mean or standard and not being an antisocial outlier – can only be seen as virtuous if the point on the scale around which cosiness occurs has some rationale. The challenge here is not variation per se: it is trying to discover where cosiness should occur, and the extent to which it is a virtue.

The Referral Decision-making Process

Cummins et al. were the first to suggest that individual GPs might have a unique 'referral threshold' combining all those characteristics which might have a bearing on a referral decision: training, experience, tolerance of uncertainty, sense of autonomy and personal enthusiasms (Cummins et al., 1981). Dowie suggested that a substantial part of the reason for variation in referral rates lay in GPs' cognitive processes including: confidence in their clinical judgement; awareness of the chances of life threatening events occurring; their current medical knowledge; and the need to sustain the esteem of consultant colleagues (Dowie, 1983). This model concentrated on decisions to refer for a diagnostic uncertainty and was developed using referrals for acute and more serious conditions, not with the chronic or non-serious conditions that GPs often refer. Thus, Wilkin and Smith developed an alternative model for the referral decision which tried to include all possible reasons for wanting to refer, including the need for treatment, advice or management (Wilkin and Smith, 1987a).

These models developed a theoretical framework highlighting the complexity of each referral decision taken by a GP. A number of studies have since tried to determine what factors influence the actual referral decisions taken by GPs (Aulbers, 1985; Newton et al., 1991; Healey and Ryan, 1992; Evans, 1993; Kennedy and McConnell, 1993; Mahon et al., 1993; Wright and Wilkinson, 1996; Clemence, 1998). These have identified four broad groups of factors that GPs felt influenced their decision to refer (Figure 10.2):

* GP associated factors;
* patient associated factors;

Source: Newton et al., 1991.

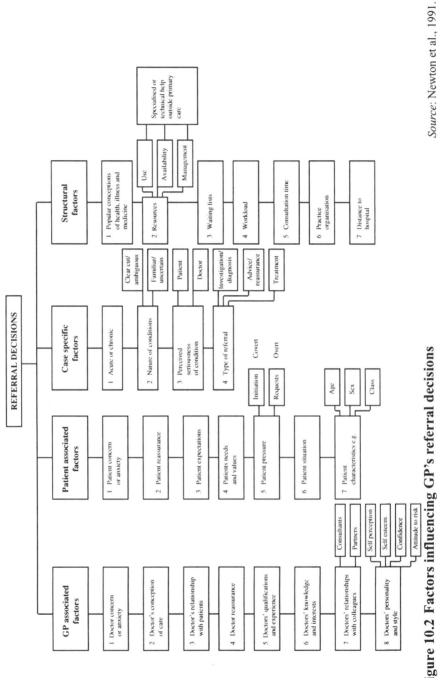

Figure 10.2 Factors influencing GP's referral decisions

- case specific factors;
- structural factors.

Two groups compared the decision-making process of high and low referring GPs (Evans, 1993; King et al., 1994; Bailey et al., 1994). High referring GPs were more likely to respond to a patient's request for a referral (Evans, 1993), consistent with Armstrong's work in which GPs with high referral rates reported significantly greater perceived pressure from patients to refer (Armstrong et al., 1991). Bailey suggested that GPs with high referral rates were less tolerant of uncertainty in their decision-making (Bailey et al., 1994).

Thus, referral decision-making is a complicated process, with no right or wrong approach. Relationships with patients, response to patient pressure and tolerance of uncertainty are clearly important factors in determining if a referral decision is made.

Modifying Referral Behaviour

Attempts to influence referral behaviour include audit and the production of locally agreed guidelines (Emmanuel and Walter, 1989; Madeley et al., 1990; de Marco et al., 1993; Fertig et al., 1993). An evaluation of the feedback of practice referral rates, together with information on local norms, found that GPs disregarded the information. This was due mainly to a lack of confidence in the accuracy of the data and the lack of consensus on a link between quality of care and referral rates (de Marco et al., 1993). However, this approach has been more acceptable elsewhere (Emmanuel and Walter, 1989; Madeley et al., 1990).

Improved communication with consultant colleagues was highlighted as an important area (McColl et al., 1994). One initiative addressing this was the development of a service called 'Boneline', where orthopaedic consultants made themselves available for telephone consultations with GPs at specified times (Roland and Bewley, 1992). Uptake of the service was poor, although GPs using the service reported that they had definitely avoided referral in 22 per cent of cases. However, there was no difference in the mean number of requests for outpatient appointments before and after the service was initiated.

Locally developed guidelines are often suggested as the way to alter referral patterns (McColl et al., 1994). However, there is no clear evidence to suggest that guidelines are effective in modifying referral behaviour (Fertig et al., 1993).

Given the lack of consensus regarding what an appropriate referral is and the lack of a clear link between referrals and quality of care, it is questionable whether much effort should be spent in attempting to modify referral behaviour. Instead, it may be better to concentrate activity on using referrals to bridge the primary-secondary care interface.

Referrals – the Way Forward

The development of clinical governance has implications for the interface between primary and secondary care. Primary care groups, trusts and local health care cooperatives will be required to monitor their performance, promote audit and develop programmes of continuing professional development (Gillam and Coulter, 1998). It has been suggested that they will also have to examine the factors influencing variation and attempt to modify these through feedback of data and educational initiatives (Majeed and Malcolm, 1999).

Attempts are now being taken to move beyond the simple counting and feeding back of information on referrals. In particular, referrals are being used to stimulate dialogue between primary and secondary care, with attempts to use them to develop meaningful performance indicators (Elwyn et al., 1999). This may be difficult as performance indicators relating to gatekeeping have been rated as unacceptable by both GPs and health authority managers (Campbell et al., 1998).

In April 2000, the National Institute for Clinical Excellence (NICE) will publish its first series of referral protocols. Areas covered include psoriasis, back ache, glue ear and menorrhagia (National Institute for Clinical Excellence, 2000). Development of the protocols will use national guidelines, coupled with discussions with a specialists, patient representatives and GPs. How these protocols are then used is important. If they are merely distributed to GPs, they are unlikely to be useful. Worse still would be the development of a culture in which GPs use of these protocols are monitored, with no account taken for the social and demographic characteristics of the area in which the GP practises. Referral and subsequent admission is a three-way process. The development of integrated educational initiatives based around these protocols, taking account of the views of GPs, hospital clinicians and patients, may help everyone involved to better appreciate the reasons for local variation, rather than trying to monitor and change it.

Conclusions

GP-initiated referrals are only one part of the process of care which may, or may not, lead to hospital admission. Variation in referral rates exists, as in most areas of clinical activity. The gatekeeper role of the GP is generally held to be highly efficient in comparison with other national systems and there is a danger that, in focusing on variations within one part of the system, the benefits of the whole system will be overlooked.

Variation remains largely unexplained, with patient, practice and GP characteristics explaining no more than half of the observed variation. Intrinsic psychological variables, such as a GP's willingness to take risks and their tolerance of uncertainty, may be as important. The role of secondary care in this equation is even less well known. Hospital supply factors appear to influence the referral rate, but the role of these factors in influencing variation in referral rates is unknown.

There is a lack of consensus about what an appropriate referral is and little evidence about long-term outcomes for patients following referral. In addition, there is no information on the 'near-referrals', i.e. those patients whom a GP considered referring, but did not. Given this situation, it is difficult to be sure that those practices which sit around the 'average' referral rate are delivering the most appropriate care, far less being concerned about those who are above or below the 'average'. It may be that under-referral is a greater problem than over-referral, although there is little evidence to support or refute this argument.

In conclusion, it is clear that variation does exist and that a large proportion of it cannot be easily explained. However, until the underlying issues are better understood the use of referral rates to measure GP performance will be misguided. Pressure on GPs to review their referral behaviour and the use of referral guidelines may reduce their willingness to tolerate uncertainty and manage problems in primary care, resulting in an increase in the number of referrals to secondary care. Instead, referral rates may be better used as a catalyst to stimulate dialogue and joint working between primary and secondary care colleagues. Such an approach may not reduce the number of referrals per se, but could result in more appropriate use of secondary care facilities and improved outcomes for patients.

Acknowledgements

I wish to thank Professor Graham Watt, Department of General Practice for his helpful discussions throughout the development of this paper; Dr David Gordon, Lanarkshire Health Board for earlier discussions; Dr Robin Dowie, Health Economics Research Group, Brunel University, for lending me a copy of her book on outpatient referrals; Ms Michere Beaumont for secretarial assistance; Lanarkshire Health Board for commissioning the review on which this work is based.

References

Accounts Commission for Scotland (1998), *Managing Hospital Admissions and Discharges*, HMSO, Edinburgh.

Armstrong, D., Britten, N. and Grace, J. (1988), 'Measuring General Practitioner Referrals: Patient workload and list size effects', *Journal of the Royal College of General Practitioners*, 38, pp. 494–7.

Armstrong, D., Fry, J. and Armstrong, P. (1991), 'Doctors' Perceptions of Pressure from Patients for Referral', *British Medical Journal*, 302, pp. 1186–8.

Aulbers, B.J.M. (1985), 'Factors Influencing Referrals by General Practitioners to Consultants', in M. Sheldon, J. Brooke and A. Rector (eds), *Decision-making in General Practice*, Stockton Press, London, pp. 131–9.

Bailey, J., King, N. and Newton, P. (1994), 'Analysing General Practitioners' Referral Decisions. II. Applying the analytical framework: Do high and low referrers differ in factors influencing their referral decisions?', *Family Practice*, 11, pp. 9–14.

Blatchford, O., Capewell, S., Murray, S. and Blatchford, M. (1999), 'Emergency Medical Admissions in Glasgow: General practices vary despite adjustment for age, sex and deprivation', *British Journal of General Practice*, 49, pp. 551–4.

Bowling, A. and Redfern, J. (2000), 'The Process of Outpatient Referral and Care: The experiences and views of patients, their general practitioners, and specialists', *British Journal of General Practice*, 50, pp. 116–20.

Calman, N.S., Hyman, R.B. and Licht, W. (1992), 'Variability in Consultation Rates and Practitioner Level of Diagnostic Certainty', *The Journal of Family Practice*, 35, pp. 31–8.

Campbell, J.L. and Elton, R.A. (1994), 'Consultation, Waiting, Prescribing, and Referral Patterns: Some methodological considerations', *Family Practice*, 11, pp. 182–6.

Campbell, S.M., Roland, M.O., Quayle, J.A., Buetow, S.A. and Shekelle, P.G. (1998), 'Quality Indicators for General Practice: Which ones can general practitioners and health authority managers agree are important and how useful are they?', *Journal of Public Health Medicine*, 20, pp. 414–21.

Christensen, B., Sorensen, H.T. and Mabeck, C.E. (1989), 'Differences in Referral Rates from General Practice', *Family Practice*, 6, pp. 19–22.

Clemence, L. (1998), 'To Whom do you Refer?', *Health Services Journal*, pp. 26–7.

Coulter, A. (1998), 'Managing Demand at the Interface between Primary and Secondary Care', *British Medical Journal*, 316, pp. 1974–6.

Coulter, A. and Bradlow, J. (1993), 'Effect of NHS Reforms on General Practitioners' Referral Patterns', *British Medical Journal*, 306, pp. 433–7.

Coulter, A., Bradlow, J., Agass, M., Martin-Bates, C. and Tulloch, A. (1991a), 'Outcomes of Referrals to Gynaecology Outpatient Clinics for Menstrual Problems: An audit of general practice records', *British Journal of Obstetrics and Gynaecology*, 98, pp. 789–96.

Coulter, A., Bradlow, J., Martin-Bates, C. and Tulloch, A. (1991b), 'Outcome of General Practitioner Referrals to Specialist Outpatient Clinics for Back Pain', *British Journal of General Practice*, 41, pp. 450–3.

Coulter, A., Noone, A. and Goldacre, M. (1989), 'General Practitioners' Referrals to Specialist Outpatient Clinics. I. Why general practitioners refer patients to specialist outpatient clinics', *British Medical Journal*, 299, pp. 304–6.

Coulter, A., Roland, M. and Wilkin, D. (1991), 'GP Referrals to Hospital. A Guide for Family Health Services Authorities', Centre for Primary Care Research, Department of General Practice, Manchester.

Coulter, A., Seagroatt, V. and McPherson, K. (1990), 'Relation between General Practices' Outpatient Referral Rates and Rates of Elective Admission to Hospital', *British Medical Journal*, 301, pp. 273–6.

Crombie, D.L. (1984), 'Social Class and Health Status Inequality or Difference', Royal College of General Practitioners (Occasional Paper 25), Exeter.

Crombie, D.L. and Fleming, D. (1988), 'General Practitioner Referrals to Hospital: The financial implications of variability', *Health Trends*, 20, pp. 53–6.

Cummins, R.O., Jarman, B. and White, P.M. (1981), 'Do General Practitioners have Different "Referral Thresholds"?', *British Medical Journal*, 282, pp. 1037–9.

de Marco, P., Dain, P., Lockwood, T. and Roland, M. (1993), 'How Valuable is Feedback of Information on Hospital Referral Patterns?', *British Medical Journal*, 307, pp. 1465–6.

Delnoij, D.M.J. and Spreeuwenberg, P.M.M. (1997), 'Variation in GPs' Referral Rates to Specialists in Internal Medicine', *European Journal of Public Health*, 7, pp. 427–35.

Dowie, R. (1983), *General Practitioners and Consultants. A study of outpatient referrals*, King's Fund, London.

Elwyn, G.J., Rix, A., Matthews, P. and Stott, N.C.H. (1999), 'Referral for "Prostatism": Developing a "performance indicator" for the threshold between primary and secondary care?', *Family Practice*, 16, pp. 140–2.

Elwyn, G.J. and Stott, N.C.H. (1994), 'Avoidable Referrals? Analysis of 170 consecutive referrals to secondary care', *British Medical Journal*, 309, pp. 576–8.

Emmanuel, J. and Walter, N. (1989), 'Referrals from General Practice to Hospital Outpatient Departments: A strategy for improvement', *British Medical Journal*, 299, pp. 722–4.

Evans, A. (1993), 'A Study of the Referral Decision in General Practice', *Family Practice*, 10, pp. 104–10.

Fertig, A., Roland, M., King, H. and Moore, T. (1993), 'Understanding Variation in Rates of Referral among General Practitioners: Are inappropriate referrals important and would guidelines help to reduce rates?', *British Medical Journal*, 307, pp. 1467–70.

Fleming, D., Crombie, D. and Cross, K. (1991), 'An Examination of Practice Referral Rates in Relation to Practice Structure, Patient Demography and Case Mix', *Health Trends*, 23, pp. 100–4.

Gillam, D.M. (1985), 'Referral to Consultants – the National Health Service versus Private Practice', *Journal of the Royal College of General Practitioners*, 35, pp. 15–18.

Gillam, S. and Coulter, A. (1998), 'Evaluating Primary Care Groups', *British Journal of General Practice*, 48, pp. 1640–41.

Giuffrida, A., Gravelle, H. and Roland, M. (1999), 'Measuring Quality of Care with Routine Data: Avoiding confusion between performance indicators and health outcomes', *British Medical Journal*, 319, pp. 94–8.

Grace, J. and Armstrong, D. (1987), 'Referral to Hospital: Perceptions of patients, general practitioners and consultants about necessity and suitability of referral', *Family Practice*, 4, pp. 170–5.

Greenhalgh, T. (1998), 'Effective Prescribing at Practice Level can and should be Identified and Rewarded', *British Medical Journal*, 316, pp. 750–4.

Haikio, J.-P., Linden, K. and Kvist, M. (1995), 'Outcomes of Referrals from General Practice', *Scandinavian Journal of Primary Health Care*, 13, pp. 287–93.

Hartley, R.M., Charlton, J.R., Harris, C.M. and Jarman, B. (1987), 'Patterns of Physicians' Use of Medical Resources in Ambulatory Settings', *American Journal of Public Health*, 77, pp. 565–7.

Healey, A. and Ryan, M. (1992), 'Factors Influencing General Practitioners' Decisions to Refer: A preliminary step towards explaining variations in GP referrals', Health Economics Research Unit, University of Aberdeen (HERU Discussion Paper 06/92), Aberdeen.

Helliwell, P.S. and Wright, V. (1991), 'Referrals to Rheumatology', *British Medical Journal*, 302, pp. 304–5.

Hippisley-Cox, J., Hardy, C., Pringle, M., Fielding, K., Carlisle, R. and Chilvers, C. (1997a), 'The Effect of Deprivation on Variations in General Practitioners' Referral Rates: A cross sectional study of computerised data on new medical and surgical outpatient referrals in Nottinghamshire', *British Medical Journal*, 314, pp. 1458–61.

Hippisley-Cox, J., Hardy, C., Pringle, M., Carlisle, R., Fielding, K. and Chilvers, C. (1997b), 'Effect of Deprivation on General Practitioner's Referral Rates', *British Medical Journal*, 315, pp. 884.

Hippisley-Cox, J., Hardy, C., Pringle, M., Fielding, K., Carlisle, R., Chilvers, C. and Avery, A. (1997c), 'Are Patients who Present Late with Cancer Registered with Low Referring Practices?', *British Journal of General Practice*, 47, pp. 731–2.

Hobbs, R. (1995), 'Rising Emergency Admissions', *British Medical Journal*, 310, pp. 207–8.

Hungin, A.P.S., Bramble, M.G. and O'Callaghan, H. (1995), 'Reasons for Variations in the Use of Open Access Gastroscopy by General Practitioners', *Gut*, 36, pp. 180–2.

Jankowski, R. (1999), 'What do Hospital Admission Rates Say about Primary Care?', *British Medical Journal*, 319, pp. 67–8.

Jankowski, R.F. (1993), 'Performance Indicators in General Practice', *British Medical Journal*, 307, pp. 1356.

Jankowski, R.F. and Mandalia, S. (1993), 'Comparison of Attendance and Emergency Admission Patterns at Accident and Emergency Departments in and out of London', *British Medical Journal*, 306, pp. 1241–3.

Jarman, B. (1983), 'Identification of Underprivileged Areas', *British Medical Journal*, 286, pp. 1705–9.

Jarman, B. (1984), 'Underprivileged Areas: Validation and distribution of scores', *British Medical Journal*, 289, pp. 1587–92.

Jones, D.T. (1987), 'A Survey of Hospital Outpatient Referral Rates, Wales, 1985', *British Medical Journal*, 295, pp. 734–6.

Kennedy, F. and McConnell, B. (1993), 'General Practitioner Referral Patterns', *Journal of Public Health Medicine*, 15, pp. 83–7.

King, N., Bailey, J. and Newton, P. (1994), 'Analysing General Practitioners' Referral Decisions. I. Developing an analytical framework', *Family Practice*, 11, pp. 3–8.

Knottnerus, J.A., Joosten, J. and Daams, J. (1990), 'Comparing the Quality of Referrals of General Practitioners with High and Average Referral Rates: An independent panel review.', *British Journal of General Practice*, 40, pp. 178–81.

Madeley, R.J., Evans, J.R. and Muir, B. (1990), 'The Use of Routine Referral Data in the Development of Clinical Audit and Management in North Lincolnshire', *Journal of Public Health Medicine*, 12, pp. 22–7.

Madeley, R.J., Evans, J.R. and Muir, B. (1990), 'The Use of Routine Referral Data in the Development of Clinical Audit and Management in North Lincolnshire', *Journal of Public Health Medicine*, 12, pp. 22–7.

Mahon, A., Whitehouse, C., Wilkin, D. and Nocon, A. (1993), 'Factors that Influence General Practitioners' Choice of Hospital when Referring Patients for Elective Surgery', *British Journal of General Practice*, 43, pp. 272–6.

Majeed, A. (1999), 'Adapting Routine Information Systems to Meet the Requirements of Primary Care Groups', *Public Health Medicine*, 1, pp. 4–11.

Majeed, A. and Malcolm, L. (1999), 'Unified Budgets for Primary Care Groups', *British Medical Journal*, 318, pp. 772–6.

Marinker, M., Wilkin, D. and Metcalfe, D.H. (1988), 'Referral to Hospital: Can we do better?', *British Medical Journal*, 297, pp. 461–4.

McColl, E., Newton, J. and Hutchinson, A. (1994), 'An Agenda for Change in Referral – Consensus from General Practice', *British Journal of General Practice*, 44, pp. 157–62.

Mooney, G. and Andersen, T.F. (1990), 'Challenges Facing Modern Health Care', in T.F. Andersen and G. Mooney (eds), *The Challenges of Medical Practice Variations*, Macmillan, London, pp. 192–200.

Moore, A.T. and Roland, M.O. (1989), 'How Much Variation in Referral Rates among General Practitioners is Due to Chance?', *British Medical Journal*, 298, pp. 500–2.

Morrell, D.C., Gage, H.G. and Robinson, N.A. (1971), 'Referral to Hospital by General Practitioners', *Journal of the Royal College of General Practitioners*, 21, pp. 77–85.

Moss, J.G., Ross, N.B. and Small, W.P. (1984), 'Sources of Referral and Letter content of Acute Surgical Emergencies Referred to One General Surgical Unit', *Health Bulletin*, 42, pp. 126–31.

Newton, J., Hayes, V. and Hutchinson, A. (1991), 'Factors Influencing General Practitioners' Referral Decisions', *Family Practice*, 8, pp. 308–13.

NHS Executive (1998), 'The New NHS, Modern and Dependable: A national framework for assessing performance', Department of Health, London.

Noone, A., Goldacre, M., Coulter, A. and Seagroatt, V. (1989), 'Do Referral Rates Vary Widely between Practices and Does Supply of Services Affect Demand? A study in Milton Keynes and the Oxford region', *Journal of the Royal College of General Practitioners*, 39, pp. 404–7.

Office of Population Censuses and Surveys (1981), *The Registrar General's Classification of Occupations 1980*, HMSO, London.

Office of Population Censuses and Surveys, Royal College of General Practitioners and Department of Health and Social Security (1974), 'Morbidity Statistics from General Practice: Second national study 1970–71', HMSO (Studies on Medical and Population Subjects: no. 26), London.

Rashid, A. and Jagger, C. (1990), 'Comparing Trainer and Trainee Referral Rates: Implications for education and allocation of resources', *British Journal of General Practice*, 40, pp. 53–5.

Reid, F.D.A., Cook, D.G. and Majeed, A. (1999), 'Explaining Variation in Hospital Admission Rates between General Practices: Cross-sectional study', *British Medical Journal*, 319, pp. 98–103.

Reynolds, G.A., Chitnis, J.G. and Roland, M.O. (1991), 'General Practitioner Outpatient Referrals: Do good doctors refer more patients to hospital?', *British Medical Journal*, 302, pp. 1250–2.

Roland, M. (1992a), 'Measuring Referral Rates', in M. Roland and A. Coulter (eds), *Hospital Referrals*, Oxford University Press, Oxford, pp. 62–75.

Roland, M. (1992b), 'Measuring Appropriateness of Hospital Referrals', in M. Roland and A. Coulter (eds), *Hospital Referrals*, Oxford University Press, Oxford, pp. 136–49.

Roland, M. and Bewley, B. (1992), 'Boneline: Evaluation of an initiative to improve communication between specialists and general practitioners', *Journal of Public Health Medicine*, 14, pp. 307–9.

Roland, M., Holden, J. and Campbell, S. (1998), 'Quality Assessment for General Practice: Aupporting clinical governance in primary care groups', National Primary Care Research and Development Centre, University of Manchester, Manchester.

Roland, M. and Morris, R. (1988), 'Are Referrals by General Practitioners Influenced by the Availability of Consultants?', *British Medical Journal*, 297, pp. 599–600.

Roland, M.O., Bartholomew, J., Morrell, D.C., McDermott, A. and Paul, E. (1990), 'Understanding Hospital Referral Rates: A user's guide', *British Medical Journal*, 301, pp. 98–102.

Royal College of General Practitioners, Office of Population Censuses and Surveys and Department of Health and Social Security (1986), 'Morbidity Statistics from General Practice 1981–82; Third national study', (Series MB5: No. 1) HMSO, London.

Samantha, A. and Roy, S. (1988), 'Referrals from General Practice to a Rheumatology Clinic', *British Journal of Rheumatology*, 27, pp. 74–6.

Scrivener, G. and Lloyd, D. (1997), 'Effect of Deprivation on General Practitioner's Referral Rates. Jarman score measures workload not deprivation', *British Medical Journal*, 315, pp. 883.

Secretaries of State for Health, Wales, Northern Ireland and Scotland (1989), *Working for Patients*, HMSO, London.

Sladden, M.J. and Graham-Brown, R.A.C. (1989), 'How Many GP Referrals to Dermatology Outpatients are Really Necessary?', *Journal of the Royal Society of Medicine*, 82, pp. 347–8.

Starfield, B. (1994), 'Is Primary Care Essential?', *The Lancet*, 344, pp. 1129–33.

Sturdy, P., Pereira, F., Hull, S., Carter, Y., Naish, J. and Harvey, C. (1997), 'Effect of Deprivation on General Practitioner's Referral Rates. Analyses should take age and sex into account', *British Medical Journal*, 315, pp. 883–4.

Sullivan, F.M., Hoare, T. and Gilmour, H. (1992), 'Outpatient Clinic Referrals and their Outcome', *British Journal of General Practice*, 42, pp. 111–5.

Surender, R., Bradlow, J., Coulter, A., Doll, H. and Stewart Brown, S. (1995), 'Prospective Study of Trends in Referral Patterns in Fundholding and Non-fundholding Practices in the Oxford Region, 1990–4', *British Medical Journal*, 311, pp. 1205–8.

The National Institute for Clinical Excellence (1999), 'NICE to Produce Primary Care Referral Guidelines', http://www.nice.org.uk/updates/press/2909pr.htm.

The National Institute for Clinical Excellence (2000), 'Update on Referral Protocol Project', http://www.nicw.org.uk/clin-guide/urpp.htm.

Townsend, P., Phillimore, P. and Beattie, A. (1988), *Health and Deprivation: Inequality and the North,* Croom Helm, London.

Vehvilainen, A.T., Kumpusalo, E.A., Voutilainen, S.O. and Takala, J.K. (1996), 'Does the Doctor's Professional Experience Reduce Referral Rates? Evidence from the Finnish referral study', *Scandinavian Journal of Primary Health Care,* 14, pp. 13–20.

Wilkin, D. (1992), 'Patterns of referral: explaining variation', in M. Roland and A. Coulter (eds), *Hospital Referrals,* Oxford University Press, Oxford, pp. 76–91.

Wilkin, D. and Dornan, C. (1990), 'General Practitioner Referrals to Hospital. A review of research and its implications for policy and practice', University of Manchester, Manchester.

Wilkin, D., Metcalfe, D.H. and Marinker, M. (1989), 'The Meaning of Information on GP Referral Rates to Hospitals', *Community Medicine,* 11, pp. 65–70.

Wilkin, D. and Smith, A. (1987a), 'Explaining Variation in General Practitioner Referrals to Hospital', *Family Practice,* 4, pp. 160–9.

Wilkin, D. and Smith, A.G. (1987b), 'Variation in General Practitioners' Referral Rates to Consultants', *Journal of the Royal College of General Practitioners,* 37, pp. 350–3.

Williams, T., Jackson, A. and Turbitt, D. (1997), 'Effect of Deprivation on General Practitioners' Referral Rates. Study should have used deprivation index that is independent of age', *British Medical Journal,* 315, pp. 882–3.

Wright, J. and Wilkinson, J. (1996), 'General Practitioners' Attitudes to Variations in Referral Rates and How these Could be Managed', *Family Practice,* 13, pp. 259–63.

Chapter Eleven

Going Public on Clinical Performance: Lessons from the USA

Martin N. Marshall

Introduction

We live in an information-rich society. When we go shopping in a supermarket we can choose to buy genetically modified, low sodium or fat-free foods – the products are clearly marked to allow us to do so. When we buy a new car, we can choose between the looks, performance and safety profile – again on the basis of reasonably reliable information. Even when we use public transport, information about the punctuality of the service is provided for us to make a judgement about how well the transport company is doing.

Health care, however, is one of the few remaining black boxes in modern society. If someone who has diabetes mellitus moves into a new town and has a choice of registering with any one of several local general practices, he or she has no way of knowing which practices provide better diabetic care. This is despite plenty of evidence that there is wide variation even in some of the most basic process of diabetic care, and despite evidence linking poor care to significant life-threatening complications (Butler et al., 1997). If someone with ischaemic heart disease needs a coronary artery bypass graft, neither the patient, nor their general practitioner, nor even the referring cardiologist have any objective information about the success rates of potential surgeons or operating departments – again despite evidence that the patient might be as much as twice as likely to die in one hospital as in another (Hannan et al., 1994).

Until recently, this lack of information has been acceptable to the general public. In part, this resulted from the strong sense of trust in the health service and in the health professionals who provide care (Davies and Shields, 1999). This trust was based on a confidence in medical training and a belief, usually

Quality in Health Care: Strategic Issues in Health Care Management, H.T.O. Davies, M. Tavakoli and M. Malek (eds), Ashgate Publishing Ltd, 2001.

implicit, that there were no systematic problems with the quality of care provided – of course, mistakes happened, but these were just bad luck; everyone was doing their best and the best was more than acceptable.

There is an increasing body of evidence that this trust is poorly founded and that there is, in fact, wide and unacceptable variation in the quality of care provided for patients. This variation is apparent in all countries and in all types of health systems that have been studied. Some of the evidence goes back a long way. In the 1860s Florence Nightingale identified significant differences in the mortality rate of London teaching hospitals (Nightingale, 1863). In 1917 an American surgeon berated his colleagues for their unwillingness to share information about their success rates; he claimed that this was because they might be embarrassed about their results (Codman, 1996). More recently we hear almost daily stories of incompetent or dangerous surgeons, murdering or predatory general practitioners and lackadaisical or poorly-managed hospitals. The media are now painting a picture of a health system and medical profession that has no idea of how well it is doing and does not seem to care anyway.

In the United Kingdom, as in many other countries, the government is making it clear that this is no longer acceptable. They are both reflecting and leading public concerns by demanding greater accountability from health care organisations and from individual professionals. Those providing care will have to be accountable not only for attaining minimum standards, but also for showing a commitment to continuously improving their performance. We are now moving into an environment of active performance management. It is clear that this will be based to a large extent on hard comparative data, which will be made publicly available (Marshall and Davies, 2000). This demand for the public disclosure of comparative performance data represents a major challenge both to the health system, which has operated largely data-free since it was established, and to health professionals who have never before had to demonstrate the quality of the care that they provide.

There have been some limited examples of public disclosure in the United Kingdom in recent years, the best example being the publication of hospital outcome data in Scotland (Dilner, 1994). However, this and other examples, such as comparative in-vitro fertilisation rates and renal transplant success rates have not been given a high public profile. In 1999 the UK government launched a major new initiative as part of their quality improvement agenda for the National Health Service. The National Performance Assessment Framework (NPAF) presents comparative data at the level of hospitals and health authorities in six areas of activity, health improvement, fair access, effective delivery of appropriate health care, efficiency, patient/carer experience and health outcomes of NHS care (NHS Executive, 1999).

The results of the first set of performance indicators were published as part of this framework in early 1999 (ibid.). The data showed a wide variation in performance between different hospitals and regions but the government urged caution in the interpretation of the results. As a consequence, the public and media response was muted and relatively balanced and there were whisperings that the government was disappointed that the data did not achieve a greater impact. The second round of indicators were released in the summer of 2000 (NHS Executive, 2000) and this time the government presented the data in more of a 'league table' format. It is too early to determine the impact this might have on future performance.

Whilst the UK, and several other countries, are just starting to release comparative data, the United States has a long history of public disclosure. Comparative data has been produced in the form of 'report cards', 'consumer reports' or 'provider profiles' for nearly 15 years. The purpose of this paper is to review the history of disclosure in the US, evaluate the use and impact of the published data and suggest ways that other countries could learn from the US experience.

The Report Card Movement in the US

The Health Care Financing Administration was the first organisation to publish comparative performance data in the US on a large scale (Vladeck et al., 1988). The in-hospital mortality data for Medicare patients, dubbed by the media the 'death lists', was first produced in 1987. The data were crude and poorly risk-adjusted. Those who opposed public release received the news that the institution with the worst mortality rate was, in fact, a hospice with great mirth. The discredited initiative was halted in 1992 but it initiated a major report card movement and spawned a multi-million dollar industry. A wide variety of public and private organisations now produce report cards, including state and federal organisations, employers, consumer advocate groups, the media and coalitions of interested parties (Marshall et al., 2000b). The information is highly variable in terms of its scientific rigour.

Report cards are usually published as short glossy brochures (Pacific Business Group on Health, 1999) but Internet publication is becoming increasingly common (Pennsylvania Cost Containment Council, 1999). Information is available about structural aspects of quality (for example, the number of clinical staff or waiting times for an appointment), process issues (for example prescribing rates or adherence to technical process of care for disease management) and outcome measures (for example mortality rates or patient satisfaction data). The data are usually presented in a tabular format, comparing performance across a number of institutions. Percentage scores, star charts or even smiling faces have been used to present the results.

There are a number of high profile public reporting initiatives in the US. The Health Plan Employer Data Information Set (HEDIS) is produced by a non-profit coalition between private purchasers, health plans and consumers. Quality data submitted by volunteer Health Maintenance Organisations is published annually in *Quality Compass* (National Committee for Quality Assurance, 1999). The self-selected nature of contributing organisations and the relatively crude process measures of quality have received some criticism (Epstein, 1998) but the reporting system has been improved year-on-year and is now well established.

The New York Cardiac Surgery Reporting System (CSRS) is one of the most highly developed and most studied of the reporting systems (Hannan et al., 1994; Chassin et al., 1996). The system publishes in-hospital mortality data following coronary artery bypass surgery at the level of hospitals and individual surgeons. Detailed administrative and clinical data is used to construct a multivariate risk adjustment model. Similarly rigorous report cards have been produced in Pennsylvania (Sirio and McGee, 1996) and in California (Romano et al., 1995) and other states are now following suit.

Evaluating the US Experience of Public Disclosure

Despite the almost frantic activity producing report cards, driven to a large extend by business interests (Davies and Marshall, 1999), there has been remarkably little desire to evaluate the use and impact of the information. However, researchers in the RAND Health Program and the Centre for Health Policy and Evaluation, United Health Group recently completed a review of public disclosure in the US (Marshall et al., 2000a, 2000b, 2000c, 2000d). The approach and findings are summarised here.

Methods

The evaluation was based on an extensive review of US published and unpublished information and expert opinion that was conducted between

October 1998 and February 1999. The published international peer-reviewed literature was accessed through Medline and Embase electronic databases. Searches using MeSH headings <report cards> <public performance reports> <provider profiling> <public/consumer/patient information> <consumer reports> were conducted independently by myself and by a professional librarian. Original articles and commentaries were reviewed. The reference lists of all articles were searched. Authors of published studies and other experts in the field were asked to recommend relevant published and unpublished studies. In addition, documents and websites prepared by the Agency for Health Policy and Research, General Accounting Office, Health Care Financing Administration, Institute of Medicine, National Committee for Quality Assurance and State organisations were reviewed.

To build on this written evidence, semi-structured interviews were conducted with experts in the field who were asked for their opinions about public disclosure and to recommend other data sources. Key informants included academics, policy advisors and others working in the public and private sector involved in the public release of performance data. In addition, media coverage of the public release of performance data was reviewed by studying news and editorial articles written in response to major disclosures. In particular, report cards published in *Newsweek, U.S. News and World Report* and *Consumer Reports* were studied. Finally a sample of report cards was reviewed.

Results

The most striking result was the paucity of hard evidence supporting the report card movement. There are several hundred different reporting systems in the US but at the time of the review only seven of them have been subject to any formal evaluation published in the peer-reviewed literature. A total of only 21 studies related to these seven reporting systems. The studies largely employed descriptive or observational methodologies; only one randomised controlled trail was found and this related to consumer use of comparative cost data, rather than clinical quality data (Hibbard and Weeks, 1989).

(i) Use of information by consumers Consumers in the US say that they want greater access to comparative data (Edgman-Levitan and Cleary, 1996; Hibbard and Jewett, 1997; Robinson and Mollyann, 1997). Their demands for information are varied and sometimes contradictory. However, when the data is made available it seems that consumers rarely search for the information,

do not understand it, do not trust it and fail to make use of it (Hibbard and Weeks, 1989; Robinson and Mollyann, 1997; Schneider and Epstein, 1998; Vladeck et al., 1988; Mennemeyer et al., 1997). In one study only 12 per cent of patients who had undergone a coronary artery bypass graft had been aware that comparative mortality data was available and less than a quarter of these stated that it had any significant impact on their choice of surgeon (Schneider and Epstein, 1998). An awareness of the report was associated with younger age, college education and high pre-operative health status.

Several possible reasons have been put forward to explain the lack of use of performance reports. Both consumers and group purchasers have complained that the data is inaccessible, too detailed and ambiguous (Hibbard et al., 1997; Mennemeyer et al., 1997). Others complain that they do not trust the data – either because they think that the hospitals will not submit data that shows them in a bad light, or because the report cards are financed by employers, who are more interested in cost than in quality (Robinson and Mollyann, 1997). Some suggest that the opportunity to exercise choice on the basis of the data is limited and that the time from accessing the information to having to make a decision based on it is too short for consumers to make effective use of the report cards (Schneider and Epstein, 1998).

(ii) Use of information by physicians Unlike consumers, physicians in the United States are acutely aware of the existence of the reports and are sensitive to them. However, they respond largely in a negative fashion (Hannan et al., 1997; Schneider and Epstein, 1996; Vladeck et al., 1988; Borowsky et al., 1997). Most commonly, physicians discredit the reports, claiming that they discourage surgeons from operating on high-risk patients and that the data are easy to manipulate or misrepresent. Only a small percentage of physicians uses the reports to influence their referring behaviour. An even smaller proportion share the information with their patients. It appears that objective information has little impact on established patterns of behaviour.

(iii) Use of information by provider organisations Whilst consumers and physicians appear to make little use of report cards, provider organisations (principally referring to hospitals in the US) are highly sensitive and responsive to them (Bentley and Nash, 1998; Rosenthal et al., 1998; Longo et al., 1997; Hannan et al., 1995). There is evidence that publication of comparative data encourages organisations to put more effort into monitoring physician performance, benchmark their performance against other hospitals in the area and introduce new services. In addition, hospitals put more emphasis on

marketing their products. Hospitals operating in competitive markets are more likely to respond to the published information. Hospitals that are shown by the data to be under-performing are more likely to respond in a dysfunctional manner, in particular by discrediting the data. However, even these organisations tend to act upon the results. Nevertheless, significant complaints are made by hospitals about the quality of the data, the tendency to focus narrowly on mortality data and the costs of producing the data and responding to the challenges presented by report cards.

(iv) Impact on quality of care outcomes Whilst the use of report cards is of interest, the most fundamental question is whether public disclosure of performance data influences outcomes of care. There is some evidence from observational studies that public disclosure is associated with improved outcomes (Hannan et al., 1994; Longo et al., 1997; Peterson et al., 1998), though there is considerable controversy about how important the disclosure element of comparative data is, and whether the benefits outweigh the problems (Chassin et al., 1996; Omogigui et al., 1996; Topol and Califf, 1994; Ziegenfuss, 1996).

The New York CSRS is the most rigorously studied system for public disclosure of performance data. Hannan et al. (1994) studied all the patients undergoing isolated CABG surgery who were discharged from the New York State hospitals performing the procedure between 1989 and 1992. The risk adjusted mortality decreased from 4.17 per cent in 1989 to 2.45 per cent in 1992; a reduction of 41 per cent. This was considerably greater than the national average.

This study resulted in considerable debate among academics. The main criticism was that the release of data in New York State could have reduced access to CABG surgery by forcing sicker patients to seek surgery outside the State or by surgeons refusing to operate on high-risk patients. Peterson et al. (1998) examined this issue by observing trends in the percentage of New York residents aged 65 years or more who received out-of-state surgery before and after the publication of the report cards. They also examined procedure use by elderly patients with myocardial infarctions within the state to determine whether high risk patients were being refused treatment. Contrary to a previous study (Omogigui et al., 1996), they found that the percentage of New York residents receiving out-of-state bypass operations decreased and that the likelihood of bypass surgery following a myocardial infarction actually increased.

What can Other Countries Learn from the US Experience?

It is tempting to ignore what is happening in the US health care system; after all, the structure of health care and the consumerist culture are so different from most other countries. Whilst it is sensible to be cautious, it would be a mistake to re-invent the wheel as other countries start to introduce their own systems for public disclosure (Klein, 1997; Davies and Marshall, 2000). Some of the lessons learnt (or not learnt) in the US are potentially relevant to non-US countries. The following policy implications are derived from the literature review described above and from interviews conducted with key informants in the US (Marshall et al., 2000b):

- *public disclosure should be seen as an evolutionary process.* Some observers claim that information should not be released to the public until the data on which it is based is totally valid and reliable. The methodological problems and cost of producing perfect data make this an unrealistic expectation. The comparative data must be good enough to be credible to those who use the information and fair to those who are affected by it, but it does not have to be perfect. However, there should be a clear commitment on the part of those controlling data release to improve the quality of the information year on year;
- *health professionals should be involved in the process.* Using public disclosure as a stick to beat the majority of hard working health professionals will have a negative effect on their moral and performance. Those who will be affected by the information should be brought on board at an early stage and actively involved in the content and design of the reports, the collection of the data and the interpretation and subsequent response to the results;
- *both the costs and the benefits of report cards should be considered.* The potential benefits of public disclosure are clear – greater openness and accountability, better informed members of the public and purchasers, encouragement to focus on quality improvement and better outcomes. However, there are real costs and unintended consequences to public disclosure. The financial cost of producing and disseminating the information and rectifying any deficiencies demonstrated by the data are likely to be significant. If a policy on public disclosure is seen primarily as a way of improving quality, then the opportunity costs of using resources in this way should be considered. Dysfunctional responses to the publication of comparative performance data have also been described (Smith, 1995;

Davies et al., 1999). These range from a short term preoccupation with the indicators being measured, an inappropriate focus on the easily measurable and 'massaging' or fabrication of the data. Most of the dysfunctional consequences are an inevitable consequence of criterion-based assessment and can be minimised or actively managed;

• *publish different types of quality indicator.* There is a tendency to regard the publication of risk-adjusted outcome indicators as the ultimate aim for those involved in public disclosure. Process indicators are often discredited as relating more to activity than to performance or quality. For a wide variety of reasons, process indicators are, however, often a more sensitive, immediate and credible measure of quality (Crombie and Davies, 1997; Davies and Crombie, 1987; Orchard, 1994), though it is clearly important that the processes can be related to outcomes by scientific evidence (McColl et al., 1998);

• *provider organisations are the key audience.* The limited evidence described above suggests that neither consumers, purchasers nor physicians are likely to respond significantly or positively to report cards in their current format, or in the current environment. Provider organisations (largely hospitals in the US, but there is no reason why the evidence should not be transferable to primary care organisations) seem to be the most likely audience to respond to the data. This has implications for the content and publication format of the reports. It also has implications for the subsequent support required to encourage providers to respond positively to the information. This does not mean that consumers and health professionals are unimportant in the process but it is important that those who produce the data are aware of the primary audience and purpose of the data;

• *consider the benefits and the costs of risk adjustment.* The case mix and risk adjustment debate is often heated but usually poorly informed. Theoretically, risk adjustment is important to ensure that meaningful conclusions are drawn when comparing the apparent differences in performance of two organisations (Iezzoni, 1997). This is particularly true when outcome measures are used but can also be important for process indicators; In practice, however, the factors that influence risk are often not well understood and risk adjustment is expensive, complicated and time consuming. It can also be misleading, resulting in important determinants of variation in quality being 'cancelled out' by statistical manipulation. There is a very real compromise to be made between the benefits, the cost and the risks of adjustment and these should be taken into consideration when deciding on the level and type of adjustment required;

- *information should be released as part of an educational package.* The most likely initial response to comparative data is a poorly informed and dysfunctional one. Comparative health data is easy to misinterpret and misrepresent. It is important to teach all stakeholders – the public, the media, professionals, managers and politicians – how to make the best and most appropriate use of the data. This would include possible explanations for the variation demonstrated and specific advice about how to improve measured performance;
- *more research and development is required.* A policy on public disclosure is most likely to be effective if it is guided by empirical evidence. At present there is little evidence in the US, despite much activity, and even less evidence in other countries. A specific R&D programme to encourage work in this field should be adequately supported and funded.

Conclusion

A higher level of public disclosure of comparative health care information is inevitable in a modern society that values accountability and choice based on objective information. However, the pursuit of such a policy is not without risks. In summary, what is the balance between the potential benefits and the problems of the release of information?

As far as the benefits are concerned, introducing greater public disclosure will reflect societal expectations for greater accountability and promote the ongoing shift of information (and therefore power) from the professions to the laity. This is an inevitable, and most would say desirable, trend that would be futile to resist. Greater openness on the part of health systems and professionals would help to maintain public trust at a time when this is under threat. Certainly, withholding information at such a sensitive time would have a detrimental effect on the relationship between the public and the medical profession.

There is some evidence that public disclosure can lead to quality improvement activity and to improved outcomes. In countries with poor information systems, it can also help to focus attention on improving the quality of the data. Finally, the information might encourage an informed public debate about the reasons for variation in performance, possible solutions and the kind of health system that a country wants to have, and is willing to pay for.

Some of the potential problems of disclosure are the mirror image of the benefits. Greater openness about under-performance could have a detrimental effect on public trust in a health system and on staff morale (Davies and Shields, 1999). It can be difficult and time consuming to manage the response to the published information and costly to produce and disseminate the data. It may also be costly to act on the results when required, and even more costly to raise expectations but then do nothing about them. Finally, there are significant methodological problems associated with producing valid and reliable data, including the risk adjustment debate described above, the most appropriate level of reporting and the inevitable time delay between collecting the data and getting it into the public domain.

On balance the benefits of public disclosure must outweigh the risks in a modern, democratic society. However, the evidence presented in this paper suggests that in the US at least, the benefits have been overestimated and the costs, risks and unintended consequences given insufficient credence. Countries that wish to learn from the US experience might wish to adopt a more balanced approach to the implementation of such a far-reaching policy.

Acknowledgements

I would like to thank the Nuffield Trust, London who funded and supported the project on which this paper is based. The work was conducted at the RAND Corporation, Santa Monica, California, where I was based as a Harkness Fellow in Health Care Policy, supported by the Commonwealth Fund of New York. I would particularly like to acknowledge the contribution of Bob Brook, Paul Shekelle and Sheila Leatherman to the conduct of the project and Huw Davies who contributed to the development of many of the ideas.

References

Bentley, J.M. and Nash, D.B. (1998), 'How Pennsylvania Hospitals Have Responded to Publicly Released Reports on Coronary Artery Bypass Graft Surgery', *Joint Commission Journal for Quality Improvement*, 24, pp. 40–9.

Borowsky, S.J., Davis, M.K., Goertz, C. and Lurie, N. (1997), 'Are all Health Plans Created Equal? The Physician's View', *Journal of the American Medical Association*, 278, pp. 917–21.

Butler, C., Smithers, M., Stott, N. and Peters, J. (1997), 'Audit-enhanced District-wide Primary Care for People with Diabetes Mellitus', *European Journal of General Practice*, 3, pp. 23–7.

Chassin, M., Hannan, E. and DeBuono, B. (1996), 'Benefits and Hazards of Reporting Medical Outcomes Publicly', *The New England Journal of Medicine*, 334, pp. 394–8.

Codman, E.A. (1996), *A Study in Hospital Efficiency (Boston, 1917)*, Oakbrook Terrace, Illinois; reprinted by the Joint Commission on Accreditation of Healthcare Organisations.

Crombie, I.K. and Davies, H.T.O. (1997), 'Beyond Health Outcomes: The advantages of measuring process', *Journal of Evaluation in Clinical Practice*, 4, pp. 31–8.

Davies, H.T.O. and Crombie, I. K. (1987), 'Interpreting Health Outcomes', *Journal of Evaluation in Clinical Practice*, 3, pp. 187–99.

Davies, H.T.O., Crombie, I.K. and Mannion, R. (1999), 'Performance Indicators in Health Care: Guiding lights or wreckers' lanterns?', *Managing Quality and Controlling Cost: Strategic issues in health care management*, Ashgate Publishing Ltd, Aldershot.

Davies, H.T.O. and Marshall, M.N. (1999), 'Public Disclosure of Performance Data: Does the public get what the public wants?', *Lancet*, 353, pp. 1639–40.

Davies, H.T.O. and Marshall, M.N. (2000), 'Divided by a More than a Common Language; Can we learn from the US health system?', *The Lancet*, 355, p. 336.

Davies, H.T.O. and Shields, A. (1999), 'Public Trust, and Accountability for Clinical Performance: Lessons from the media reporting of the Bristol enquiry', *Journal of Evaluation in Clinical Practice*, 5, pp. 335–42.

Dilner, L. (1994), 'Scottish Death Rates Published with Health Warning', *British Medical Journal*, 309, pp. 1599–600.

Edgman-Levitan, S. and Cleary, P. (1996), 'What Information Do Consumers Want And Need?', *Health Affairs*, 15, pp. 42–56.

Epstein, A.M. (1998), 'Rolling Down the Runway The Challenges Ahead for Quality Report Cards', *Journal of the American Medical Association*, 279, pp. 1691–6.

Hannan, E.L., Kilburn, H., Racz, M., Shields, E. and Chassin, M.R. (1994), 'Improving the Outcomes of Coronary Artery Bypass Surgery in New York State', *Journal of the American Medical Association*, 271, pp. 761–6.

Hannan, E.L., Siu, A.L., Kumar, D., Kilburn, H.J. and Chassin, M.R. (1995), 'The Decline in Coronary Artery Bypass Graft Surgery Mortality in New York State', *Journal of the American Medical Association*, 273, pp. 209–13.

Hannan, E.L., Stone, C.C., Biddle, T.L. and DeBuono, B.A. (1997), 'Public Release of Cardiac Surgery Outcomes Data in New York: What do New York state cardiologists think of it?', *American Heart Journal*, 134, pp. 55–61.

Hibbard, J.H. and Jewett, J.J. (1997), 'Will Quality Report Cards Help Consumers', *Health Affairs*, 16, pp. 218–28.

Hibbard, J.H., Jewett, J.J., Legnini, M.W. and Tusler, M. (1997), 'Choosing A Health Plan: Do Large Employers Use the Data?', *Health Affairs*, 16, pp. 172–80.

Hibbard, J.H. and Weeks, E.C. (1989), 'Does Dissemination of Comparative Data on Physician Fees Affect Consumer Use of Services?', *Medical Care*, 27, pp. 1167–74.

Iezzoni, L.I. (1997), 'The Risks of Risk Adjustment', *Journal of the American Medical Association*, 278 (19), pp. 1600–7.

Klein, R. (1997), 'Report From the Field Learning from Others: Shall the last be the first?', *Journal of Health Politics Policy and Law*, 22, pp. 1267–78.

Longo, D.R., Land, G. et al. (1997), 'Consumer Reports in Health Care: Do they make a difference in patient care?', *Journal of the American Medical Association*, 278, pp. 1579–84.

Marshall, M.N. and Davies, H.T.O. (2000), 'Performance Measurement and Management of Healthcare Professionals', *Disease Management and Health Outcomes*, 7, pp. 305–14.

Marshall, M., Shekelle, P., Brook, R. and Leatherman, S. (2000a), 'Public Reporting of Performance: Lessons from the USA', *Journal of Health Services Research and Policy*, 5, pp. 1–2.

Marshall, M.N., Shekelle, P.G., Leatherman, S. and Brook, R.H. (2000b), *The Public Disclosure of Performance Data in Health Care: Learning from the US experience*, Nuffield Trust, London.

Marshall, M.N., Shekelle, P.G., Leatherman, S. and Brook, R.H. (2000c), 'Public Disclosure of Performance Data: Learning from the US experience', *Quality in Health Care*, 9, pp. 53–7.

Marshall, M.N., Shekelle, P.G., Leatherman, S. and Brook, R.H. (2000d), 'What do we Expect to Gain from the Public Release of Performance Data? A Review of the Evidence', *Journal of the American Medical Association*, 283, pp. 1866–74.

McColl, A., Roderick, P., Gabbay, J., Smith, H. and Moore, M. (1998), 'Performance Indicators for Primary Care Groups: An evidence based approach', *British Medical Journal*, 317, pp. 1354–60.

Mennemeyer, S.T., Morrisey, M.A. and Howard, L.Z. (1997), 'Death and Reputation: How consumers acted upon HCFA Mortality', *Inquiry*, 34, pp. 117–28.

National Committee for Quality Assurance (1999), www.ncqa.org.

NHS Executive (1999), *The NHS Performance Assessment Framework*, London.

NHS Executive (1999), 'Quality and Performance in the NHS – Performance Indicators', www.doh.gov.uk/nhsperformanceindicators/index.htm.

NHS Executive (1999), *Quality and Performance in the NHS: High level performance indicators and clinical indicators*, London.

NHS Executive (2000) 'Quality and Performance in the NHS – Performance Indicators', www.doh.gov.uk/nhsperformanceindicators/index.htm.

Nightingale, F. (1863), *Notes on Hospitals*, 3rd edn, Longman, Green, Longman, Roberts and Green, London.

Omogigui, N.A., Miller, D.P. et al. (1996), 'Outmigration For Coronary Bypass Surgery in an Era of Public Dissemination of Clinical Outcomes', *Circulation*, 93, pp. 27–33.

Orchard, C. (1994), 'Comparing Healthcare Outcomes, *British Medical Journal*, 308, pp. 1493–6.

Pacific Business Group on Health (1999), *Healthscope: A guide to choosing the right health care for you and your family*, Pacific Business Group on Health, San Francisco.

Pennsylvania Cost Containment Council (1999), www.phc4.org.

Peterson, E.D., DeLong, E.R., Jollis, J.G., Muhlbaier, L.H. and Mark, D.B. (1998), 'The Effects of New York's Bypass Surgery Provider Profiling on Access to Care and Patient Outcomes in the Elderly, *Journal of the American College of Cardiology*, 32, pp. 993–9.

Robinson, S. and Mollyann, B. (1997), 'Understanding the Quality Challenge for Health Consumers: The Kaiser/AHCPR Survey', *Joint Commission Journal for Quality Improvement*, 23, pp. 239–44.

Romano, P.S., Zach, A. et al. (1995), 'The California Hospital Outcomes Project: Using administrative data to compare hospital performance', *Joint Commission Journal for Quality Improvement*, 21, pp. 668–82.

Rosenthal, G.E., Hammer, P.J., Way, L.E. et al. (1998), 'Using Hospital Performance Data in Quality Improvement, *Joint Commission Journal for Quality Improvement*, 24, pp. 347–60.

Schneider, E.C. and Epstein, A.M. (1996), 'Influence of Cardiac-Surgery Performance Reports on Referral Practices and Access to Care: A survey of cardiovascular specialists', *New England Journal of Medicine*, 335, pp. 251–6.

Schneider, E.C. and Epstein, A.M. (1998), 'Use of Public Performance Reports', *Journal of the American Medical Association*, 279, pp. 1638–42.

Sirio, C.A. and McGee, J.L. (1996), 'Public Reporting of Clinical Outcomes – the Data Needs of Health Stakeholders', *American Journal of Medical Quality*, 11, S78–S81.

Smith, P. (1995), 'On the Unintended Consequences of Publishing Performance Data in the Public Sector', *International Journal of Public Administration*, 18, pp. 277–310.

Topol, E.J. and Califf, M.R. (1994), 'Scorecard Cardiovascular Medicine: Its impact and future directions', *Annals of Internal Medicine*, 120, pp. 65–70.

Vladeck, B.C., Goodwin, E.J., Myers, L.P. and Sinisi, M. (1988), 'The HCFA "Death List"', *Health Affairs*, 7, pp. 122–5.

Ziegenfuss, J.T.J. (1996), 'Editorial: Health Care Quality Report Cards Receive Grade-Incomplete', *American Journal of Medical Quality*, 11, pp. 55–6.

Chapter Twelve

On the Limitations and Pitfalls of Performance Measurement Systems in Health Care

Russell Mannion, Maria Goddard and Peter C. Smith

Introduction

Formal performance measurement systems are increasingly a prominent feature of health systems concerned with raising quality and containing costs. The UK NHS has proved no exception and recent government policy has increased dramatically the role of formal performance measurement and external audit. Whereas the 1991 internal market reforms gave supply side competition the central role in securing performance improvements, the key instrument for managing performance in the new NHS is the provision of quantitative information in the form of a Performance Assessment Framework.

Although formal performance measurement systems may exhibit a range of strengths in relation to monitoring performance they may also be characterised by a number of weaknesses which should be taken carefully into account when designing formal measurement schemes such as the Performance Assessment Framework. In this chapter we focus on two potential limitations of formal measurement systems: the inability of performance indicators to capture adequately important aspects of performance which defy or are resistant to quantification: and the potential for formal performance systems to induce a range of unintended and dysfunctional behaviour in organisations and staff. As well as reviewing the theoretical literature on these topics we also draw on the findings of an empirical study into the types of information used to assess the performance of NHS hospital Trusts.

The chapter is arranged as follows. In the next section we describe the rise of performance indicators in the NHS. This is followed by an outline of

Quality in Health Care: Strategic Issues in Health Care Management, H.T.O. Davies, M. Tavakoli and M. Malek (eds), Ashgate Publishing Ltd, 2001.

the methodology used in our empirical study. We then examine the role of 'hard' and 'soft' information in assessing hospital performance and explore the possible unintended and adverse consequences associated with the use of performance indicators. In the final section we discuss the key policy implications arising from the theoretical review and empirical study.

Policy Context

Whilst the publication of performance data can be traced back at least as far as Florence Nightingale, historically, the NHS has not invested heavily in its information base or given performance information a particularly prominent role. Over the last two decades, however, there has been an unprecedented proliferation in the collection, use and dissemination of such information. The use of performance indicators at a national level within the NHS began in 1983 when over 100 indicators were reported for each health district. The emphasis of these data was on costs and activity rather than outcome and they facilitated internal control rather than public accountability. In 1991, coinciding with the introduction of the internal market, these data were renamed Health Service indicators, and the focus shifted from administrative, geographical areas to hospitals and other providers. A year later the emphasis moved towards the use of performance data for promoting public accountability when the Patient's Charter was introduced which focuses on various measures of waiting times for health care. These are released annually and individual hospitals are rated on a five point scale for the a range of standardised services.

Performance management is now a central plank of the UK government's public sector modernisation programme. The latest NHS reforms comprise a three pronged approach to securing quality and performance improvements; setting of clear national standards; establishment of dependable local delivery systems; and development of new systems of monitoring and performance assessment (Figure 12.1).

- *Setting standards* – the National Institute for Clinical Excellence (NICE) now promotes clinical and cost-effectiveness through guidance and audit, and advice on best practice. National Service Frameworks are used to set standards and define service models for individual care groups.
- *Delivering standards* – at the local level new systems of clinical governance are being developed. These local frameworks for ensuring accountability for clinical quality and performance are to be augmented by new systems

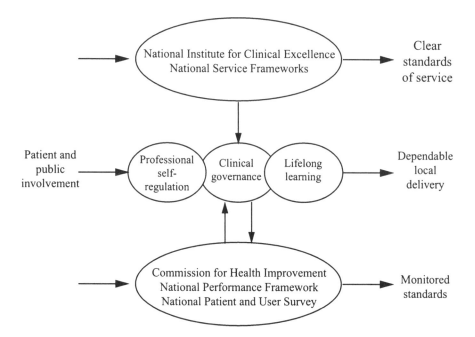

Figure 12.1 The new system for monitoring quality and performance

of professional self-regulation and lifelong learning to ensure that national standards and guidance are reflected in the local delivery of services.

*   *Monitoring standards* – the Performance Assessment Framework replaced the Purchaser Efficiency Index in April 1999 and focuses on six areas of activity and outcome: health improvement; fair access; effectiveness; efficiency; patient/ care experience; and the health outcomes of NHS care. Targets for progress against these six areas are now built into local Health Improvement programmes; accountability agreements between devolved levels of the NHS, and the agreements between commissioners and providers of health care. The Commission for Health Improvement has been established to undertake local reviews to check that systems to monitor, assure and improve clinical quality are working effectively.

Background and Study Design

The research was based on case studies of eight English NHS Trusts. Two NHS Executive regional offices were approached and senior staff responsible for provider finance and performance were asked to nominate four hospitals exhibiting what they considered to be a wide range of performance. We limited the choice to district general hospitals in order to make our sample as homogenous as possible. The Chief Executive of each of the selected Trusts was contacted and invited to participate in the research. Within each Trust, semi-structured interviews were undertaken with the chief executive, the medical director, a nurse manager and a junior doctor. One junior doctor did not attend for interview, so we undertook a total of 31 interviews within Trusts. In addition we interviewed the finance director for the local health authority for each Trust (the Trust's main purchaser). We asked the finance director to include any other relevant staff in the interviews and in half the cases, additional people attended. At the regional office we interviewed staff responsible for provider finance and performance. These external organisations added a further 10 interviews to the data set and thus in total the study is based on the results from 41 interviews.

Evidence on the Use of Hard and Soft Information

Information of all kinds plays a key role in facilitating and mediating relationships in any economic system and the NHS is no different in this respect. However, it should be noted that information is not a homogenous commodity but comprises a variety of different types of data, emanating from a range of sources and transmitted via a variety of channels. One of the key issues investigated was the extent and ways in which 'soft' information is used by a variety of stakeholders to form judgements on hospital performance. Analytically, it is difficult to define precisely what the terms 'hard' and 'soft' information represent as they are on a continuum rather than being polar opposites (Goddard et al., 1999). For ease of exposition in presenting our findings we make a rather crude distinction between hard, quantitative information emanating from official channels (e.g. Patients' Charter data) and soft, qualitative information transmitted via a variety of informal channels and professional networks. However, we recognise that in practice there is often no clear distinction between these types of information as the various stages of gathering, processing, disseminating and interpreting data will normally involve a blend of hard and soft approaches.

Soft Information as a Complement to Quantitative Indicators

A clear and dominant theme arising from our study is that hard information, used in isolation, is seen as an inadequate and sometimes misleading indicator of Trust performance. Regional office staff reported that they examined closely the hard financial information provided by individual Trusts in order to assess whether they are meeting their targets. However, hard information is not used in isolation from the knowledge of other factors affecting the Trust and this was reflected in their selection of Trusts to be included in the study. Those characterised by regional office staff as being at the lower end of performance were not necessarily the ones which on paper had the worst financial performance and vice versa. The main factor found to influence views on financial stability of Trusts was the degree to which the Trust acknowledges the fact that a problem exists and takes action to deal with it. Some of the judgements about the degree to which the Trust acknowledges the existence of a financial problem are based on hard data such as the existence of a recovery plan or willingness to sign up to an agreement with the health authority to tackle a financial deficit. However, we found that to a large extent the views of regional staff were influenced by the attitude of the Trust management. If regional staff perceive such attitudes are positive (based on personal exchange) they are far less concerned about the objective evidence of performance in terms of the Trust to meeting financial targets.

Judgements on Trust performance are also influenced by assessments of the quality of clinician–management relationships. Whilst some hard data exist around clinical process and outcome measures, the burden of the evidence suggests that regional offices and health authority staff are more concerned with the nature of clinical–managerial relationships within Trusts. NHS Trusts viewed as having 'cracked' the involvement of clinicians in management, were without exception classed as being good performers. Again, the nature of information on which such judgements are based is a mixture of hard and soft data. For example both regional offices and health authority staff noted the presence or absence of medical representation at key meetings with Trusts. However, the vast majority of information is in the form of soft intelligence gathered through informal networks. Regional office staff also reported that they routinely gather knowledge on the quality of local hospital services and individual clinical performance from the Deans of local medical schools and via special secondments of senior medical staff to advisory positions at the regional office.

Soft Information as a Substitute to Quantitative Indicators

Hard data are either not available or fail to capture all the areas which are seen as important factors in forming a judgement on Trust performance. We identified circumstances where external stakeholders relied on softer information for making assessments of Trust performance. For example, the regional office staff felt that its was important that Trust Chief Executives and chairman possessed charisma and vision and that they were skilled at networking and forging collaborative and strategic alliances within the local health economy. Such judgements are inevitably based on personal experiences and relationships and subjective accounts obtained from staff and through information relayed via professional networks. Similarly, many aspects of clinical care defy simple quantification and we found that medical directors and consultants often relied on informal knowledge of colleagues (including 'whistle-blowing'), rather than official clinical indicators to monitor the performance of clinicians. Moreover, we found that staff often viewed soft information as more timely than figures emanating from official sources which were often years out of date.

Limitations of Soft Information

Although soft information appears to play an important role in performance assessment it would be misleading to suggest it has no drawbacks. One of the main issues raised by respondents in our study was the potential for obtaining biased or distorted views, largely because soft information is often collected via conversations with individuals. This was seen to be particularly important in relation to views held by GPs. Trust chief executives were aware that the relationship between Trusts and GPs was one of the major criteria on which they were assessed by health authorities, but some expressed concern about this as they felt the evidence used was anecdotal. To some degree this was confirmed by comments made health authority staff who noted that often when they investigate negative views expressed by GPs, they find the GP was basing his or her view on anecdotes from other GPs rather than personal experience. Many Trusts felt that their reputations could be unfairly damaged in this way.

Another potential drawback of soft information is that it is not perceived as having the credibility of hard information and therefore it is more difficult to use this type of information to implement significant change. For example we found that it was easier for health authority staff to initiate discussion at a

Trust about why it does not meet Patient's Charter standards, than to base discussion on why it feels that relationship between management and clinicians in the Trust needs attention. Although the latter may well emerge as the underlying cause of the problem, it is easier to use the hard data as a 'can opener'. Regional office and health authority staff noted that hard information could 'kick start' such discussions and that soft data were rarely a sufficient basis for implementing strategic change.

Finally, it appears that hard data will always be required at strategic levels of the organisation as they facilitate comparisons and allow a summary of system performance to be made. The use of soft data is also likely to generate an unwieldy amount of information, which cannot be summarised or digested easily. Most importantly, the UK Treasury is unlikely to be convinced of arguments for increased funding for the NHS without some sort of summary quantitative evidence relating to improvements in performance.

Unintended and Adverse Consequences of Performance Indicators

Most of the external organisations and staff believed that the range of performance indicators in operation at the time of the study had provided some impetus for achieving some gains in improving performance. To this extent these data had the desired impact. However, many staff also highlighted areas where these data induced a range of unintended and adverse side effects.

Following Smith (1995) it is possible to examine the unintended and adverse consequences of performance indicator programmes under a number of headings. In our study we found examples of the following:

- *tunnel vision*: concentration on areas that are included in the performance indicator scheme, to the exclusion of other important but unmeasured areas. We found that the priority placed on reducing waiting times and lists was frequently cited as diverting attention and resources away from other important areas of activity;
- *sub-optimisation*: the pursuit of narrow local objectives by managers, at the expense of the objectives of the origination as a whole. We found that although each Trust had corporate objectives, personal and organisational incentive structures were not always closely aligned with strategic goals and objectives. In particular, problems were identified with aligning corporate financial objectives with clinical priorities. Issues were also raised concerning the alignment of Trust objectives with those of the wider health

economy, especially problems around 'bed blocking' with social services departments;

* *myopia*: concentration on short term issues to the exclusion of long-term criteria that may not show up in performance measures for many years. Many respondents felt that they were sometimes pushed to deliver short term targets (e.g. reductions in management costs or to balance Trust expenditure) without a view to longer term consequences;
* *misrepresentation*: the deliberate manipulation of data including 'creative accounting' and fraud so that reported behaviour differs from actual behaviour. Our study elicited many examples of staff stating that they had or knew of other staff who had knowingly engaged in misrepresentation routine performance data. Examples cited included double counting of Finished Consultant Episodes when a patient is referred to another consultant within the same hospital and excluding the least favourable cases when compiling data for performance audits;
* *gaming*: altering behaviour to obtain strategic advantage. The most frequently cited example of gaming concerned the efficiency index. Some respondents reported that they would be reluctant to achieve high gains one year for fear that they would be expected to deliver even higher gains the next. The ratchet effect was a common feature of the former soviet economic system where successful managers were 'punished' for good performance by having even higher target set in the subsequent years plan.

Discussion and Implications for the NHS

The key themes emerging from our study, which highlight the importance of soft intelligence and the potential pitfalls associated with a reliance solely on hard data as the informational base of a system of performance measurement, suggest that such systems will at best only ever give a partial view of performance of NHS Trusts, and at worst may give a distorted view or even induce a range of unintended and adverse consequences.

The extent to which soft information is used as a complement or substitute to hard data in Trust performance suggests that even in the 'performance-led NHS' it will be impossible to rely solely on a formal system of performance assessment. The use of soft information performs a number of important roles. It enriches the overall picture of Trust performance by providing information that covers dimensions of performance that defy simple quantification. In many instances this incorporates areas that external organisations view as crucial to forming a rounded assessment of Trust performance (e.g. the quality of management–clinician relationships) but about which they would have no formal information. Moreover, it avoids misjudgements about performance which can easily be made in the absence of contextual information, sometimes indicating that a Trust is a good performer despite the apparent problems suggested by the hard data, and sometimes working in the opposite direction to indicate the existence of underlying problems in an apparently well performing Trust.

Therefore, in order for the new system of monitoring to bear fruit, it is important that the Performance Assessment Framework does not suppress or distort this valuable flow of soft intelligence. In this respect it is important to resist the temptation to try to capture all the soft data by incorporating them within a formal system. This has been tried (with some success) in the private sector with the development of performance management tools such as the 'balanced scorecard' which go beyond the traditional financial focus to incorporate 'softer' measures of organisational performance such as such as employee satisfaction and commitment and customer views (Kaplan and Norton, 1992, 1996).

Informal social networks should be valued in their own right as a form of 'social capital' which as been shown to be a vital lubricant of complex economic relationships (Granovetter and Swedberg, 1992; Burt, 1995). Research has indicated that network-based styles of management and organisation are of substantial and increasing importance in the NHS, but may be difficult to sustain in a performance oriented organisation with a focus on quantitative target setting (Gabbay and Stewart , 1987; Ferlie and Pettigrew, 1996). There is a real danger that an overemphasis on measures of effectiveness and efficiency may have a detrimental effect on social networks, turning social capital into 'sour' capital with a corresponding deterioration in efficiency, effectiveness and consumer satisfaction (Bulder and Flap, 1996).

However, a note of caution should be added as excessive reliance on soft and informal networks may give rise to a range of problems. In particular, there is a danger that inaccurate information may be used to build up a reputation (good or bad) which is not justified. The importance of reputation and reputational capital as an intangible asset in the context of asymmetrical information and incomplete contracts has been well rehearsed in both the public and private sectors (Milgrom and Roberts, 1997; Tirole, 1989; Davies and Walker, 1998). The NHS provides a prime example of a situation where it is often difficult for a user (the patient) and their agent (the purchaser) to make fully informed decisions about the quality of the supplier or service provided. It is therefore likely that in the NHS, the attribution of a good (beacon) or poor (laggard) reputation will influence heavily the decisions concerning where to purchase services and invest in excellence. If the use of soft information facilitates the manipulation of reputation, this will provide misleading signals for those with responsibility for making purchasing decisions. In particular, there is the very real danger that a reliance solely on quantified data for making judgements on hospital performance may lead to a suboptimal solution either by wrongly condemning a high performing hospital (Type I error) or wrongly condoning a poorly performing hospital (Type II) error. We therefore suggest that a balanced combination of hard and soft intelligence, tailored to local circumstances may prove an optimal information strategy.

We have also highlighted the importance of ensuring that attention is paid to the potential unintended and dysfunctional consequences induced by a system of formal performance measurement. It is clear that performance measures do not always effect the desired changes in behaviour. The unintended consequences of some measures may actually encourage people to behave in ways, which are directly contradictory to what was expected.

Techniques to mitigate some of the specific unintended consequences highlighted by respondents have been suggested and it is also possible to identify a number of general strategies that address the dysfunctional consequences as noted by Smith (1995). Not all of these strategies will help address very problem, some may exacerbate other problems and they may in some circumstances be contradictory. Judgements may have to be made about the relative importance of different adverse outcomes, and these are likely to vary from one application to another. The choice of instrument is therefore likely to depend on the particular aspect of organization under consideration

The first three strategies address a large number of problems, and so are likely to be applicable in most situations:

1 involving staff at all levels in the development and implementation of performance measurement schemes;
2 retaining flexibility in the use of performance indicators, and not relying on them exclusively for control purposes;
3 keeping the performance measurement system under constant review.

The importance of the next three strategies is more dependent on the particular aspect of performance being measured, being most relevant when objectives are poorly defined and measurement of output difficult:

4   measuring client satisfaction;
5   seeking expert interpretation of the performance indicator scheme
6   maintaining careful audit of the data.

The final three strategies are designed to address specific difficulties – myopia, misrepresentation and gaming – and so should be considered when any of these is especially important:

7   nurturing long–term career perspectives among staff;
8   keeping the number of indicators small;
9   developing performance benchmarks independent of past activity.

In conclusion, we advocate a cautious approach to the use of performance indicators in the NHS. Our research has highlighted some of the limitations and drawbacks associated with the use of such formal measurement systems and these issues should be taken into careful consideration when developing measurement programmes such as the Performance Assessment Framework.

Acknowledgement

Much of the material presented here is derived from the following journal articles: Goddard, M., Mannion, R. and Smith, P. (1999), 'Assessing the Performance of NHS Hospital Trusts: the role of "hard" and "soft" information', *Health Policy*, 48, pp. 119–34; Goddard, M., Mannion, R. and Smith, P. (2000), 'Enhancing Performance in Health Care: A theoretical perspective on agency and the role of information', *Health Economics*, 9, pp. 95–107.

References

Bulder, B., Leeuw, F. and Flap, H. (1996), 'Networks and Evaluating Public Sector Reforms', *Evaluation*, 2 (3), pp. 261–76.
Burt, R. (1995), *Structured Holes: The social structure of competition*, Harvard University Press, Cambridge, Mass.
Davies, H. and Walker, B. (1998), 'Trust and Competition: Blue collar services in local government', in A. Coulson (ed.), *Trust and Contracts: Relationships in local government*, *Health and Public Services*, Policy Press, Bristol, pp. 159–82.

Ferlie, E. and Pettigrew, A. (1996), 'Managing through Networks: The issues and implications for the NHS', *British Journal of Management*, 7 (special issue), S81–S99.

Gabbay, J. and Stewart, R. (1987), 'Knowledge Needs Nurture', *Health Services Journal*, 23 July, p. 852.

Goddard, M., Mannion, R. and Smith, P. (1999), 'Assessing the Performance of NHS Trusts: the use of hard and soft information', *Health Policy*, 48, pp. 119–32.

Goddard, M., Mannion, R. and Smith, P. (2000), 'Enhancing Performance in Health Care: A theoretical perspective on agency and the role of information', *Health Economics*, 9, pp. 95–107.

Granovetter, M. and Swedberg, R. (1992), *The Sociology of Economic Life*, West View Press, Oxford.

Kaplan, R. and Norton, D. (1992), 'The Balanced Scorecard – Measures that Drive Performance', *Harvard Business Review*, Jan–Feb., pp. 71–9.

Kaplan, R. and Norton, D. (1996), 'Using the Balanced Scorecard as a Strategic Management System', *Harvard Business Review*, Jan–Feb, pp. 75–85.

Milgrom, P. and Roberts, J. (1989), *Economics, Organisation and Management*, Prentice-Hall, New Jersey.

Smith, P. (1995), 'On the Unintended Consequences of Publishing Performance Data in the Public Sector', *International Journal of Public Administration*, 18, pp. 277–310.

Tirole, J. (1989), *The Theory of Industrial Organisation*, 3rd edn, MIT, Massachusetts.

SECTION FOUR
INCORPORATING USER
VIEWS

Chapter Thirteen

What do Older People Expect from Health and Social Care in the Community?

P. Kliempt, D. Ruta, S. Ogston and M. McMurdo

Introduction

Community care is a vital component of care for older people (The Scottish Office, 1998) and the need to evaluate the outcomes of health and social care has become increasingly important. Many patient based outcome measures have been developed or adapted for use in elderly populations (Department of Health 1998; Kliempt, Ruta, and McMurdo, 1999a, 1999b, 1999c; McDowell and Newell, 1996; Sheikh et al., 1991). However, few health care researchers have asked the key question: 'which outcomes of health and social care are the most appropriate, important, and relevant for the quality of life of older people living in the community?'

In a recent consultation document for 'The New NHS', the government recognized that to assess performance, a priority should be to listen to local doctors and nurses, because they are *in the best position to know what patients need* and *will be in the driving seat in shaping services* (Department of Health, 1998). However, patients and health professionals have been shown to have very different perspectives with regard to the experience of illness (Parkerson, Broadhead, and Tse, 1992). It has also been recognised that patients may define a successful outcome and a good quality of life differently from professionals (Neuberger 1998). In a community care context there is no evidence that older people and their professional carers necessarily agree on the desired outcomes of care.

In this study we aimed to identify the outcomes of community care that people aged 75 and over consider most important for their overall quality of

Quality in Health Care: Strategic Issues in Health Care Management, H.T.O. Davies, M. Tavakoli and M. Malek (eds), Ashgate Publishing Ltd, 2001.

life. A second aim was to see how the views of older people compared with the views of professional carers.

Subjects and Methods

To identify an initial set of outcomes we began by conducting 10 in-depth interviews with people aged between 75–97 years, living in their own homes, and randomly selected from a district nurse caseload. We used an unstructured interview approach and asked people about the health and social care they had been receiving and about the factors they considered most important and relevant to their quality of life. The interviews were recorded on tape and lasted up to two hours. They were then transcribed and the data examined for outcomes relevant to the research question. In other words similar statements were compiled in broad categories of outcomes or themes.

Six important desired outcomes of care emerged from the qualitative analysis. These were: company (e.g. somebody to talk to); mobility (being physically mobile, but also having access to public transport); pain relief; personal hygiene (e.g. help with bathing); safety (having rails and bath seats but also door chains and spy holes); and social support (e.g. having people to help in times of need with tasks like shopping or housework).

These outcomes were incorporated into a survey questionnaire for older people and health and social care professionals. Respondents were asked to rank the six quality of life outcomes by placing them in one of six numbered boxes, where box number one represented 'area that [patients/clients] I feel is most important to my quality of life, and where I think that help would most benefit me [them]', and box number six represented 'area that I feel is least important'. However, both groups were given the option to include outcomes other than the six listed in the questionnaire if they considered them more important. The questionnaire for older people was piloted with a group of older people who were also asked to make comments on the wording and layout.

The questionnaires were posted to 165 people aged 75 and over living in the community in North East Fife, Scotland, who were randomly selected from all 12 general practices in this region. One hundred and fifty-seven questionnaires were posted to all community health and social care professionals working in North East Fife (nine community mental health nurses, 16 district nurses, 46 general practitioners, 19 health visitors, nine home care managers, 19 occupational therapists (health and social work), 15 physiotherapists, 14 social workers, and 10 voluntary workers). One reminder letter including a copy of the questionnaire and a return envelope was sent to both staff and older people after three weeks, if no questionnaire was returned. Patients and staff were both given the option to return the questionnaire blank if they did not want to take part, which would avoid sending unnecessary reminders.

Data were entered using EPI 6 and analysed in Microsoft Excel, version 7.0. The outcome that was ranked as most important was given a value of 6, and subsequent outcomes were scored 5, 4, 3, and 2, with 1 for the outcome ranked as least important. If a respondent did not include an outcome in the rankings, it was excluded from the analysis and the remaining ranks adjusted so that the respondent's average was the same as for respondents who ranked all the outcomes. This ensured that any comparison of older person and professional mean values for the importance of each outcome to overall quality of life was not biased by differences in the prevalence of experience of outcomes in the older person population.

Results

Of the 165 older people, 120 (72 per cent) returned a questionnaire. Fifty-four (32 per cent) returned the questionnaire completed, 66 (40 per cent) returned the questionnaire blank, seven (4 per cent) failed to complete it satisfactorily, and two (1 per cent) were deceased. Of the 157 health and social care professionals, 100 (64 per cent) returned their questionnaires completed, and eight (5 per cent) blank. Many older people who returned their questionnaires blank did, however, include personal comments often explaining why they did not complete the questionnaire. The most common reasons given were: that they were healthy and not in need of any health or social care; that family members or friends cared for them; or that the six outcomes stated in the questionnaire were not applicable to them at present. Neither the older people nor health and social work professionals offered any other items than the six listed. The ages of the 100 female patients ranged from 76–93 years with a mean age of 80.1 years, and the ages of the 65 male patients ranged from 75–95 years with a mean age of 80.0 years. There were no differences detectable in the age ranges and mean ages between the patients returning the questionnaire completed and the patients returning the questionnaire blank.

The majority of older people who responded felt that all six outcomes were relevant to their quality of life, with only 30 per cent completing less than six boxes in the questionnaire. Three outcomes were not listed by about a fifth of respondents (social support, pain relief and personal hygiene), and three were omitted by about 10 per cent of respondents (mobility, company and safety). However, there was substantial variation within both the older people and staff samples over the relative importance of the six outcomes. Each outcome was ranked highest by some respondents and lowest by others. This explains why a mean of less than two rankings separates the most important outcome from the least important for both older people and staff (Figure 13.1).

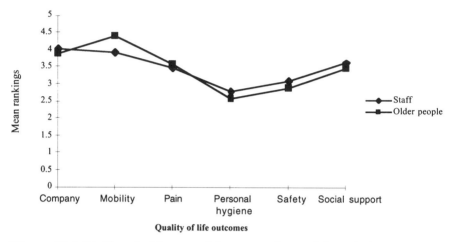

Figure 13.1 Staff and older people's perceptions of the relative importance of six quality of life outcomes

A non-parametric test, Kendall's W was conducted for staff and older people to determine whether any statistically significant differences occurred between the mean rankings of the six outcomes. The mean rankings for both staff ($p<0.001$) and older people ($p<0.001$) across the six outcomes were significantly different. Paired sample t-tests were then used to identify any significant differences between the individual outcomes within each group and to calculate 95 per cent confidence intervals. Statistically significant differences in the means of older people's rankings were obtained when comparing company with personal hygiene ($p=0.001$, CI=-2.22:-0.66) and safety ($p=0.028$, CI=-2.07:-0.12), mobility with pain relief ($p=0.016$, CI=-1.57:-0.17), personal hygiene ($p<0.001$, CI=-2.55:-1.29), social support ($p=0.015$, CI=-1.71:-0.19) and safety ($p<0.001$, CI:-2.22:-0.83), pain relief and personal hygiene ($p=0.007$, CI=-1.81:-0.30) and personal hygiene and social support ($p=0.039$, CI=0.04:1.71). A comparison of the mean staff rankings produced statistically significant results for company with personal hygiene (p<0.001, CI=-1.80:-0.76) and safety (p=0.002, CI=-7.49:-0.34), mobility with personal hygiene (p<0.001, CI=-1.64:-0.57) and safety (p=0.002, CI=-1.34:-0.31), pain relief with personal hygiene (p=0.014, CI=-1.13:-0.13) and personal hygiene with social support (p<0.001, CI=-0.38:1.30).

On average, however, a consistent pattern emerges which is similar for older people and staff: mobility and company are perceived as relatively more important for a good quality of life, while personal hygiene and safety are perceived as relatively less important.

While this pattern holds true for all professional groups taken together, when the various professions are analysed separately, differences in perceived importance emerge (Figure 13.2). Thus occupational and physical therapists appear to value perceived safety much more highly than other professional groups. Social workers and nurses on the other hand attach much greater importance to personal hygiene.

Discussion

Several studies have looked at the ingredients older people consider important for their overall quality of life. Bowling, for example, compared responses from older and younger age groups in a UK national interview survey (Bowling, 1995a, 1995b). The five most important life areas for older people were: own health; relationships with family; financial security/standard of living; health of someone close; and social life/leisure (Bowling, 1995b). She found people over the age of 75 years were more likely than younger people to mention their own health, and less likely to mention relationships with family and other relatives, as the first most important area of life (Bowling, 1995a). Bowling's findings were confirmed by Farquhar (1995). O'Boyle et al., using a well-validated individualised quality of life assessment tool, the SEIQoL (Hickey et al., 1996; O'Boyle et al., 1992), found that quality of life for older people was generally higher than for younger age groups (Browne et al., 1994). Similar ingredients emerged amongst the five most important areas for overall quality of life, with the notable exception that religion replaced 'health of someone close'. Although these studies provide a valuable insight into the factors influencing perceived quality of life of older people, they have one important limitation. They do not ask specifically about those areas of life where health and social care provision may be of benefit. The latter is arguably the more relevant question when the aim is to identify the appropriate desired outcomes of care for older people.

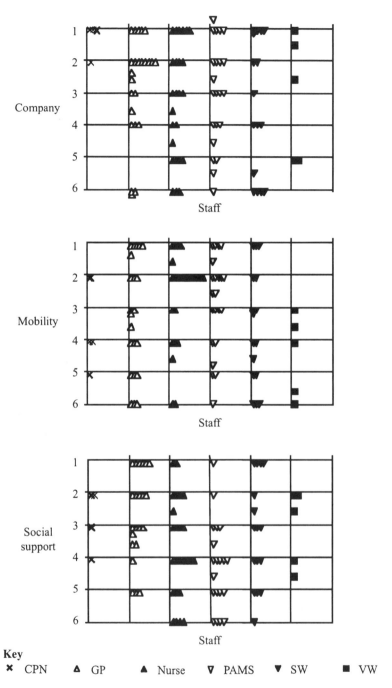

Key
✗ CPN   ▵ GP   ▲ Nurse   ▽ PAMS   ▼ SW   ■ VW

Figure 13.2 Staff rankings of six quality of life outcomes

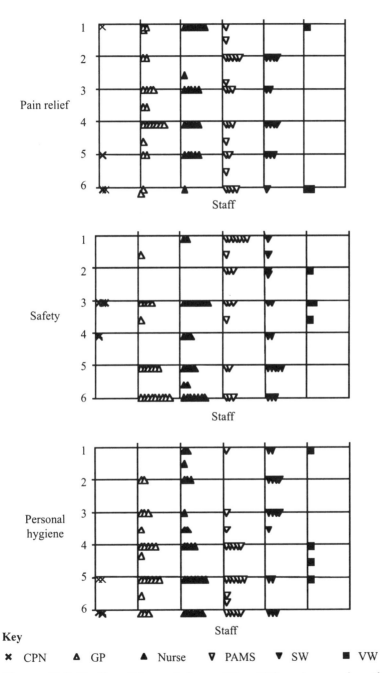

Figure 13.2 Staff rankings of six quality of life outcomes (continued)

Roberts et al. looked specifically at the appropriateness of 12 possible performance measures for geriatric services, and compared hospital specialists' views with those of their patients (Roberts, Khee, and Philip, 1994). They found that both geriatricians and patients gave high priority to reducing disability and improving quality of life. However, the candidate performance measures for the survey were selected by geriatricians not by care recipients, and included a mix of clinical, patient satisfaction, and process of care outcomes. The nature of desired improvements in quality of life were not specified.

Our study asks the relevant question – 'which areas do you feel are most important to your quality of life, and *where help would most benefit you?*'. It quantifies the relative importance of these areas and directly compares the perceptions of care recipients with staff. It provides evidence that six areas of life – company, mobility, pain relief, personal hygiene, safety, and social support – are considered to be both important to a good quality of life by people over 75 years living in the community, and the key desired outcomes of the health and social care they receive.

We are aware of only one other published study that asked the same question of older people living in the community. Qureshi et al. looked specifically at home care clients. Through interviews and focus groups (Qureshi et al., 1998) they identified five desired outcomes. These were: meeting of basic physical needs; personal safety and security; being able to live in a clean and tidy environment; keeping alert and active; and access to social contact and company. The similarities with the outcomes identified in our study are striking, even though Qureshi's study was concerned exclusively with the outcomes of social care. It is perhaps not surprising that recipients of home care in Qureshi's study did not identify 'pain relief' as a desired outcome, since the alleviation of pain is clearly the province of health care professionals.

Although the relative importance of desired quality of life outcomes identified in our study was found to differ between individuals, on average both older people and their professional carers tend to value mobility and company most highly. However considerable inter-professional differences appeared in the responses of staff. This suggests that professionals tend to focus on those aspects of quality of life that can be improved as a direct result of the services they provide.

Most of the older people felt that all six outcomes were relevant to them and the postal survey failed to identify any additional quality of life outcomes. This may be taken as confirmatory evidence that the desired outcomes of health and social care are comprehensively encompassed by these six categories. It is possible, however, that our survey design may have deterred respondents from adding or substituting other outcomes.

Some have argued against the use of self-administered postal questionnaires in an older population (O'Mahoney et al., 1998; Owens and Batchelor, 1996). Others have shown that postal surveys amongst older people can achieve high response rates in certain settings, or where the survey is seen as directly relevant to respondent's interests and concerns (Jones and Lester, 1994; Victor, 1988). Given the exploratory nature of our research and the complexity of our open survey question, a completion rate of 32 per cent is not unexpected. With hindsight however, if we had avoided sending questionnaires to patients who did not feel they needed health and social care we might have achieved a better completion rate. For example a third of respondents returning a blank questionnaire attached comments indicating that they did not consider the survey to be relevant to their needs or concerns. If the survey were to be repeated, we would recommend that a screening question be included asking whether people are currently receiving any health or social care. This would differentiate those patients returning a blank questionnaire because they did not wish to take part in the study from those who were not eligible because they were not in receipt of community services.

We are aware of at least 75 different health or health-related quality of life instruments that have been used in older populations. Many of these instruments include questions or scales designed to assess one or more of the quality of life outcomes identified in our study. For example at least four instruments – the Barthel Index (Mahoney and Barthel, 1965), the Activities of Daily Living Scale (Katz and Akpom, 1976), the Townsend Disability Scale (Townsend, 1962), and the Physical Maintenance Scale (Lawton and Brody, 1969) – measure mobility and personal hygiene. However, we could find no instrument or scale in the literature specifically designed to assess perceived safety. The Royal College of Physicians of London and the British Geriatrics Society recently used the domains for assessment in the elderly recommended by the World Health Organisation (WHO, 1989) to select a set of standardised assessment scales for older people (Research Unit of the Royal College of Physicians and the British Geriatrics Society, 1992). Their recommended scales do not include any assessment of three of the quality of life outcomes identified in our study – pain relief, company, and perceived safety.

We believe our findings have important implications for evaluating the outcomes of care for older people in community settings. Any package of outcome measures intended for use in such settings must, at the very least, provide an assessment of the six quality of life outcomes that are most important and relevant to older people.

Acknowledgements

We gratefully acknowledge the help of all health and social work professionals and older people who participated in this survey. The survey was part of an ongoing three year long outcomes project which is funded by Perth & Kinross Health Care Trust.

References

Bowling, A. (1995a), 'The Most Important Things in Life. Comparisons between older and younger population age groups by gender. Results from a national survey of the public's judgements', *International Journal of Health Sciences*, 6(4), pp. 169–75.

Bowling, A. (1995b), 'What Things are Important in People's Lives? A survey of the public's judgements to inform scales of health related quality of life', *Social Science and Medicine*, 41(10), pp. 1447–62.

Browne, J.P., O'Boyle, C.A., McGee, H.M., Joyce, C.R.B., McDonald, N.J., O'Malley, K. and Hiltbrunner, B. (1994), 'Individual Quality of Life in the Healthy Elderly', *Quality of Life Research*, 3, pp. 235–44.

Department of Health (1998), 'The New NHS, Modern, Dependable: A national framework for assessing performance', NHS Executive.

Farquhar, M. (1995), 'Elderly People's Definitions of Quality of Life', *Social Science and Medicine*, 41(10), pp. 1439–46.

Hickey, A.M., Bury, G., O'Boyle, C.A., Bradley, F., O'Kelly, F.D. and Shannon, W. (1996), 'A New Short Form Individual Quality of Life Measure (SEIQoL-DW): Application in a cohort of individuals with HIV/AIDS', *British Medical Journal*, 313, pp. 29–33.

Jones, D. and Lester, C. (1994), 'Hospital Care and Discharge – Patients' and Carers' Opinions', *Age and Ageing*, 23, pp. 91–6.

Katz, S. and Akpom, C.A. (1976), 'Index of ADL', *Medical Care*, XIV(5), pp. 116–18.

Kliempt, P., Ruta, D., McMurdo, M. (2000), 'Measuring the Outcomes of Care in Older People: A non-critical review of patient-based measures. I General health status and quality of life instruments', *Reviews in Clinical Gerontology*, 10, pp. 33–42.

Kliempt, P., Ruta, D. and McMurdo, M. (2000), 'Measuring the Outcomes of Care in Older People: A non-critical review of patient-based measures. II Mental status, depression, and psychological wellbeing instruments', *Reviews in Clinical Gerontology*, 10, pp. 123–32.

Kliempt, P., Ruta, D. and McMurdo, M. (2000), 'Measuring the Outcomes of Care in Older People: A non-critical review of patient-based measures. III Pain, physical disability& handicap, and social health measures', *Reviews in Clinical Gerontology* (in press).

Lawton, M.P. and Brody, E.M. (1969), 'Assessment of Older People: Self-maintaining and instrumental activities of daily living', *Gerontologist*, 9, pp. 179–86.

Mahoney, F.I. and Barthel, D.W. (1965), 'Functional Evaluation: The Barthel index', *Rehabilitation*, pp. 61–5.

McDowell, I. and Newell, C. (1996), *Measuring Health. A Guide to Rating Scales and Questionnaires*, Oxford University Press, New York.

Neuberger, J. (1998), 'Primary Care: Core values. Patients' Priorities', *British Medical Journal*, 317, pp. 260–2.

O'Boyle, C.A., McGee, H., Hickey, A., O'Malley, K. and Joyce, C.R.B. (1992), 'Individual Quality of Life in Patients Undergoing Hip Replacement', *Lancet*, 339, pp. 1088–91.

O'Mahoney, P.G., Rodgers, H., Thomson, R.G., Dobson, R. and James, O.F.W. (1998), 'Is the SF-36 Suitable for Assessing Health Status of Older Stroke Patients'?, *Age and Ageing*, 27, pp. 19–22.

Owens, D.J. and Batchelor, C. (1996), 'Patient Satisfaction and the Elderly', *Social Science and Medicine*, 42(11), pp. 1483–91.

Parkerson, G.R. Jr, Broadhead, W.E. and Tse, C.-K.J. (1992), 'Quality of Life and Functional Health of Primary Care Patients', *Journal of Clinical Epidemiology*, 45(11), pp. 1303–13.

Qureshi, H., Patmore, C., Nicholas, E. and Bamford, C. (1998), 'Overview: Outcomes of social care for older poeple and carers', in SPRU, The University of York (ed.), *Outcomes in Community Care Practice*, University of York Printing Unit, York.

Research Unit of the Royal College of Physicians and the British Geriatrics Society (1992), *Standardised Assessment Scales for Older People*, The Royal College of Physicians of London and The British Geriatrics Society, London.

Roberts, H., Khee, T.S. and Philip, I. (1994), 'Setting Priorities for Measures of Performance for Geriatric Medical Services', *Age and Ageing*, 23, pp. 154–7.

Sheikh, J.I., Yesavage, J.A., Brooks, J.O., Friedman, L. and Gratzinger, P. (1991), 'Proposed Factor Structure of the Geriatric Depression Scale', *International Psychogeriatrics*, 3(1), pp. 23–8.

The Scottish Office (1998), *Modernising Community Care. An Action Plan*, HMSO.

Townsend, P. (1962), *The Last Refuge*, Routledge and Kegan Paul, London.

Victor, C.R. (1988), 'Some Methodological Aspects of using Postal Questionnaires with the Elderly', *Archives of Gerontology and Geriatrics*, 7, pp. 163–72.

WHO (1989), *Health for the Elderly*, World Health Organisation, Geneva.

Chapter Fourteen

Serving *all* the Community? The Views and Preferences of Lesbian and Gay Consumers of Health Care

Yaniv Poria, Adrian Coyle and Terry Desombre

Introduction

Organisations wishing to ensure that they provide appropriate and high quality services need to understand their entire 'customer' base (Kotler, 1997). One strategy for doing this is to segment their customer/consumer base, on the assumption that consumers are not homogeneous (Beane and Ennis, 1987) and that it is useful to identify groups of consumers on the basis of certain shared distinguishing characteristics which may influence their views of services and their patterns of service consumption (Morgan and Pritchard, 1998). Segmentation can be based on various characteristics and can yield valuable data for service provision and service development.

This chapter contributes to the process of ascertaining the views and preferences of one segment of the consumer base of physical health care services, i.e., lesbians and gay men. 'Lesbian' and 'gay' are terms used to describe people 'whose sexual and emotional feelings and behaviours are exclusively or predominantly directed towards others of the same sex' (Coyle, 1998, p. 164). However, this segment of the population has been variously defined, for example, in terms of lifestyle (Hughes, 1997) and the visibility of their relationships (Jacobson and Samdahl, 1998). Additionally, marketing research has already identified that this group has certain characteristics relevant to marketing such as a relatively high disposable income (Wood, 1999) (although this is greater among gay men than lesbians), a high level of education (Oleck, 1995) and a high level of brand loyalty (Pitts, 1999). This information has been used to segment lesbians and gay men in the context of

Quality in Health Care: Strategic Issues in Health Care Management, H.T.O. Davies, M. Tavakoli and M. Malek (eds), Ashgate Publishing Ltd, 2001.

other domains of service consumption such as in tourism (Hughes, 1997; Pitts, 1999).

The research presented in this chapter is based on the assumption that the sexuality of consumers will influence their views and preferences in relation to health care services. This assumption arises from the recognition that the use of health care services can call for the explicit or implicit disclosure or management of potentially sensitive information which may influence the nature of subsequent interactions between the patient and health care professionals. This includes information about patients' sexuality. For lesbian and gay patients, this may create particular dilemmas because lesbian and gay sexualities are often subject to social disapproval, prejudice and discrimination (Snape et al., 1995; Herek, 1998). This situation may mean that lesbian and gay patients have particular views and preferences regarding the provision of health care services and the ways in which their sexuality is dealt with in health care contexts. However, it is acknowledged that many other factors, such as gender, will also shape their views and preferences so that these views and preferences will sometimes represent the outcome of an interaction between sexuality and other factors.

Lesbian and gay sexualities have already been considered and studied in the context of health care, largely in terms of health care staff's (perceived) attitudes towards and interactions with lesbian and gay patients and patients' openness about their sexuality in interactions with staff (for example, Dardick and Grady, 1980; Douglas et al., 1985; Paroski, 1987; Webb, 1987, 1988; Rudolph, 1988; Hellman and Stanton, 1989; Faugier and Wright, 1990; Eliason and Randall, 1991; Irwin, 1992; Annesley and Coyle, 1995). Much work has also been conducted in the specific context of staff attitudes to gay men with HIV/AIDS (for example, Scherer et al., 1991; Siminoff et al., 1991; Wadsworth and McCann, 1992; Vermette and Godin, 1996). In addition, studies have been conducted which have reported lesbian women's and gay men's experiences and evaluations of mental health services (Proctor, 1994; Golding, 1997; Annesley and Coyle, 1998; McFarlane, 1998; Milton and Coyle, 1999). All of this work points to some positive but many negative experiences of care. Although recommendations have been produced by professional bodies regarding the care of lesbian and gay patients (for example, Royal College of Nursing 1994, 1998a, 1998b), the extent to which these are currently reflected in health care practice is debatable.

It was hoped that, in ascertaining the views and preferences of a group of lesbian and gay (potential) consumers of health care services, the present study would contribute to this body of work and would produce findings that could be used by providers of health care services to improve service provision to lesbians and gay men. By attending to the research findings, providers could thus be helped to work towards ensuring that health care services respond to the needs of the whole community.

Method

Participants

Forty self-identified lesbians and gay men (16 lesbians and 24 gay men) took part in interviews in the UK (in the Guildford area in Surrey) and in Israel (in Tel Aviv and Jerusalem). Six lesbians and seven gay men participated in interviews in the UK; 10 lesbians and 17 gay men took part in interviews in Israel. Data were gathered from two countries in an attempt to reduce the risk of producing findings that were specific to a particular health care system. The countries in question were chosen on the grounds of convenience to the researchers.

Participants were recruited through lesbian and gay groups and organisations, through personal contacts of the researchers and by approaching individuals in lesbian and gay pubs and meeting places. This sample was extended by 'snowballing', i.e., asking interviewees to recruit additional participants from their social networks who might provide a different perspective on the research topic. Being a qualitative study, the aim of this sampling strategy was to obtain diverse rather than representative perspectives on the research topic.

Procedure

Interviews took place in lesbian and gay pubs and meeting places using a semi-structured interview format (Smith, 1995). These locations were chosen partly for practical reasons and partly because it was felt that they would enable interviewees to feel at ease. Although the interviews focused upon participants' views and preferences (as lesbians or gay men) in relation to physical health care services, ample scope was provided for participants to discuss issues which were relevant to this topic but which were not included on the interview schedule. To illustrate their views, participants were encouraged to draw upon their personal experiences of health care and their friends' experiences.

While 15 interviews were conducted on a one-to-one basis (eight in the UK, seven in Israel), participants often subsequently involved friends and others in the ensuing discussions in a quasi-focus group format. These additional participants (n=25) contributed their own viewpoints and experiences. The interviews in the UK were conducted in English; the interviews in Israel were conducted in Hebrew.

Ordinarily in qualitative research, interviews are tape recorded in order to afford the researcher a detailed record of the data. However, in this case, tape-recording proved impossible due to the high level of background noise in the interview locations. The interviewer (YP) therefore made detailed notes during the interviews, summarising the content of participants' responses and recording their actual words when they made points which seemed especially pertinent to the research questions. These notes were then elaborated immediately after the interviews.

Analysis

These notes were subjected to thematic content analysis to illuminate underlying themes in participants' talk (Smith, 1995). The analysis was not guided by specific prior hypotheses but instead allowed key themes to 'emerge' from the data, the aim being to gain an account of participants' own views and preferences. However, the adoption of a semi-structured interview approach to data collection means that data are at least partly shaped by the core questions asked of all participants. The analytic process involved the careful rereading of the interview notes by one researcher (YP) to discern common themes and differences in the accounts provided by the participants. A preliminary set of themes was developed and illustrative quotations were noted. This was subsequently checked by the other researchers to ensure that themes were consonant with and grounded in the data (see Elliott et al., 1999, on the importance of these procedures for ensuring the legitimacy of qualitative research). In addition, the translation of those quotations which were originally in Hebrew has been checked by a native Hebrew speaker who is also fluent in English and who was not part of the research team. In the quotations that follow, empty square brackets (i.e. [ ]) indicate where material has been omitted and material within square brackets has been added for clarification.

Results

Background Information on Participants

Some basic background information was gathered from the 15 lesbians and gay men who participated in one-to-one interviews. Participants' mean age was 25.4 years (range 16–40); the mean age of the UK group was 25.2 years (range 19–40) and the mean age of the Israeli group was 25.6 years (range 16–34). Eight participants (three in the UK; five in Israel) were currently involved in at least one sexual and emotional relationship; seven (four in the UK; three in Israel) did not currently have a partner. In terms of the extent to which others in their social world knew about their sexuality, 13 participants (all eight UK participants and five Israeli participants) said that some people knew: 10 said that only those 'who should know' knew about their sexuality; more specifically, three said that only those who were close to them knew (for example, family and close friends). Two participants (both Israeli) said that everyone in their social worlds knew. Due to the informal nature of the interviews with the other 25 participants, it was not possible to gather background information from them.

The analysis of the interview data centred around three major themes, relating to a perceived need for health care staff to develop an awareness that patients might be lesbian or gay, preferences regarding the gender of health care staff who are providing treatment and the non-desirability of having health care services specifically for lesbians and gay men. No systematic differences were observed between the data from UK participants and the data from Israeli participants, even though the data were analysed in two groups based on participants' nationality.

The Need for Staff Awareness

The situation that was most commonly identified as problematic for lesbian and gay patients in health care contexts concerned the failure of health care staff to consider that patients might be lesbian or gay (see also Dardick and Grady, 1980) and that a person of the same gender accompanying a patient might be their partner. In specific terms, many participants spoke of situations where a patient was taken for a medical examination and – without consulting the patient – health care staff asked their partner to leave the room. This was said to have arisen from staff's failure to consider that two people of the same gender could be a couple. For example:

There is one thing in particular that I find uncomfortable and this is the fact that the doctor did not ask my partner if she wants me to stay in the room. Immediately they make the assumption that we are friends and not a couple and I think that they should be aware of that (lesbian woman: Israel).

What makes me angry is the fact that he [the doctor] did not ask me. He did not even think that maybe we are a couple – he thought that we are just friends. At least he could ask (lesbian woman: Israel).

One participant expressed bewilderment at why this should occur:

Why are there no procedures that ask the doctor to ask the patient [ ] 'Do you want him or her to stay in the room?'. Is it so complicated? (gay man: UK)

As Kitzinger and Coyle (1995) have observed, lesbian and gay relationships are routinely unacknowledged and rendered invisible in many social contexts. When this occurs in what may be anxiety-provoking health care contexts, it is not surprising that it should lead to strong, negative emotional reactions. Even those participants who had not experienced inpatient or outpatient services after having developed a lesbian or gay identity identified this lack of acknowledgement as a situation that could cause them most concern. Regardless of the reasons for staff's failure to consider that two people of the same gender could be a couple, participants interpreted this in terms of discrimination against lesbians and gay men.

When asked to reflect upon how health care staff could improve services for lesbian and gay patients, all participants recommended that staff should develop their awareness of lesbian and gay sexualities, specifically in terms of considering that two people of the same gender might be a lesbian or gay couple. For example:

Just to be aware that if there are two men, it is not necessary that they are just good friends. They can be a couple (gay man: Israel).

One participant pointed out that staff should not make assumptions about the nature of the relationship between patients and those accompanying them, regardless of their gender:

They should ask every couple – does not matter what their genders are – if they are together. How do they know if a man and a woman coming together are a couple? Maybe they are brother and sister (gay man: UK).

Preferences Regarding the Gender of Health Care Staff

Although a range of views were expressed concerning preferences for male or female health care staff, many participants did express preferences concerning the gender of health care staff who might be involved in their care. These preferences were mostly related to situations where health care professionals would be required to conduct examinations of 'intimate' areas of the body (such as in breast, testicular, gynaecological and rectal examinations) or to engage in close, sustained contact with the patient's body (such as when providing massage in physiotherapy).

Some participants related their preferences to their sexuality. Some explained that they preferred to be examined by a health care professional of a different gender because they would not want to risk finding the staff member sexually attractive and becoming sexually aroused during the examination; it was feared that this could lead to embarrassment and social discomfort for both the patient and the member of staff. However, it was felt that this was unlikely to occur in gynaecological examinations because of the physical discomfort involved in these procedures.

Other participants invoked their sexual identity in different ways. Some participants expressed the view that heterosexual men are more favourably disposed towards lesbians than towards gay men and that heterosexual women are more favourably disposed towards gay men than towards lesbians ('Men are not friendly to gays and women are not friendly to lesbians' – lesbian woman: Israel) (see Kite, 1984 and Herek, 1994 on this). This led them to prefer receiving treatment from a health care professional of a different gender, which seemed to be based on an assumption of universal heterosexuality among health care staff.

Some lesbian women said that they would prefer to be examined by a woman because they did not trust men. This distrust was not specifically related to their sexual identity and arose from considerations that might be shared by some heterosexual women:

> I just do not trust men. Maybe he [the doctor] just wants to touch my breast because I am another sex attraction for him (lesbian woman: UK).

Other preferences for male or female health care staff that were not related to the patient's sexual identity were based on assumed connections between the gender of the staff member and the quality of the treatment they could provide. For some, these connections centred on the assumption that a professional would be better able to understand the body and feelings of a patient of the same gender. For example:

> The only thing I can think about where I would prefer a woman to a man is when you need to shave your [pubic] hair because she has to do it for herself so she may take more care. She will know what the results can be if you do it the wrong way (lesbian woman: Israel).

> [In a breast examination] it will be easier for her [a female staff member] to understand what I am feeling and my way of thinking. A man, I think, could not understand what it is for a woman to lose a breast (lesbian woman: Israel).

> I would prefer a woman gynaecologist because she has something like this [gynaecological concerns] at home (lesbian woman: Israel).

Other participants' preferences were based on (assumptions about) gender-specific physical qualities that were felt to influence the quality of treatment. For example, male health care professionals were assumed to be physically stronger than females which, in some areas of health care such as orthopaedics, was seen as advantageous; one woman's preference for a female gynaecologist was based on the fact that women have smaller hands than men and so would be able to offer a more comfortable examination.

Some other participants did not express preferences regarding the gender of health care staff involved in their treatment. Although some thought that they would have positive or negative reactions to male or female staff, these participants felt that these reactions were immaterial and that the quality of treatment was more important than the gender of the staff who were providing the treatment. In discussing their views, these participants sometimes bracketed their sexual identity and gender in startling ways:

> When I am going to a hospital, I am like a piece of meat that needs some treatment and I do not think that my identity – the fact that I am lesbian – should be taken into account (lesbian woman: Israel).

Health Care Services Specifically for Lesbians and Gay Men

It might be assumed that one way of ensuring that the health care needs and preferences of lesbians and gay men are properly addressed would be to develop health care services specifically for lesbians and gay men. However, none of the participants felt that this would be desirable. Their rejection of this idea was based on a desire to avoid becoming ghettoised and marginalised – a fear that lesbians and gay men would become 'separate [ ] from the community' and be seen as negatively different. Participants felt that the development of separate health care services would create the impression that 'being gay is a disease' or dangerous and that lesbians and gay men need to be separated from the rest of the population for fear of contagion. When discussions explored the desirability of developing specific services for lesbians and gay men in other contexts (such as hotel services), resistance was much less marked because it was felt that such a development would not carry the same connotations of disease, danger and contagion.

Discussion

In common with other research with lesbians and gay men and other qualitative research, this study has certain limitations. Firstly, it is impossible to determine the representativeness of samples of lesbians and gay men because the parameters of these populations are unknown. Instead, research with lesbians and gay men tends to aim for a diversity of participants with the intention of exploring the research phenomenon from multiple perspectives (for example, see Davies et al., 1993). This study deliberately sought such diversity by recruiting participants from two countries and by ensuring that both lesbian and gay perspectives were adequately represented. However, the core sample could have been more diverse in terms of age, which might have provided access to more varied outlooks that reflected age- and development-related differences.

Secondly, although the sample is sizeable for a qualitative study, no conclusions can be drawn concerning the generalisability of the findings. When researching a relatively sensitive topic with a specific group, it is often necessary to build up an increasingly comprehensive picture through a series of small-scale, complementary studies, with each extending the insights gained from previous work. In relation to the exploration of the views and preferences of lesbian and gay consumers of health care services, the present study may be seen as contributing to the development of a comprehensive knowledge base. Other researchers may wish to extend this process by conducting studies with lesbians and gay men whose voices are missing from the present study (for example, older lesbians and gay men; lesbians and gay men who are less involved with lesbian and gay communities; and lesbians and gay men from ethnic minority communities) and whose position might have led to a different set of views and preferences from those reported here. In addition, further research might usefully attempt to identify differences between the views and preferences of lesbian women and gay men. It might also be worth considering service providers' conceptualisations of the needs and preferences of lesbian and gay consumers of health services and their views concerning the feasibility of developing services in accordance with these needs and preferences.

It is noteworthy that the themes reported in this chapter demonstrated both unity and diversity among the participants. Calls for greater awareness and knowledge among health care staff of lesbian and gay sexualities – specifically in terms of considering that two people of the same gender might be a lesbian or gay couple – and resistance to the creation of health care services specifically for lesbians and gay men were universal. On the other hand, all shades of viewpoint were represented on the question of participants' preferences regarding the gender of health care staff involved in their care.

Although further research is required before policy and practice can be developed or revised, provisional recommendations can be offered concerning the universally-acknowledged need for the development of staff awareness. This can be achieved in various ways, such as by ensuring that lesbian and gay sexualities and lifestyles are addressed in an informed and integrated way in the curricula of all education and training programmes in health care and by providing post-qualification training for health care staff. This could be usefully located within a broader framework of considering the needs and preferences of patients from diverse backgrounds, which would avoid singling out and problematising lesbians and gay men and would permit useful parallels to be drawn with other social groups (such as ethnic minority groups) which may suffer discrimination. Educational interventions could include both information-giving and opportunities (perhaps through structured exercises) for staff to reflect upon their attitudes towards lesbians and gay men and their feelings about providing health care services to lesbian and gay patients (see Irwin, 1992 and Taylor and Robertson, 1994 for further recommendations). However, due to the uncertain relationship between attitude change and behaviour change (Ajzen and Fishbein, 1980), attention would need to be paid to the question of how to increase the likelihood of increased awareness being translated into practice. This may involve role-playing scenarios with lesbian and gay patients that are akin to real-life practice contexts and/or providing opportunities for staff to reflect on their practice some time after receiving educational interventions.

By increasing staff awareness of lesbian and gay patients, the situations which participants described in which their partnerships were not recognised might be more easily avoided (see Royal College of Nursing, 1998a for recommendations on how to address 'next-of-kin' issues with lesbian and gay patients). Health care professionals might then be able to involve partners in the care of patients as a resource for providing support (Dardick and Grady, 1980). An awareness of the possibility that two people of the same gender might be partners may also obviate the need for patients and partners to disclose their sexual identity explicitly to staff, which they may not wish to do. Instead, if staff are attuned to the possibility that two people might be partners, interactions between staff, patients and partners can be based on a tacit recognition of the relationship, which may subsequently enable patients and/ or partners to feel sufficiently comfortable to disclose their sexuality and discuss their relationship in more explicit terms. More generally, it could be hypothesised that heightened staff awareness and sensitivity could promote the development of a positive relationship between staff and patients, which is a vital component in good psychological care (Nichols, 1993).

Provisional recommendations can also be offered on the issue of patients' preferences regarding the gender of health care staff who are involved in their care. Given the diversity of views expressed in this study, it may be beneficial for health care staff to recognise that some patients may have particular preferences and to ascertain these preferences before treatment commences, with the aim of taking patient preferences into account during treatment, where possible. These recommendations are, of course, not specific to lesbian and gay patients. Indeed, if this procedure were routinely applied to all patients, it might lead patients to feel that they were being respected and might enhance their perceptions of the quality of their care.

It could be said that the provision of high quality care for lesbian and gay patients involves the same general principles that shape high quality care for any patient group, including knowledge of, sensitivity to and respect for patients and their needs and preferences. This research can therefore be seen as contributing to that body of work which reminds health care staff of the importance of these principles and identifies some specific ways in which they can be expressed to ensure that lesbian and gay patients receive high quality health care services.

Acknowledgements

We would like to express our gratitude to all our participants, to Naama Poria and to the Open House in Jerusalem, the Other Ten Per Cent at the Hebrew

University in Jerusalem, BLH (the main lesbian, gay and bisexual organisation in Israel) and the managers of the Elm Tree pub in Guildford and the Minerva pub in Tel Aviv for their assistance and cooperation in this study.

References

Ajzen, I. and Fishbein, M. (1980), *Understanding Attitudes and Predicting Social Behavior*, Prentice-Hall, Englewood Cliffs, New Jersey.
Annesley, P. and Coyle, A. (1995), 'Clinical Psychologists' Attitudes to Lesbians', *Journal of Community & Applied Social Psychology*, 5, pp. 327–31.
Annesley, P. and Coyle, A. (1998), 'Dykes and Psychs: Lesbian women's experiences of clinical psychology services', *Changes: An International Journal of Psychology and Psychotherapy*, 16, pp. 247–58.
Beane, T.P. and Ennis, D.M. (1987), 'Market Segmentation: A Review', *European Journal of Marketing*, 21(5), pp. 20–42.
Coyle, A. (1998), 'Developing Lesbian and Gay Identity in Adolescence', in J. Coleman and D. Roker (eds), *Teenage Sexuality: Health, risk and education*, Harwood Academic, London.
Dardick, L. and Grady, K.E. (1980), 'Openness Between Gay Persons and Health Professionals', *Annals of Internal Medicine*, 93, pp. 115–19.
Davies, P.M., Hickson, F.C.I., Weatherburn, P. and Hunt, A.J. (1993), *Sex, Gay Men and AIDS*, Falmer Press, London.
Douglas, C.J., Kalman, C.M. and Kalman, T.P. (1985), 'Homophobia among Physicians and Nurses: An empirical study', *Hospital and Community Psychiatry*, 36, pp. 1309–11.
Eliason, M. and Randall, C. (1991), 'Lesbian Phobia in Nursing Students', *Western Journal of Nursing Research*, 13, pp. 363–74.
Elliott, R., Fischer, C.T. and Rennie, D.L. (1999), 'Evolving Guidelines for Publication of Qualitative Research Studies in Psychology and Related Fields', *British Journal of Clinical Psychology*, 38, pp. 215–29.
Faugier, J. and Wright, S. (1990), 'Homophobia, Stigma and Aids: An issue for all health care workers', *Nursing Practice*, 3(2), pp. 27–8.
Golding, J. (1997), *Without Prejudice: MIND lesbian, gay and bisexual mental health awareness research*, MIND Publications, London.
Hellman, R.E. and Stanton. M. (1989), 'Treatment of Homosexual Alcoholics in Government-Funded Agencies: Provider training and attitudes', *Hospital and Community Psychiatry*, 40, pp. 1163–8.
Herek, G.M. (1994), 'Assessing Heterosexuals' Attitudes Toward Lesbians and Gay Men: A review of empirical research with the ATLG Scale', in B. Greene and G.M. Herek (eds), *Lesbian and Gay Psychology: Theory, research, and clinical applications*, Sage, Thousand Oaks, California.
Herek, G.M. (ed.) (1998), *Stigma and Sexual Orientation: Understanding prejudice against lesbians, gay men, and bisexuals*, Sage, Thousand Oaks, California.
Hughes, H. (1997), 'Holiday and Homosexual Identity', *Tourism Management*, 18, pp. 3–7.
Irwin, R. (1992), 'Critical Re-Evaluation Can Overcome Discrimination: Providing equal standards of care for homosexual patients', *Professional Nurse*, 7, pp. 435–8.

Jacobson, S. and Samdahl, D.M. (1998), 'Leisure in the Lives of Old Lesbians: Experiences with and responses to discrimination', *Journal of Leisure Research*, 30, pp. 233–55.

Kite, M.E. (1984), 'Sex Differences in Attitudes Towards Homosexuals: A meta-analytic review', *Journal of Homosexuality*, 10, pp. 69–81.

Kitzinger, C. and Coyle, A. (1995), 'Lesbian and Gay Couples: Speaking of difference', *The Psychologist*, 8, pp. 64–9.

Kotler, P. (1997), *Marketing Management*, Prentice-Hall, Englewood Cliffs, New Jersey.

McFarlane, L. (1998), *Diagnosis: Homophobic. The Experiences of Lesbians, Gay Men and Bisexuals in Mental Health Services*, PACE, London.

Milton, M. and Coyle, A. (1999), 'Lesbian and Gay Affirmative Psychotherapy: Issues in theory and practice', *Sexual and Marital Therapy*, 14, pp. 41–57.

Morgan, N. and Pritchard, A. (1998), *Tourism, Promotion and Power*, John Wiley, Chichester.

Nichols, K. (1993), *Psychological Care in Physical Illness* (2nd edn), Chapman and Hall, London.

Oleck, J. (1995), 'The Gaying of America', *Restaurant Business*, 94(5), pp. 42–51.

Paroski, P.A. (1987), 'Health Care Delivery and the Concerns of Gay and Lesbian Adolescents', *Journal of Adolescent Health Care*, 8, pp. 188–92.

Pitts, B.G. (1999), 'Sports Tourism and Niche Markets: Identification and analysis of the growing lesbian and gay sports tourism industry', *Journal of Vacation Marketing*, 5, pp. 31–50.

Proctor, G. (1994), 'Lesbian Clients' Experience of Clinical Psychology: A listener's guide', *Changes: An International Journal of Psychology and Psychotherapy*, 12, pp. 290–8.

Royal College of Nursing (1994), *The Nursing Care of Lesbians and Gay Men: An RCN statement – Issues in Nursing and Health No. 26*, RCN, London.

Royal College of Nursing (1998a), *Guidance for Nurses on 'Next-of-Kin' for Lesbian and Gay Patients and Children with Lesbian or Gay Parents – Issues in Nursing and Health No. 47*, RCN, London.

Royal College of Nursing (1998b), *Sexual Orientation and Mental Health: Guidance for nurses – Issues in Nursing and Health No. 48*, RCN, London.

Rudolph, J. (1988), 'Counsellors' Attitudes Toward Homosexuality: A selective review of the literature', *Journal of Counselling and Development*, 67, pp. 165–8.

Scherer, Y.K., Haughey, B.P. and Wu, Y.W.B. (1991), 'AIDS and Homophobia among Nurses', *Journal of Homosexuality*, 21, pp. 17–27.

Siminoff, L.A., Erlen, J.A. and Lidz, C.W. (1991), 'Stigma, AIDS and Quality of Nursing Care: State of the Science', *Journal of Advanced Nursing*, 16, pp. 262–9.

Smith, J.A. (1995), 'Semi-Structured Interviewing and Qualitative Analysis', in J.A. Smith, R. Harré and L. van Langenhove (eds), *Rethinking Methods in Psychology*, Sage, London.

Snape, D., Thomson, K. and Chetwynd, M. (1995), *Discrimination Against Gay Men and Lesbians: A study of the nature and extent of discrimination against homosexual men and women in Britain today*, Social and Community Planning Research, London.

Taylor, I. and Robertson, A. (1994), 'The Health Needs of Gay Men: A discussion of the literature and implications for nursing', *Journal of Advanced Nursing*, 20, pp. 560–6.

Vermette, L. and Godin, G. (1996), 'Nurses' Intentions to Provide Home Care: The impact of AIDS and homosexuality', *AIDS Care*, 8, pp. 479–88.

Wadsworth, E. and McCann, K. (1992), 'Attitudes Towards and Use of General Practitioner Services among Homosexual Men with HIV Infection or AIDS', *British Journal of General Practice*, 42, pp. 107–10.

Webb, C. (1987), 'Nurses' Knowledge and Attitudes about Sexuality: Report of a study', *Nurse Education Today*, 7, pp. 209–14.

Webb, C. (1988), 'A Study of Nurses' Knowledge and Attitudes about Sexuality in Health Care', *International Journal of Nursing Studies*, 25, pp. 235–44.

Wood, L. (1999), 'Think Pink: Attracting the pink pound', *Insights*, 10, A107–A110.

Chapter Fifteen

Strategic Health Care Policy and Development for Maori, the Indigenous People of New Zealand

Lynette Stewart, Louise Davis and Sharon Shea

Maori – The Indigenous People of New Zealand

It is generally accepted that the eponymous ancestors of Maori arrived in *Aotearoa* (New Zealand) in 800AD and were of Melanesian/ Polynesian descent (Walker, 1990).

Significant European or *Pakeha* settlement and colonisation of New Zealand occurred in the nineteenth century. There was strong competition between France, Britain and other European countries to secure governance of New Zealand. Eventually Britain prevailed and on 6 February 1840, representatives of Queen Victoria signed a treaty with Maori entitled *Te Tiriti o Waitangi* or the Treaty of Waitangi (the Treaty).

Although the Treaty is recognised by the New Zealand Government as the 'founding' document of New Zealand, there is less consensus regarding the interpretation of the Treaty and its practical application today.

With regard to interpretation, there are three key areas of dissension. First, Maori believe the Treaty guaranteed *Tino Rangatiratanga* or supreme sovereignty to the Maori people whilst allowing the *Pakeha* the right to *Kawanatanga* or to govern only. For simplicity we refer to this interpretation as the *sovereignty issue*.

Second, Maori believe that the Treaty confirmed their right to retain their authority or chieftainship over their lands, villages and all *taonga* or treasures in exchange for giving the Crown pre-emptive land sale rights. For simplicity we refer to this interpretation as the *authority issue*.

Third, Maori believe the Treaty confirmed that the Crown would protect the Maori (and other) people in New Zealand by conveying upon them the

Quality in Health Care: Strategic Issues in Health Care Management, H.T.O. Davies, M. Tavakoli and M. Malek (eds), Ashgate Publishing Ltd, 2001.

same rights and duties enjoyed by the people of Britain. Equality has not been achieved in practice however. Consequently, Maori seek equitable redress for the social, economic and cultural imbalances in New Zealand society created by colonisation. For simplicity we refer to this interpretation as the *equity issue*.

Since 1840, the Crown (represented by the New Zealand government) and Maori have disputed the interpretation and consequent prudent practical implementation of the Treaty. The result is that both 'partners' have frequently requested the Court to adjudicate on matters related to recognising the Treaty and applying it in good faith and for the benefit of the Maori people.

Over time a body of case law has developed which sets out specific Treaty principles. These now underpin the government's response to Maori. The principles are, briefly, partnership, cooperation, active protection of Maori interests, equity and utmost good faith.

The divergence of opinion between the Crown and Maori over the last 160 years has exacted a toll on the Maori people. Irrespective of the sovereignty, authority and equity rights Maori believe are guaranteed by the Treaty, the following key facts paint a dismal picture.

Why is Maori Health a Priority for New Zealand?

As with many indigenous and ethnic cultures, Maori suffer the consequences of significant disparities and inequitable health status compared with other New Zealanders (non-Maori). This fact is not widely known outside New Zealand, as New Zealand is perceived as a First World country with First World characteristics.

At the last New Zealand Census in 1996 (Health Funding Authority, 1998), the Maori population was 523,269 or 14.5 per cent of the total New Zealand population of 3,617,586. *Pakeha* New Zealanders make up the largest population group at 71.7 per cent. Maori have a very young population compared with non-Maori, with 37.5 per cent of Maori aged 15 years and under. Conversely, Maori aged 65 years and older constitute only 3 per cent of the Maori population. We understand the Maori population age structure is similar to a structure more commonly associated with third world countries.

From a health status perspective (Health Funding Authority, 1998), life expectancy for Maori men and women is eight and nine years less than non-Maori respectively, and Maori fertility rates are declining. Maori mortality rates for cancer, cerebrovascular disease, chronic obstructive respiratory disease and unintentional injury are considerably higher than the rates for the rest of New Zealand's population. Maori men have twice the mortality rate for coronary heart disease and 50 per cent higher rates from respiratory disease, compared to non-Maori. Maori women have nearly three times the mortality rate from lung cancer as non-Maori women, and four times the mortality rate from cervical cancer (aged 45–64 years). The rate of diabetes in Maori women and men (aged 65+) is five times higher than that for non-Maori.

From a socioeconomic perspective (Health Funding Authority, 1998), 41.4 per cent of Maori smoke regularly compared with 20 per cent of *Pakeha*, 11.4 per cent of Maori are unemployed compared with 3.6 per cent of *Pakeha*, and 46 per cent of Maori collect government welfare support compared with 36 per cent of *Pakeha*. Only 2.6 per cent of the Maori population have a tertiary qualification.

The preceding statistics illustrate the poor state of Maori health. They also highlight the obligation on the New Zealand government to prioritise and action health improvements for Maori, and eliminate the health disparities between Maori and non-Maori. The titanic challenge is, how will New Zealand's government achieve Maori health gain and development?

Key Development Themes

We argue that the designers and implementers of any strategy or policy targeting indigenous or ethnic development must recognise and incorporate the following themes:

- capacity;
- partnership;
- equity;
- social, economic, and cultural determinants of health;
- innovation versus status quo;
- building upon successes;
- inter-sectoral integration;
- relativity.

Capacity

Capacity refers to the current capacity of the available workforce in overall terms, and specifically the indigenous or ethnic workforce. Capacity also concerns the willingness and collective accountability of the overall workforces' ability to eliminate disparities.

Many issues affect capacity and the ability to effect developmental change (e.g. education, experience, knowledge and use of indigenous culture). Perhaps the most important influence on ability is an individual's capability to mitigate and not be effected by the psychological and sociocultural impact of racism. We define racism as 'the power to put prejudice into practice'.

Partnership

Partnership is a major strategic development theme, which can provide powerful opportunities for robust participation and direct benefits. Effective partnerships must ensure the ability to participate in decision-making, actioning decisions, sharing information, accessing appropriate resources and agreeing lines of accountability and authority. Partnership principles include reciprocity; mutual respect; commitment; good faith; and transparency. In New Zealand, the Treaty obligates the Crown to enter into partnerships with Maori.

Later in this chapter, we outline our practical experience in a health funding partnership referred to as *the MAPO strategy*, and share successes and lessons for future development.

Equity

Equity is one of the more difficult development themes as its practical implementation constantly challenges the status quo. Equity is not equality nor should it be applied in a narrow sense.

We advocate that for indigenous or ethnic development, equity is defined and must be applied as follows:

• the recognition and full acceptance of historical injustice;
• the commitment to eliminate injustice and its effects;
• the provision and agreed application of appropriate resources (human, technological, financial and structural) to an equitable level;
• the provision of sufficient capacity to ensure indigenous peoples can effect equitable solutions.

From a health specific point of view, we also advocate that equity is not simply about ensuring that health disparities are eliminated, it concerns equity in every sense at every level.

For example, equity principles should apply to participation (e.g. equitable Maori participation at governance and operational levels) and information (e.g. as a minimum any information available to *Pakeha* should be made available to Maori with an emphasis on providing targeted Maori specific information for Maori gain).

With respect to equitable funding, we believe it can be achieved by ensuring that, as a minimum, funds should be targeted to Maori health gain. The overall amount of funds targeted should at least equate to the Maori population of 15 per cent. However, the New Zealand health sector currently expends less money per capita on Maori than it does on others. The total funds expended on Maori are estimated to be 11.4 per cent, or NZD$612 million of a total NZD$5.35 billion (Health Funding Authority, 1999).

Social, Economic and Cultural Determinants of Health

It is generally accepted in New Zealand that social and economic factors are determinants of health. What has only recently become recognised is that culture is also an important determinant of health.

We argue that colonisation has contributed to cultural deprivation, which in turn has impacted negatively upon Maori health status. This is due to the nexus between Maori culture and Maori health status. The simplest way to describe this nexus is to illustrate the relationship between Maori culture and the Maori definition of health and well-being.

Maori culture is often described as holistic in nature. Put simply, family, tribe, spiritual, cultural and physical elements of the Maori world all inter-react and affect each other. Accordingly, Maori apply equally holistic definitions to health and wellbeing. An example is the *Whare Tapa Wha* Maori health model, also known as the four cornerstones of Maori health. The model describes four dimensions which contribute to health and wellbeing: *te taha wairua* (spiritual aspects); *te taha hinengaro* (mental and emotional aspects); *te taha whanau* (family and community aspects); and *te taha tinana* (physical aspects) (Pomare et al., 1995). 'Good' Maori health and wellbeing is dependent upon the equilibrium of these dimensions.

Innovation versus Status Quo

As with equity, the strength, and the threat of innovation is that it challenges the status quo. For many, the status quo is firmly set within their 'comfort zone' and the element of change inherent within innovation, particularly if it is targeted to an indigenous population, can be uncomfortable. However, this is where capacity is so important, because the concepts of commitment, willingness and the ability to not be influenced by prejudice are liberating factors for success.

Building Upon Successes

Some innovation creates success and some does not. A carefully planned and strategic response will ensure that successes are built upon and the 'best of the best' is retained for continued and sustainable growth.

Historically, sector reform has tended to be total. This type of upheaval can exact a heavy and unnecessary toll. When you have limited capacity for indigenous development the price of change usually impacts more on the indigenous population. This is not acceptable if development and eliminating disparities is an objective. Therefore, robust indigenous participation in any new design and/or redevelopment is absolutely crucial as this will serve to mitigate the desire for total change with limited regard to indigenous successes to date.

Inter-sectoral Integration

To honour the Maori definition of health, recognition of inter-sectoral integration as a development theme is very important. Health initiatives must be seen as part of an overall development strategy informed by the need to strengthen the community, family and tribal group as a whole.

Integration brings with it many difficulties. However, we firmly believe that to improve Maori health, wellbeing and development, well-resourced initiatives need to occur across multiple sectors.

Relativity

The relativity theme is often overlooked in a development sense. We argue this theme is a powerful tool to mitigate the psychological effects of racism towards indigenous or ethnic populations.

Often, and particularly in the media, relative or proportionate responses to the failure of an indigenous initiative in comparison with a mainstream initiative, are rare. We associate the phrase 'negative sensationalism' with these types of media reports. Such media reporting contributes to negative public perceptions and reaction to indigenous development. This in turn perpetuates the myth that indigenous people either do not know what they are doing, or that funding should not be invested in their development as it is wasteful. This creates a 'limited value' emphasis upon indigenous development which results in a 'glass ceiling' approach to capacity, commitment, investment and willingness. However, when the opportunity to introduce relativity is available, people's perceptions can be changed.

Recognising and Incorporating Development Themes – a Prudent Risk Management Approach

If each theme is not recognised and therefore not built into the overall development strategy, indigenous development is more likely to fail, irrespective of the good intent. These themes are fundamental to ensuring that indigenous gains through active participation are not only a possibility but also a real opportunity.

The Development Themes and New Zealand Maori Health Strategy

Generally, the preceding development themes have been recognised and incorporated into the three major strategies for Maori health gain and development, which have dominated New Zealand's national and regional strategic and operational health developments over the last five years.

The three major strategies are:

- greater Maori participation at all levels of the health sector;
- Maori provider and workforce development;
- mainstream (or sector) enhancement.

The objective of greater Maori participation is to encourage the participation of Maori in the benefits of the publicly funded health and disability support sector by preserving Treaty-based rights (the sovereignty and authority issues) and compensating, where and when required, for disparities originating within the sector (the equity issue). This strategy attempts to identify and utilise the potential contribution of *Whanau* (family), *Hapu* (sub-tribe) and *Iwi* (main tribe) in all aspects of the health sector and to counterbalance disparities that adversely affect choice, access, and needs-based utilisation of services (Health Funding Authority, 1998).

The objective of Maori provider and workforce development is to support the establishment, consolidation and continuation of quality Maori health service providers and health professionals within the sector (Health Funding Authority, 1998).

The objective of mainstream (or sector) enhancement is to encourage and provide incentives to mainstream (non-Maori) providers to fully comprehend and respond to Maori needs in an appropriate manner (Health Funding Authority, 1998).

The remainder of this chapter concentrates upon the practical implementation of the greater Maori participation strategy as this underpins the other two major strategies and we believe it is the most crucial for successful Maori development.

Implementing the Greater Maori Participation Strategy

In New Zealand, some innovative initiatives have been created which enable Maori participation to occur at each level of the health sector, that is, at the funder, provider and consumer levels. The following specific examples relate to participation at the health funder level.

Participation with and within the Funder

From a developmental point of view, effective Maori participation must be both internal and external. Internal participation means Maori participation at governance and operational levels of the funder to ensure that the funder has sufficient internal or employed Maori expertise and capacity to respond to Maori health need.

External participation means Maori participation in partnership with the Funder through an adequately resourced Maori owned and representative organisation, which operationalises the partnership commitment entrenched within the Treaty; assists the funder to respond to Maori health need; engages in local provider development; mainstream enhancement; and consultation with Maori.

Internal Participation – Modelling Indigenous Matrix Management and Strategic Policies

The capacity of a mainstream organisation to respond to Maori health gain and development is enabled by an appropriate management structure that creates collective accountability and responds to and prioritises Maori development.

In New Zealand, two key structural developments have occurred within the government-owned health funder. First, the introduction of what has been called an Indigenous Matrix Management system. Second, the creation of strategic policies that promote collective organisation-wide commitment to Maori development.

Indigenous Matrix Management Indigenous Matrix Management provides for the strategic placement of Maori personnel within an organisation's operational structure to promote prioritisation of Maori health gain and development through horizontal and vertical organisation-wide integration of Maori issues.

From 1998–2000, this concept was implemented within New Zealand's government-owned health Funder, the Health Funding Authority (HFA). A dedicated Maori Health Group (the Group) exists as part of the overall HFA structure. The Group's role is to fund, monitor and manage Maori specific health and disability services across New Zealand, develop national HFA Maori health strategy and policy, and matrix across the entire HFA in order to promote and monitor the organisation's responsiveness to Maori health needs. Importantly, the Group has a general manager who is an integral and influential part of the HFA senior management ream. At the same time, other operating groups within the HFA employ Maori and some are placed in influential national positions within these mainstream groups. There is also Maori specific representation on the HFA Board.

The HFA is expected to conform to a national Maori health strategic plan which was drafted by the Maori Health Group, and is owned by the entire organisation. This plan contributes to the benchmarks by which all HFA Groups are measured and monitored in terms of Maori health and development performance.

Collective Accountability Organisation-wide strategies and policies targeting Maori health gain and development support the matrix management approach.

The HFA Board adopted an HFA Maori health policy which is designed to demonstrate that the Funder is capable of developing policies and practices that encourage Maori to perceive the HFA as a culturally responsive and supportive funding body. This in turn encourages Maori to engage with the Funder in health partnerships which focus upon the provision of quality health care services (Health Funding Authority, 1998).

The policy is divided into two sections. The first section deals with getting the funder 'into shape' by providing the Funder with high-level Maori specific policy for internal ownership purposes. The second section outlines policy positions regarding dealings with external parties (e.g. mainstream and Maori health service providers and stakeholders) and is designed to display the internal responsiveness of the funder.

For example, internal ownership policy requires Maori specificity in all HFA planning documents; the identification of funding spent and/or dedicated to Maori health with a concomitant directive to move towards equitable funding; HFA staff member commitment to Maori health through specific clauses and performance measures in employment contracts; collective accountability through Maori specific performance measures for the entire organisation; and an internal Maori workforce development human resource policy which promoted active recruitment, retention and training.

External policy requires the HFA to build relationships with Maori that provided opportunities for participation; promotes Maori provider and workforce development in a sustainable manner; identifies and targets revenue dedicated to Maori health development; and fully implements mainstream enhancement activities via contract specificity, dialogue and effective monitoring, evaluation and audit.

Summary of successes and learning points The experience of indigenous matrix management and the creation of organisation-wide, Maori specific, change management policies delivered successes never before seen in New Zealand's health sector. For example, for the first time in New Zealand's history, funding spent on Maori health was identified and quantified, thus enabling better planning for further Maori health development. In addition, the HFA introduced nationally consistent Maori health specificity into contract documentation for all government funded health providers. Every provider must develop a Maori health strategic and business plan with an emphasis on partnerships with Maori and utilising Maori specific quality parameters. The HFA is, in our opinion, the first and only government agency to adopt such a systematic internal strategic change management policy response to Maori.

As with any change, there are lessons to be learnt. The major lessons relate to strategy and policy design; monitoring and enforcement; keeping up and risk managing the pace of change; capacity; and what we call the 'comfort zone blues'.

In regard to strategy and policy design, an important overall point is that each of these lessons needs to be taken into account in the original design phase and included as part of the management and implementation of strategy and policy.

Monitoring and enforcement relates to managing compliance with the strategy and policy. This should be a crucial component in terms of organisation-wide implementation and performance. In our experience, enforcement in the New Zealand health sector is not a common practice generally, and when you add the dynamic of Maori health, enforcement is even less likely to occur. Put simply, no monitoring or enforcement means no incentive to perform.

Keeping up and risk managing the pace of change is an important lesson. First, keeping up or maintaining the momentum of change requires constant monitoring, evaluation, and feedback at all levels of the organisation. When the implementation pace is not being maintained, the organisation should have a pre-designed early warning system, which in turn promotes enforcement.

Second, risk managing the pace of change is very important in terms of human resource capacity and moving to the 'next step'. With respect to human resources, the change agent function is very stressful. The change agent needs to have clear authority to matrix across the organisation. The agent must also have an effective communication mechanism. This must include congruent and constant communication about the importance of implementing the strategy and policy from the Board, to the Chief Executive, through to senior managers and their respective staff.

Third, the 'next step' needs to be designed and defined so any developmental change is clear from beginning to end. At the same time, such change must be staged, and coordinated organisation-wide capacity must be developed to accommodate the various stages of change.

Clarity and capacity are crucial parts of risk managing what we call the 'comfort zone blues'. Change and innovation challenge the status quo and the 'safe' environment. One of the risks of Maori or any indigenous and ethnic development is that the environment of constant change often becomes the status quo. For some people, this is perceived as 'unsafe' and therefore outside their 'comfort zone'.

The 'blues' can be manifested through multiple signs such as no evident commitment; constant irritation; overt tension; making excuses; creating 'stumbling blocks'; and non-performance. We believe the 'blues' can be mitigated through the application of the principles of partnership, monitoring and enforcement and through transparent transitional plans that are clearly communicated and acted upon. The commitment to change must be owned and evident throughout the organisation and not displayed solely by Maori who are usually the principal change agents. The burden of change is too great for small numbers of individuals to bear alone and can lead to the loss or 'burn-out' of the most crucial development resource.

External Participation – Modelling Indigenous Partnerships with Mainstream Organisations – The MAPO Strategy

The MAPO strategy is a practical example of external Maori participation that was designed primarily to operationalise the Treaty of Waitangi in the health sector. Consequently, the Partnership concept dominates the design.

During 1995/6 three Maori organisations, known as 'MAPO' (an acronym for Maori Co-Purchasing Organisation) were established in the northern part of New Zealand's North Island. The government funder for the region (at that time one of four regional health authorities) developed Treaty-based partnerships with these external, Maori owned and representative organisations.

Health sector reforms of the government funder from 1996–2000 have seen the partnership relationship transfer three times – from the Regional Health Authority, to the Transitional Health Authority to the Health Funding Authority. Through out the three MAPO have remained constant.

The funder supported a one-off establishment grant to set-up the MAPO infrastructure on a commercially viable basis. The MAPO have operational contracts comprising of a Memorandum of Understanding and a Deed of Partnership. The Memorandum outlines the Treaty-based partnership principles and relationship. The Deed confirms the operational functions and funding for the MAPO.

The operational functions of the MAPO include co-funding; co-planning; co-monitoring; consultation; provider and workforce development; mainstream enhancement and co-management of multiple health service contracts (held by mainstream and Maori providers).

The MAPO structure includes a Board and a small operational team led by a Chief Executive Officer. The MAPO team usually consists of policy analysis, clinical, financial, project management and administrative expertise.

A joint committee of the funder's Board was established and comprised representatives from the three MAPO Boards and the funder's Board. This joint committee was delegated the full rights and responsibilities of the funder's Board regarding all functions associated with the funding of services for Maori health gain and development. All members participated in a partnered manner with decisions being managed through a consensus process.

At an operational level, the MAPO teams have complete access to the funder's administrative and core business systems. All operational groups of the funder were directed by the joint committee to operationalise the MAPO

Strategy by ensuring full MAPO team participation in core business activity.

MAPO and funder staff were trained in funder core business activity and relationship management. Reciprocal performance measures were agreed between the MAPO and the funder with a view to the MAPO having as much right to monitor the funder, as the funder had to monitor the MAPO.

Summary of successes and learning points Based on the authors' current practical experience implementing the MAPO strategy and working within a MAPO, we believe the strategy and it's strategic themes and intent, are by far, the most comprehensive opportunity Maori have had to operationalise Treaty-based partnerships in New Zealand. Maori are participating and influencing at all levels of the health sector.

By way of specific example, key successes directly attributable to the authors' MAPO between 1996–2000 include a 500 per cent increase in the number of sustainable and robust Maori health service providers; the growth of Maori health employment from less than 10 to over 300 people; a 300 per cent growth in dedicated Maori health funding; the growth of targeted training for the Maori health workforce which has resulted in almost 400 Maori health personnel being trained since 1997; the explicit recognition of the MAPO Strategy by key mainstream health stakeholders evidenced by repeated requests for strategic advice and guidance from the MAPO; and most importantly, evident Maori health gains (e.g. the Maori health service provider immunisation rate for Maori children is approximately 95 per cent compared with the mainstream provider figure of under 50 per cent).

The major lessons learnt in the past four years relate to strategy and policy design; capacity; partnership realities; transitional arrangements; and recognition.

In hindsight, capacity could have been improved with more rigorous emphasis placed by both partners on planned training and development. As an example, both partners could operate an internship programme where MAPO staff work and train within the funder for a defined period and vice versa, rather than non-contextual training sessions held on dislocated days. The reciprocal advantages would include an in-depth knowledge of internal operations; a 'stepped', rather than 'steep' learning curve; the creation and embedding of operational working relationships, and a more 'hands-on' opportunity to learn the core business.

In regard to partnership realities, lessons learnt include the introduction of better mechanisms for information sharing and exchange; transparency concerning all of the funder's activities, as they all potentially impact on Maori health; and an evident equitable commitment at all levels to the partnership.

A clear and agreed transition timeframe and process for sustainable MAPO growth was and is required. Unclear transition timeframes and processes lead to uncertainty in many areas. Failure to plan for this event is a serious risk management issue for both partners as it can create an unnecessary hiatus in continued strategic development.

To mitigate the above, when indigenous development strategy is being designed, where practicable, each stage of development should be defined and agreed as part of the overall strategy. The partners should also continually review the current position and capacity of the strategy and it's 'people' to evolve and grow, and the designers must ensure that flexibility is an integral part of the strategic design and implementation.

Indigenous development is unique and demanding and there is no easy-to-follow 'instruction book'. Put simply, no developmental strategy should be static, nor will static strategists create the change required.

Finally, recognition is always a struggle for any new organisation but this issue is heightened when it relates to an indigenous organisation or initiative. We discussed the issues of relativity and recognition earlier in this chapter and those concepts impact directly here.

The process to achieve recognition should not be underestimated. Every effort should be taken to ensure that during the design and implementation phases of development strategy and policy, the partners must give their full support.

Maori Health and Strategic Development in the New Millennium

The new millennium presents both challenges and opportunities. We are committed to ensuring the implementation of the development themes that build upon successes to create ongoing positive change and developments for Maori. We have highlighted innovative partnerships and internal and external participation models, successes and lessons learnt in this chapter. We believe these can form the building blocks for successful strategic development models across all sectors and indigenous and ethnic populations.

We submit that the challenge for New Zealand is to ensure collaborative, workable, Treaty-based partnership models are entrenched in New Zealand's public sector.

We do not advocate separatism. What we do advocate is the right for Maori to develop by participating and operationalising decisions that affect

212 Quality in Health Care: Strategic Issues in Health Care Management

the overall improvement of Maori status. What is most important is that Maori have the opportunity to own the results of development and not be passive receivers of decisions made predominantly by non-Maori. We believe effective partnerships are a powerful solution.

Our overall aim is to mitigate and ultimately break the 'cycle of dependency' that has burdened Maori for too long. We wish to create a strong and powerful positivism associated with being Maori. This positivism must then be entrenched within New Zealand society so that it may be enjoyed by all.

References

Health Funding Authority (1998), *National Strategic Plan for Maori Health, 1998–2001*, unpublished, New Zealand.

Health Funding Authority (1999), *Presentation to Te Tai Tokerau MAPO Annual General Meeting*, unpublished, New Zealand.

Pomare, E.P., Keefe-Ormsby, V., Ormsby, C., Pearce, N., Reid, P., Robson, B. and Watene-Haydon, N. (1985), *Hauora, Maori Standards for Health III, A Study of the years 1970–1991*, GP Print Ltd, New Zealand.

Walker, R. (1990), *Ka Whawhai Tonu Matou – Struggle Without End*, Penguin Books Ltd, New Zealand.

SECTION FIVE
CHOICE

Chapter Sixteen

Limited Access to Alternative Models of Maternity Care in the UK: Barriers to Change

J.S. Tucker, W.J. Graham and M.H. Hall

Policy Background and Evidence for Alternative Models of Maternity Care in the Early 1990s

A representative survey of antenatal care in Scotland in 1989 demonstrated a very standard package of consultant-led shared care with virtually all deliveries taking place in hospital settings (Tucker et al., 1994). In the early 1990s, alternative, devolved models of maternity care were being strongly advocated. These models varied in location but tested maternity care managed by primary carers (GPs and/or midwives). They were developed in response to both consumer pressure about medicalisation of pregnancy and childbirth (Oakley, 1991; Rodell, 1990; Collee, 1992) as well as some clinicians' concerns about potentially wasteful over-observation in the traditional care packages for women with healthy pregnancies (Hall, 1981; Hall et al., 1980; RCOG, 1982). Key questions were about how much clinical supervision was needed for normal pregnancies? Who could safely deliver that care? And could maternity services become more woman-centred and acceptable to women? Amid contentious debate even within professions (James, 1995; Walker, 1995) contemporary policy documents in Scotland (SOHHD 1993; CRAG-SCOTMEG 1995) and England and Wales, (House of Commons Health Committee, 1992; *Changing Childbirth*, 1993) specified maternity services that should more closely match women's needs (CRAG-SCOTMEG, 1995) and give women more information, choice, control and continuity (CRAG-SCOTMEG, 1995; *Changing Childbirth*, 1993).

Evaluation, in single-site and multicentre RCTs of alternative organisational models of routine maternity care, for women at low risk of pregnancy and

Quality in Health Care: Strategic Issues in Health Care Management, H.T.O. Davies, M. Tavakoli and M. Malek (eds), Ashgate Publishing Ltd, 2001.

labour complications, had taken place in Scotland and other parts of the UK with measures of:

- *clinical effectiveness* (Hundley, 1994; Tucker, 1996; Turnbull, 1996; Sikorski, 1996; Clement, 1999);
- *cost-efficiency and effectiveness* (Hundley, 1995a; Ratcliffe, 1996; Young, 1997; Henderson, 2000);
- *acceptability and satisfaction for women* (Shields, 1998; Tucker, 1996; Sikorski, 1996; Sikorski, 1995; Ryan, 1997);
- *and acceptability to staff and staff views* (Cheyne, 1995; MDU, 1995; Hundley, 1995b; Reid, 1999; Sikorski, 1995).

Ideally a new model of care would be identified as one where all the indicators in such multidimensional and multidisciplinary evaluation demonstrated gain before being adopted and offered as an option for women. These dimensions however may not be independent of each other and 'the interactions may mean that the identified goal in one dimension, may be at odds with the goals of another – making simultaneous improvement on all difficult' (Mackenzie, 1999, p. 139).

A crude summary of gains and drawbacks in each of the main evaluative dimensions of the new care models demonstrates this effect (Table 16.1). In a detailed critical appraisal of methodology of the three Scottish trials included in Table 16.1, Graham (1997) noted the difficulties raised by lack of comparability of the evaluative dimensions. The summary in Table 16.1 shows a seesaw of gains and drawbacks in different models but with no explicit values or weights available for each dimension to aid care purchaser in decision-making. Indeed the perceived relative importance of these evaluative dimensions may vary according to the role of the assessor. For example, a manager/purchaser might well choose models with highest clinical effectiveness and lowest service cost, whereas women might prefer models with high clinical effectiveness and improved levels of acceptability or access.

Conflicting Multidimensional Performance Measures in Devolved Models of Maternity Care

Table 16.1 suggests that the new devolved models of maternity care appear to be clinically as effective as traditional models for the defined patient groups, *and* that women and the primary care-givers (GPs and midwives) were more satisfied with them (Turnbull, 1996; Tucker, 1996; Hundley, 1994). All models

Table 16.1 A summary of gains and drawbacks in the main evaluative dimensions of new maternity care models

Maternity care model	Clinical effectiveness	Reported costs and interpretation	Acceptability to women and women's satisfaction	Trial care-giving profession views	Inter-professional staff views comparisons
Midwifery-managed maternity care	=/+ (Turnbull, 1996)	Higher NHS costs (Young, 1997)	+ (Shields, 1998, Turnbull, 1996)	+ (MDU, 1995)	variation (Cheyne, 1995)
Community-based GP/midwife antenatal care	=/+ (Tucker, 1996)	Lower NHS and societal costs (Ratcliffe, 1996)	+ (Tucker, 1996, Ryan, 1997)	+ (Reid, 1999)	variation (Reid, 1999)
Midwifery-managed intrapartum care	=/+ (Hundley, 1994)	Higher NHS costs (Hundley, 1995a)	+ (Hundley, 1995b)	+ (Hundley, 1995b)	not reported
Reduced schedules of routine antenatal visits	=/+ (Sikorsky,1996, Clement 1999)	Higher NHS costs (Henderson, 2000)	-/+ (Sikorsky, 1995, Sikorsky, 1996)	+ (Sikorsky, 1995)	variation (Sikorsky, 1995)

showed some improved continuity of carer (Turnbull, 1996; Tucker, 1996; Hundley, 1994). Furthermore, the societal costs in the GP/midwife antenatal care were lower (Ratcliffe, 1996) than those of traditional shared care, mainly because of the higher costs to women of attending hospital clinics compared with general practice clinics. Women appeared to value the new devolved GP/midwife care at least as well as traditional care in both a patient satisfaction survey (Tucker, 1996) and in a postal survey which used willingness-to-pay method (Ryan, 1997). In testing midwifery models of care however, it appeared that cost efficiency was reduced with reported higher NHS costs (Young, 1997; Hundley, 1995a). The higher costs were identified as due to the employment of higher grade midwives for midwifery intrapartum care in the midwife-managed unit in Aberdeen, and in Glasgow's midwifery-managed maternity care were due to higher costs in postnatal care (Hundley, 1995a; Young, 1997).

One further striking factor in Table 16.1 is the consistently variation in opinion *between* the professional groups concerning devolved and reduced models of care (Cheyne, 1995; Reid, 1999; Sikorsky, 1995). Prior to publication of results that GP/midwife community-based care was as clinically effective as consultant-led shared care, surveys of participating staff showed that obstetricians were more likely to believe that GP/midwife care would be less clinically effective. Nevertheless, in the same survey, the majority in all three professional groups (84 per cent GPs, 73 per cent midwives and 64 per cent of obstetricians) responded that they would be happy to adopt this devolved model of care for the specified patient group (Reid, 1999).

Conflicting Multidimensional Performance Measures in Reduced Schedules of Antenatal Visits

Table 16.1 shows in the UK trial of a reduced schedule of antenatal visits that the reduced schedule was clinically as effective (and improved continuity of care) compared to traditional schedules (Sikorsky, 1996). No comparison of economic costs was undertaken initially, perhaps due to presumed gains in efficiency associated with overall reduced visit number if effectiveness was maintained (ibid.). A recently reported evaluation of costs showed only a small reduction in costs for the reduced schedule of antenatal care. But when neonatal outcome care costs were introduced (3.2 per cent (infants with postnatal care in traditional schedule) versus 3.5 per cent (infants with postnatal care in new reduced schedules)) overall costs for the reduced schedule were slightly higher. (Henderson, 2000). That economic evaluation concluded that fewer routine visits for low risk women were unlikely to result in cost savings to the NHS.

Furthermore , there were at best equivocal results in women's satisfaction measures and psychosocial outcomes for reduced schedules (Sikorsky, 1996, 1995; Clement, 1999). More women were dissatisfied with the frequency of visits in the reduced schedule (40 per cent) versus the traditional schedule (6 per cent, odds ratio 11 (95 per cent CI 7–15)). They were more likely to report that gaps between visits were too long and that they lacked enough opportunities for reassurance that all was well in their pregnancy. Conversely, however, more of the women with reduced schedules (68 per cent versus 60 per cent in the traditional group) said that they would choose that schedule of visits again in their next pregnancy (Sikorsky 1996, 1995).

A similar division in staff views to those reported above for the GP/midwife trial was notable for the reduced schedule trial. The majority of all three professional groups said they supported reducing antenatal visit schedules, both before (60 per cent GPs, 71 per cent midwives, 69 per cent obstetricians) and especially after the trial (77 per cent GPs, 87 per cent midwives, 95 per cent obstetricians) (Sikorsky, 1995). But in this case GPs were significantly and consistently less enthusiastic.

Policy Support and Implementation Initiatives of Alternative Models of Care

Further impetus for implementation of alternative models of maternity care had been put in place. The 'Changing Childbirth Implementation Team' was established by the NHS-Executive in England and Wales (1994–98). In Scotland CRAG-SCOTMEG's Working Group on Maternity Services (1995) had given recommendations for planning and provision of maternity care. In these recommendations they anticipated savings in the reorganisation of maternity services and recommended that services meet women's expressed need for continuity of care, information, communication, choice, less routine interventions, and reasonable access. The Scottish Office asked for response and evidence from Health Boards in 1996/7 about how their maternity services met or would meet these recommendations.

Subsequent National Audits and Evidence of Limited Access to Different Models of Care

Lack of Access or Choice in Antenatal Care

As shown in Table 16.2, *Birth Choices* (1995) had shown 29 per cent of women were aware of having any choice of *who* could provide their antenatal care and 14 per cent recognised a choice of *where* they could go to receive it. By 1998/99 national audit reports for both England and Wales (*First Class Delivery*, Garcia, 1998) and Scotland (*Maternity Care Matters*, SPCERH, 1999) showed modest increases, to around one third of women aware of choices, particularly about place of care during the antenatal period. However, it was still a marked minority of women who reported having any options in antenatal care. Further indication of lack of diversity of antenatal service models was shown in *Maternity Care Matters* in Scotland with only four of 23 maternity units offering optional models of devolved routine antenatal care by GPs and midwives in community settings. Although only three units had achieved a named midwife coordinator for both community and hospital maternity care, there was wide variation in the reported structure and extent of 'team' midwifery at a total of 12/23 Scottish units.

Table 16.2   Evidence of choice in antenatal care in recent audits

Audit report	Number of respondents (response rate)	Report year	Choice in where antenatal check-ups would take place?	Choice in who would carry out antenatal check-ups?
Birth Choices (1995) (National Childbirth Trust survey, North Essex Thames)	792 (67%)	1995	14%	29%
National Audit in England and Wales *First Class Delivery* (Garcia et al., 1998)	2,406 (67%)	1998	34%	38%
National Audit in Scotland: *Maternity Care Matters (SPCERH, 1999)*	1,176 (70%)	1999	33%	37%

There also appeared to have been little adoption of reduced schedules of care. In 1989 the average number of routine antenatal visits was 14 (Tucker, 1994). *First Class Delivery* (Garcia, 1998) and *Maternity Care Matters* (SPCERH, 1999) reported overall averages of 11 to 12 antenatal visits with interquartile ranges of 10–15. These results suggests a small move towards the target reduced visit schedules of eight visits for primiparous women and six for multiparous.

Lack of Access or Choice in Intrapartum Care

Access to alternative care models at intrapartum has also remain limited. The recent national audits (Garcia, 1998; SPCERH, 1999) showed 98 to 99 per cent of deliveries continue to occur in hospital. In the Scottish audit (SPCERH, 1999) models of intrapartum care in separate midwife-managed delivery suites had been adopted in only six of the 23 Scottish maternity units. Six per cent of women in *Birth Choices* (1995), 13 per cent in the Audit Commission report for England and Wales (Garcia, 1998) and 23 per cent in the Scottish maternity services audit (SPCERH, 1999) reported a choice of DOMINO delivery. (DOMINO deliveries are those where community midwives care for women throughout their pregnancy, accompany them in labour to hospital and where women are discharged at around six hours postpartum to community midwife care once more.) The reported proportions (6 per cent to 23 per cent respectively) were women who acknowledged this as a theoretical choice. But a further 46 per cent of the Scottish respondents were unsure about whether they had been offered DOMINO delivery, because they did not recognise the care model being referred to in this question. By 1999 DOMINO delivery was reported by service managers as available only on request at 14 of the 23 Scottish maternity units. A total of 0.83 per cent DOMINO-deliveries, and 0.34 per cent planned home births were reported in Scotland (0.7 per cent home births occurred in total including those with hospital booking but delivery before admission), versus 2 per cent reported home births in England and Wales. The proportions of respondents who identified home birth as a theoretical choice were 17 per cent (England and Wales) and 40 per cent in Scotland.

In *First Class Delivery* (Garcia, 1998) it is also observed that what is noted as a possible or theoretical choice may not actually be available. Thus one woman's comments about her delivery plans were: 'I couldn't have the hospital of my choice as it was considered outside my catchment area. I couldn't have DOMINO, which I really wanted, due to "lack of funds".' The overall results of these national audits can be interpreted as demonstrating limited availability to women of alternative models of maternity care.

Identifying Possible Barriers to Change

In exploring the difficulties of interpreting trial evidence of clinical effectiveness and costs as well as patient and staff satisfaction in alternative models of maternity care, some of the possible barriers to implementation may have been highlighted. These may be the relatively small size of effect and the conflicting directions of effect in the different evaluative dimensions. We can speculate that some of the barriers may be:

- the perceived strength of the evidence and the generalisability of the results;
- the pre-existing strength of professional pre-held beliefs and consensus about relative clinical efficacy or appropriateness of care models;
- implicitly lower values being attached to improving women's satisfaction;
- professional groups' vested interests.

Further barriers may include issues of costs of change or diversification, or variation through time in competing priority health needs outwith maternity services, or perhaps implicit acceptance of different definitions of equity between consumers and providers.

Equity of access to a service has been described (Mackenzie, 1999) as the extent to which a service is available to those who fall within its remit, and this has also been used as an indicator of the quality of a health service. Generally women in the UK do have access to NHS maternity care, but it may not be the *type* of maternity care they want. One important barrier to implementation of alternative maternity care programmes may be that service providers hold a different definition of equity (rather than equality of access to plurality of highly-valued alternative models of maternity care).

There is no single objectively correct definition of equity (Mooney, 1992) and the *equity of access* by patient preference as described above, is only one possible definition. For example, equity in maternity services may also *mean equality of inputs per capita*, or alternatively *equality of inputs for equal clinical need*. The latter might be construed as ensuring delivery of effective care programmes or protocols for women with particular disease-specific problems arising in pregnancy, e.g. intervening appropriately for women with pregnancy induced hypertension or diabetes. It may also mean aiming at *equality of utilisation* e.g. where service provision would aim to discriminate positively to deliver maternity services to particular geographical areas or socioeconomic groups of women who might otherwise be unwilling or unable to use the existing available maternity services at all. Finally equity might mean *equality of health outcomes independent of inputs*. In this scenario input would be theoretically unlimited in efforts to gain equality between subgroups with disparate rates of adverse outcomes such as prematurity, perinatal mortality, low birthweight etc. Overall however, moves toward higher equity of access are almost inevitably associated with a fall-off in efficiency (Mooney, 1992).

The Handbook of Medical Ethics (BMA, 1980, p. 35), states that in a resource-limited NHS 'doctors have a duty to advise on equitable allocation and efficient utilisation'. If the 'equitable allocation' is based on a non-explicit egalitarian concept of equality of inputs per capita or equality of input for *clinical* need, then providing equality of access based on women's preferences may be implicitly valued as having little benefit.

Conclusions

Although maternity care policy over the last decade has urged diversification to offer women choice, make the service more woman-centred and improve their satisfaction; and alternative models of maternity care have now been tested and shown to be as clinically effective and mostly highly acceptable to women, implementation still appears limited. Recent UK audits showed limited evidence of alternative maternity care models being offered as options to women. Some barriers to implementation have been suggested. These include: dilemmas in valuation for different 'quality' perspectives; that providers may have a low valuation of women's preferences; that substantial NHS cost savings are not likely in the new devolved or reduced maternity care models; and that other organisational barriers may exist e.g. cost of change, cost of plurality of service models and professional stakeholding. Furthermore, there may be evidence in the current Department of Health 'Performance Assessment Framework Document' (1999) of further conflicting pressures against maternity policy implementation to achieve diversification and choice in maternity care. The High Level Performance Indicator (HLPI) (1999–2000) within that framework for maternity care is 'cost per maternity case' and that HLPI is located within the efficiency domain. Thus one last possible barrier may be that policy initiatives are not sustained to drive change and implementation.

NHS maternity services have been at the forefront of progress towards efficacy in health care provision (for example, Cochrane's (2000) first collaborative group on systematic review of RCTs was in the area of pregnancy and childbirth). Maternity care was also in the early front line of NHS services to feel patient pressure to change the shape of services to what consumers want. Recent government policies (SODOH, 1996, 1997) continue to seek clinical effectiveness and efficiency throughout all NHS services and also emphasise that care should be patient-focused, with improved continuity, and include the patient in choices and decision-making. The factors suggested above, which may limit the implementation of alternative models of maternity care, may similarly impede change in other NHS service lines as they seek to attain the same quality goals. The fundamental dilemma for service providers is in trying to balance efficiency and access; where access may mean developing plurality of services to match patient preference.

References

Birth Choices (1995), *Women's Expectations and Experiences*, National Childbirth Trust and North London Health Authority, London.

British Medical Association (1980), *The Handbook of Medical Ethics*, BMA, London.

Changing Childbirth (1993), *Part I: Report of the Expert Maternity Group*, Department of Health, HMSO, London (Cumberledge Report).

Cheyne, H., Turnbull, D., Lunan, C.B., Reid, M. and Greer, I. (1995), 'Working Alongside a Midwife-led Care Rnit. What do Obstetricians Think?', *British Journal of Obstetrics and Gynaecology*, 102, pp. 485–7.

Clement, S., Candy, B., Sikorski, J., Wilson, J. and Smeeton N. (1999), 'Does Reducing the Frequency of Routine Antenatal Visits have Long-term Effects? Follow up of participants in a randomised controlled trial', *British Journal of Obstetrics and Gynaecology*, 106, pp. 367–70.

Cochrane Pregnancy and Childbirth Group (2000), *Abstracts of Cochrane Reviews*, The Cochrane Library Issue 3.

Collee, J. (1992), 'Delivery Note', *The Observer* (supplement), 19 April, p. 66.

CRAG-SCOTMEG (1995), *Antenatal Care. A report of the Working Group on Maternity Services*, The Scottish Office, Edinburgh.

Department of Health (1999), *The NHS Performance Assessment Framework (1999-2000)*, Department of Health, London.

Garcia, J., Redshaw, M., Fitzsimmons, B. et al. (1998), *First Class Delivery: A national survey of women's views of maternity care*, Audit Commission and National Perinatal Epidemiology Unit, London.

Graham, W. (1997), 'Devolving Maternity Services', *Health Bulletin*, 55, pp. 265–75.

Hall, M.H. (1981), 'Is Antenatal Care Really Necessary?', *The Practitioner*, 225, pp. 126–5.

Hall, M.H., Chng, P.K. and McGillivray, I. (1980), 'Is Routine Antenatal Care Worthwhile?', *Lancet*, I, pp. 78–80.

Henderson, J., Roberts, T., Sikorski, J. et al. (2000), 'An Economic Evaluation Comparing Two Schedules of Antenatal Visits', *Health Services Research and Policy*, 5(2), pp. 69–75.

House of Commons Health Committee (1992), *Second Report, Maternity Services. Vol 1*, HMSO, London (Winterton Report).

Hundley, V., Cruikshank, F., Lang, G. et al. (1994), 'Midwife-managed Delivery Unit: A randomised controlled comparison with consultant-led care', *British Medical Journal*, 309, pp. 1400–4.

Hundley, V. et al. (1995), 'Costs of Midwife-managed Delivery Unit and a Consultant-led Labour Ward', *Midwifery*, 11, pp. 103–9.

Hundley, V., Cruikshank, F., Milne, J. et al. (1995), 'Satisfaction and Continuity of Care: Staff views in a midwife-managed delivery unit', *Midwifery*, 11, pp. 163–73.

James, J.K. (1995), 'Controversies in Management. Should Obstetricians see Women with Normal Pregnancies? Obstetricians should Focus on Problems', *British Medical Journal*, 310, pp. 37–8.

Mackenzie, K., White, D. and Paxton, D. (1999), 'Quality Here, There and Everywhere', *Health Bulletin*, 57(2), pp. 134–40.

MDU Research Group (1995), *Final Report: The establishment of a Midwifery Development Unit based at Glasgow Royal Maternity Hospital*, Glasgow Royal Maternity Hospital, Glasgow.

Mooney, G. (1992), *Economics, Medicine and Health Care* (2nd edn), Prentice Hall, Europe.

Oakley, A. (1991), 'The Changing Social Context of Pregnancy Care' in G. Chamberlain and L. Zander (eds), *Pregnancy Care in the 1990s*, Parthenon, Carnforth, Lancs.

Ratcliffe, J., Ryan, M. and Tucker, J. (1996), 'The Costs of Alternative Types of Antenatal Fare for Low Risk Women – Shared Care versus Care by General Practitioners and Midwives', *Health Services Research and Policy*, 1, pp. 135–40.

Reid, M.E., Barbour, R. and Tucker, J.S. (1999), 'Professional Views on Randomised Controlled Trials', *British Journal of Midwifery*, 7(10), pp. 637–41.

Rodell, L. (1990) 'Having a Baby? It's Easy-peasy', *The Sunday Express*, 27 May, p. 15.

The Royal College of Obstetricians and Gynaecologists (1982), *Report of the RCOG Working Party on Antenatal and Intrapartum Care*, The Royal College of Obstetricians and Gynaecologists, London.

Ryan, M., Ratcliffe, J. and Tucker, J. (1997), 'Using Willingness to Pay to Value Alternative Models of Antenatal Care', *Social Science in Medicine*, 44, pp. 371–80.

Shields, N., Turnbull, D., Reid, M. et al. (1998), 'Satisfaction with Midwife-managed Care in Different Time Periods: A randomised controlled trial of 1299 women', *Midwifery*, 14(2), pp. 85–93.

Sikorsky, J., Wilson, J., Clement, S. et al. (1996), 'A Randomised Controlled Trial Comparing Two Schedules of Antenatal Visits', *British Medical Journal*, 312, pp. 546–53.

Sikorsky, J., Wilson, J., Clement, S. et al. (1995), *Final Report: The antenatal care project*, Primary Care Development Fund, South Thames Regional Health Authority, London.

SOHHD (1993), *Provision of Maternity Services in Scotland – A Policy Review*, The Scottish Office Home and Health Department, HMSO, Edinburgh.

SODOH (1996), *The Scottish Health Service, Ready for the future*, The Scottish Office Department of Health, Scottish Office, Edinburgh.

SODOH (1997), *Designed to Care*, The Scottish Office Department of Health, Scottish Office, Edinburgh.

SPCERH (Scottish Programme for Clinical Effectiveness in Reproductive Health) (1999), *Maternity Care Matters. An Audit of Maternity Services in Scotland*, SPCERH, Edinburgh.

Tucker, J., Florey, C. du V., Howie, P. et al. (1994), 'Is Antenatal Care Apportioned According to Obstetrics Risk? The Scottish Antenatal Care Study', *Journal of Public Health Medicine*, 16, pp. 60–70.

Tucker, J.S., Hall, M., Howie, P.W. et al. (1996), 'Should Obstetricians see Women with Normal Pregnancies? A Multicentre Randomised Controlled Trial of Routine Antenatal Care by General Practitioners and Midwives Compared to Shared Care Led by Obstetricians', *British Medical Journal*, 312, pp. 554–9.

Turnbull, D., Holmes, A., Shields, N. et al. (1996), 'Randomised Trial of the Efficacy of Midwife–managed Care', *Lancet*, 348, pp. 213–18.

Walker, P. (1995), 'Controversies in Management. Should Obstetricians see Women with Normal Pregnancies? Obstetricians Should be Included in the Integrated Team', *British Medical Journal*, 310, pp. 36–7.

Young, D., Lees, A. and Twaddle, S. (1997), 'The Costs to the NHS of Midwifery Care: Midwife-managed vs shared care', *British Journal of Midwifery*, 5, pp. 465–71.

List of Contributors

Andrew B. Bindman	Associate Professor Medicine, Epidemiology and Biostastics, University of California, San Francisco and Atlantic Fellow and Visiting Professor, School of Public Policy, University College London
Ruth Boaden	Manchester School of Management, UMIST
Peter Buckley	Medipurchase Ltd, Harrow
Adrian Coyle	Department of Psychology, University of Surrey
Huw Talfryn Oakley Davies	Reader in Health Care Policy and Management, Department of Management, University of St Andrews, Scotland
Louise Davis	Project Manager/Policy Analyst, Te Tai Tokerau MAPO Trust, New Zealand
Terry Desombre	School of Management Studies for the Service Sector, University of Surrey
Victoria Doyle	Research Fellow, Liverpool School of Tropical Medicine
Rebecca Duffy	Clinical Lecturer, Tayside Centre for General Practice, University of Dundee
Mattia J. Gilmartin	Research Associate, Judge Institute of Management Studies, University of Cambridge

Quality in Health Care: Strategic Issues in Health Care Management, H.T.O. Davies, M. Tavakoli and M. Malek (eds), Ashgate Publishing Ltd, 2001.

Maria Goddard — Centre for Health Economics, University of York

W. Graham — Professor and Director, Dugald Baird Centre for Research on Women's Health, Department of Obstetrics and Gynaecology, University of Aberdeen, Aberdeen Maternity Hospital

Marion Hall — Consultant Obstetrician and Gynaecologist, Department of Obstetrics and Gynaecology, Aberdeen Maternity Hospital, Grampian University Hospital Trust

David Haran — Senior Lecturer, Liverpool School of Tropical Medicine

Paul Haywood — Manchester School of Management, UMIST

Carmel M. Hughes — Lecturer in Primary Care Pharmacy, School of Pharmacy, The Queen's University of Belfast

Petra Kliempt — Research Assistant, Ninewells Hospital and Medical School, Department of Epidemiology and Public Health, Dundee

Russell Mannion — Centre for Health Economics, University of York

Martin N. Marshall — Clinical Senior Research Fellow, National Primary Care Research and Development Centre, University of Manchester

Mary Massey — Aintree Hospitals NHS Trust

Professor M.E.T. McMurdo — Head of Section of Ageing and Health, Ninewells Hospital and Medical School, Department of Epidemiology and Public Health, Dundee

David Melzer	Senior Researcher, Institute for Public Health, University of Cambridge
Catherine A. O'Donnell	Department of General Practice, University of Glasgow
Simon Ogston	Lecturer in Statistics, Ninewells Hospital and Medical School, Department of Epidemiology and Public Health, Dundee
Yaniv Poria	School of Management Studies for the Service Sector, University of Surrey
Thomas G. Rundall	Professor of Health Policy and Management University of California, Berkeley
Danny Ruta	Senior Lecturer in Epidemiology and Health Services Research, Ninewells Hospital and Medical School, Department of Epidemiology and Public Health, Dundee
Sharon Shea	Strategic Projects Manager, Te Tai Tokerau MAPO Trust, New Zealand
Peter C. Smith	Department of Economics and Centre for Health Economics, University of York
Harry Staines	Senior Lecturer, Scottish Informatics Mathematics Biology and Statistics Centre, The University of Abertay, Dundee
Lynette Stewart	Chief Executive Officer, Te Tai Tokerau MAPO Trust, New Zealand
J.S. Tucker	Senior Researcher, Dugald Baird Centre for Research on Women's Health, Department of Obstetrics and Gynaecology, University of Aberdeen, Aberdeen Maternity Hospital

John Turner   Aintree Hospitals NHS Trust

James Watkin   St. Andrew's Hospital, Northampton